HOLLYWOOD BLUE
The Tinseltown Pornographers
by Harris Gaffin

HOLLYWOOD BLUE

The Tinseltown Pornographers

by Harris Gaffin

✴

'Anybody that came into this business with a screw loose
is going to have a bolt missing when they leave.' –Anon.

© Harris Gaffin 1997

First published 1997

All rights reserved. No part of this publication maybe reproduced,
in any form or by any means, without permission from the Publisher.

Printed by Butler & Tanner Ltd, Frome and London

Published by
B.T. Batsford Ltd
583 Fulham Road
London SW6 5BY
http://www.batsford.com

ISNN 0 7134 7906 X

A catalogue record for this book is available from the British Library

All photographs copyright Harris Gaffin/Harris from Paris.
The publishers also offer special thanks to David O'Leary ('for editorial insight'), and to Willoughby, for his determination to make this project a reality. Special thanks to Houston, for her witty letters.

The author would like to thank his family and relatives who supported him writing a book but never asked about its content.

FAX

March 30, 1995

Dear Willoughby

I've been mulling over what we discussed during our meeting at the book fair and I've decided you're right - my idea for the film book is a bit too esoteric, and probably not very marketable. But your Hollywood Blue proposal is interesting. Through previous assignments I've made a few contacts in the Hollywood porno business and no doubt the list of contacts could be expanded. My own perceptions of the business are pretty stereotyped - it would be interesting to see if they could be challenged by what I discovered. Even in just writing up the enclosed experimental chapter, I find myself looking at the subject in a new light. I would see the book's structure to be based on a series of interviews. Each interview would lead me on to the next - until I have an overview of what is, let's face it, a billion dollar American industry that few people will openly discuss. Anyway, have a look at this draft and let me know what you think.

Thanks for introducing me to your friend the agent. Apparently leaving the fair he had a nasty accident in some revolving doors and hurt his hand, so no cheque as yet.

Best regards

Harris Gaffin

Harris Gaffin

Contents

1 Hollywood Here I Come 8

2 A Boy's Own Story 13

3 Beverly Hills Bondage 16

4 A Vivid Introduction 19

5 Beginner's Luck 23

6 The Business of Porno 29

7 Casting Call:
The Gang's All Here 33

8 A Man Who Has Found
True Job Satisfaction 38

9 Keeping Up Appearances:
Houston 40

10 Total Quality Control:
Steve Hirsh 44

11 The Iverson Ranch Boys 47

12 A Day Out at Track Tech 52

13 My Way or the Highway 59

14 Down in the Alley 64

15 Cultural Exchange:
Rebecca Lord 68

16 Greg, Prince of Darkness 70

17 Where Everyone's a Winner:
The FOXE Awards 73

18 Just How Much is Your
Name Worth? 80

19 A Fresh Approach: Susan Yanetti 82

20 This Girl Scout Isn't Selling
Cookies: Kristine Imboch 83

21 Girls on Top 88

22 At the Adultdex Convention 92

23 Sexual Healing: Nina Hartley 98

24 Adam & Eve: North Carolina's
Forbidden Fruit 102

25 Ron Jeremy:
The Firm Favourite 105

26 Seaweed Salad with Al 111

✳ Frontispiece: Harris and Houston

27 Vice Squad 114

28 He's Only Doing His Job 119

29 Reuben Sturman,
Peep Show Wizard 123

30 Learn with Professor Bill 126

31 AVN: The Colour of Money 129

32 The Bottom Line at
Shadow Lane 133

33 The Gay Line: From the
Bottom to the Top 140

34 Boys' Night Out: Sailors
and Supermen 143

35 Spot the Difference 145

36 Joy King: Public Spirit 147

37 Hollywood Bowl 150

38 Wicked, Man 152

39 VCA: Porno for the Masses 156

40 Girls at Sea: Conquest 162

41 The Price is Right: Nitewatch 167

42 An Old Hand: Gourmet 171

43 Janine: You Can't Touch This 173

44 Dyanna Lauren: Family Values 175

45 Compilations:
It's All in the Detail 176

46 Time for a Reality Check 178

47 Kristine's Are For Real 180

48 A Hard Act To Follow:
Buttman 184

49 Sex and Aggression in
Los Angeles 190

50 The Dinner Party 195

51 Adultdex: The Future is On-Line 199

Afterword: Where Are They Now? 204

Index 206

CHAPTER 1
HOLLYWOOD HERE I COME

Bill Margold is a writer for the *Hollywood Press*, a tabloid newspaper found on every corner of every major intersection, advertising every variety of sexual service imaginable. I've been told this guy runs a clearing house for porno stars and is well-connected in the very lucrative porno business. So I've phoned him.

'Hello,' he answers.

What, no secretary?

'I'd like to come by for an interview,' I say.

'I have to warn you, this place is not what you imagine,' he answers.

A chill goes down my spine. The Hollywood porno business. Millions of dollars. Lewd and lascivious behavior. The Beverly Hills Playboy Mansion with its manicured lawn, iron gates, swimming pool and lavish decor was built on the soft core. My story is the real truth on the hard stuff.

I pull up to a not old, not new beige apartment building, entry up a side alley – no manicured lawn, no iron gates, not even a door bell. Obviously, an underground business requires a low-key presence.

I knock on a screen door whose bottom panel has been pushed through, probably by an escaping cat.

The door opens. I enter. There's only one person there, presumably Bill Margold, and an extremely well-fed cat. Bill is talking on his mobile while walking around the one-bedroom apartment furnished with a coat tree piled with jackets, a couch covered with cat hairs and a desk stacked with dusty piles of papers. In the corner, pictures of cats are taped to the wall by the cat's food bowl. Kitty porn.

✱ Bill Margold

The carpet is worn. Bill's short-sleeve, button-down shirt is worn. Same for the faded blue jeans worn without belt and sneakers without socks. Pre-grunge. He has thick glasses, needs a haircut and looks more like a graduate student than a business executive, film tycoon and porno star, all of which he is reported to be. And more.

His business card reads 'God created Man. Bill Margold created himself.'

Bookshelves are filled with non-sexual books. The walls are covered with non-sexual pictures including a few posters and old press clips. There's a stack of dusty old records, mostly movie soundtracks: *Around the World in 80 Days*, *The Big Country*, *Star Wars*, *American Pie*. His taste is vanilla white. It must have been years since he listened to any of them. There's no record player, no cassette or CD player, though he does have a television and tape deck.

A few hundred porno magazines are stacked in three-foot-high columns on the floor. Behind the desk hang personal autographed pictures of the Detroit Lions football team. Teddy bears line the shelves and the walls. One sits upright in a rocking chair. The apartment is dark, as in poor. Not sunny, as in successful.

'A guy's here to interview me. I'll talk to you later,' Bill hangs up.

He looks at me. I look at him.

'See,' he says. 'I told you it wasn't going to be what you expected. Do you need an apartment? There are two available next door, a one-bedroom and a two-bedroom. Two of the "kids" left. I manage the building for the owner so I get free rent.'

A couple come running up the stairs. The girl's wearing a shirt tied around her stomach and tight jeans to the knee. She has thick, messy hair and looks wild. The guy by contrast, looks tame, wearing a new chequered sports shirt and Bermuda shorts. His hair is neatly trimmed and combed, his face clean shaven, his posture straight.

Bill introduces me to the couple, Peaches Richards and Robert Herrera.

'You can interview Peaches,' Bill says. But she can't sit still.

'Peaches, show Harris your tattoo,' Robert says.

'You want to see my tattoo?' she asks with a smile.

It must be on her bum.

'Sure, why not,' I say, acting like this happens all the time.

She goes into the kitchen and returns with her jeans pulled down to her thighs. I am sitting on the couch, eye-level to where her pubic hair might have been but it's been shaved and in its place is a beautiful, full-colour tattoo of a ripe peach. I get a good look at Peaches' privates and thank her. She smiles. I smile. She returns to the kitchen, pulling up her jeans. I go to the kitchen too:

I'm interested in food. I check the fridge: bagels, cream cheese, eggs, orange juice, coffee, limes, three bottles of ketchup, one hot sauce, two mustards, one stick of butter, cheese, jam, mayonnaise. In the freezer there's eight 'Meals on Wheels', normally distributed to the homeless, and pumpkin ice cream.

Bill takes Peaches next door to see the empty apartment. Robert hands me his business card which reads 'Triple X Merchandise'.

'You make super hard-core T-shirts?' I ask.

'No, actually I specialize in extra-extra-extra large T-shirts,' he says. 'But now that I make them for the business it's kind of appropriate.'

'What's your connection?'

'Well, I'm a shy kind of guy but I like sex as much as anyone,' he says. 'I've always loved pornography and my fantasy has always been to be with one of these kind of girls. I'm a fan of theirs.'

'They must have a lot of fans but few of them ever come this close,' I say.

'I joined FOXE and was looking for a way to meet them. When the girls got busted at the Vegas show and needed help raising funds, I volunteered to make T-shirts at cost to raise funds to get them out of jail. I met Bill and we became friends.'

FOXE — Friends of X-Entertainment — is an organization Bill set up for fans to meet performers. Bill set up a porno star press conference and demonstration in Las Vegas which was busted by the police and landed everyone in jail. Charges were eventually dropped after everyone spent a fortune on lawyers' fees.

'And Peaches?'

'I'm over at Bill's discussing T-shirts and here comes Peaches, a stripper from Atlanta, new in town, no place to stay. She's 33 and at an age where her hormones are raging and she just wants to have sex all the time so she figured she may as well get paid for it. Pornography is illegal in Atlanta so she came out here. But she's a good girl. I mean, she says grace before every meal.'

Bill and Peaches return.

'So, I got a one-bedroom for $750 and a two-bedroom for $1,050,' Bill says, taking a seat on the couch.

Peaches smiles at Robert who looks kind of sheepish.

'Can I give you a check?' Robert asks. He seems reluctant to pay.

'No checks,' Bill says without hesitation. 'Cash or banker's note. First and last plus one month security. If you want, I can give you a six-month or a one-year lease.'

Peaches runs outside to get her things from the car.

Robert whispers. 'Well, OK, I mean, if things don't go so well, if she

* Peaches Richards

decides to go back home to Georgia. I'll have to go to the bank.'

'No problem, I'm not going anywhere,' Bill says.

Peaches returns with her clothes piled up in boxes and brings them into her new apartment. On the way out again, she hugs Robert, runs her hand up his rib-cage and teasingly kisses up and down his neck. He takes it like a man.

'And what about the gas, electricity, water and telephone?' Bill asks. 'We'll put it in your name?'

Peaches apparently skipped out of paying her electricity bill in Georgia so has a bad credit rating.

Robert swallows and agrees to put the bill in his name. He leaves to go to the bank.

Who gets into this business?

'Most are rebelling against their upbringing but don't understand that's why they're doing it,' he says.

What percentage are stable?

'None of them,' he answers. 'People are non-supportive of themselves. There's no safety net. The casting couch isn't always in front of the camera. A lot of guys want their dicks sucked before they get their dicks sucked.'

Margold has a degree in journalism and was doing a story on the porno world. 'If I'm going to write, I better do it,' he told himself. Do it on camera, that is. Twenty-three years later he's still doing it. He is also like a guidance counsellor for many of the porno performers. Talent can take their problems to him. He is a mentor and coach. He screens those he feels are not suited for this tough business. He has even set up an emergency hotline to help those in need.

'Who should be in this business?' I ask.

'If they're here for the sex, I tell them go away,' says Bill. 'If they're here for the money, I throw them out. But if they want to get even with their upbringing and stick it to society, I welcome them with open arms. I must see rebellion because otherwise they will become miserable.'

The phone rings. It's a dance job for Peaches.

'I can't dance good,' Peaches tells Bill.

'No, you just have to be dirty and nasty,' Bill says.

'Oh fuck, I can do that no problem,' Peaches says confidently. I believe her.

The phone rings again. This time, a video shoot. Bill coaches her on what to say and assures her she can do whatever she does best.

'She's here now. I can put her on,' he says.

Peaches jumps for the phone. Standing in the middle of the room, she twists and turns. This customer wants a refined strip-tease but this is not her style and Peaches bows out.

'I can do "down-and-dirty" but not "fine-dining",' she says. 'When you need down and dirty, call me, honey.'

An editor from *Hustler* comes into Bill's apartment. She weighs about 250 pounds, wears a sleeveless white T-shirt and jeans, and is carrying a notepad and miniature camera. She greets Bill. He grunts. She stays long enough to collect Peaches for a day of shopping.

'Don't let the cat out,' Bill shouts.

Robert returns from the bank and gives the banker's note to Bill.

'So, for $1,050 a month, you got yourself a mistress. That's a pretty good deal.'

Robert doesn't seem so sure.

Bill, Robert and myself walk up the hill one block to Sunset Boulevard to a restaurant called The Source, where lunch is on me. It would be great to get an interview with somebody eventually.

'You want to see the day-to-day world of the porno business,' Bill says, as if reading my mind. 'Well, you're looking at it.'

The Source has a clientele of single young people in the business, which means a lot of people don't have work today. One guy dressed in sleeveless T-shirt, shorts and sandals sits in the middle of the restaurant with his feet up on another chair, reading the newspaper.

Bill and Robert order the roast chicken salad. Me, the turkey burger.

'Bill, can I talk to you a minute,' says a tall man who approaches with a very attractive blonde woman. Veronica and PJ join us for lunch. On a separate tab.

Veronica's a stripper who's arrived this week from Colorado and now wants to do porno. She has fine blonde hair, long manicured fingernails, an abundant chest on a petite frame and perfect white skin. She looks frail and perhaps too innocent to be doing her line of work. The only thing that is not perfect is her mouth which she keeps twisting, either from being anxious or because she has food stuck between her teeth. PJ is an economics professor at a nearby college and is Veronica's caretaker while she gets established. Girls come into town and Bill matches them up with respectable 'fans', who hopefully keep the girls out of serious trouble. In LA, serious trouble is easy to find.

'How long have you been stripping?' I ask.

'Since I was three years old,' she answers. 'That's all I've ever wanted to do.'

Veronica's stuffed mushrooms on a bed of rice arrives and she dives into her plate, effectively ending the conversation.

'I tell my kids, "As long as you have a cunt, you'll never starve,"' Bill says.

I get a flash of my four-year-old cousin who once shouted, 'fuck' at the dinner table, giggled when all the adults gasped and cried when he got a good spanking. Nobody here gasps, or even blinks for that matter.

After lunch, Veronica and PJ head off in a Mercedes convertible and Bill, Robert and I walk back to the apartment.

'Veronica said that all her life she's wanted to be a stripper so that's what she's doing,' I said. 'She seemed very normal.'

'Any kid who does a strip-tease in front of an audience of dolls at age three is not normal,' he says.

'Is Veronica PJ's mistress?' I ask.

'No, strictly platonic,' Bill assures. 'A lot of guys like to be around beautiful sexy girls and will do anything, or sometimes nothing, to be part of the scene.'

Now that he mentions it, I noticed Bill lives alone. Surely he could have the pick of the litter.

'They're my kids,' he says. 'It wouldn't be right. I would lose their respect if I took advantage of them.'

Ethics in Hollywood? This I got to see.

CHAPTER 2

A BOY'S OWN STORY

I grew up in Dorchester, part of Boston, Massachusetts, in a relatively self-contained neighbourhood where we'd play football in the gravel parking lot, walk to school, skip to the candy store, hang out on the sidewalk, run from bullies, and sit on top of parked cars while the big kids told us about adventures in the outside world.

The neighbourhood juvenile delinquent wore a leather jacket, spit after every phrase and combed back his hair after every paragraph of his tough guy tales. He had a mean-looking, sexy girlfriend who chewed gum, teased her dyed-blonde hair and wore pink eye makeup. She was thrilling to watch but we knew even then Mama would never let her be our baby-sitter.

There was not much pornography around that I was aware of. But when the family car needed repair, I made it a point to wander into the back of the garage where the posters of naked women were pinned up on the wall.

One of my friends showed me a porno book kept hidden by his father who worked in a factory. Another found a porno book hidden by his mother, a philosophy professor. 'How come we're always told to act like adults but they hide the "Adults only" books?' I asked a friend.

'Because it's about sex.'

'Why?'

'Just because.'

As I got older, I took the subway by myself and visited the bookshop on the 'good side' of Washington Street in downtown Boston. I would browse along the Classics, Sports and Poetry sections in case I was being watched, then would settle into the Sex section. There were some great books there.

As a double precaution, I usually bought a useless book in front after making my selection in back. 'Let's see, *Windjammer Ships* is for me,' I'd mutter. 'And these are for my older brother. How much do *we* owe you?'

Down the 'bad side' of Washington Street was the 'Combat Zone' where sailors on leave spent their time and money on sexy girls on the street, and in dark bars, strip joints and more, dirty, bookstores. My favorite books had no pictures on the cover; I usually found them at the bottom of the $1 barrel. The bookstore also sold dirty magazines. My favorites had a provocative glossy cover with a cheap newspaper interior. I liked my sleaze cheap.

I wondered: Who were these people in the magazines who seemed so free? On the front page of every magazine a disclaimer stated that all scenes were fiction, all names were false and all the participants were 'models'. I didn't believe it. Nice actresses would never pose like that. It was obviously a ruse to fool the police.

I was too young to enter the strip joints but the windows outside the bar were adorned with black-and-white photos of women in classic art-class poses, wearing tassels and G-strings. I'd pass by as many times as possible, trying not to attract the bouncer's attention and muttering excuses like, 'Let's see, which way to the subway?,' or 'Darn, I forgot to get something.'

Maybe, if I got lucky, one of the girls would walk out the door. Then I could follow her sashaying down the street. Who knows where that might lead?

I wanted to be popular in high school. I wanted to meet girls. I didn't want anybody to know I had this need so I pretended I didn't want to meet girls and that I didn't want to be popular. Hopefully, by not acting needy, I would become popular and meet girls. This system seemed to have worked for Clint Eastwood and Gary Cooper but somehow it didn't work for me.

One weekend I made a pact with my friends Roger and Marc. We didn't want a relationship. We wanted to get laid. We were not going to play ridiculous social games to get what we wanted. We would each ask a girl to go to bed and we'd be straightforward about it.

Roger would ask the prettiest and most popular girl in school to go to bed with him. I was a photographer and would find talent in a working-class neighbourhood where the girls grew up fast. Marc would approach a coed at the Boston University library.

We met on Monday. We'd all failed.

Sadly, we concluded that other guys simply played the game better than us. They got sex by pretending to be in love. We still couldn't do it. Maybe we just couldn't act. Mainstream Hollywood sure can. They have 'romances' all the time. Not so the porno people. They don't need to pretend. They just fast-forward to the action.

In the meantime, I ran cross-country, a socially acceptable form of masochism. No girls watched. In fact, no one did. And we were league champions! A race was once coordinated to finish around the track at half-time during a football game. The stands were full. We won. Nobody noticed.

In the locker room, Paul, a friend of a teammate, pulls from his back pocket a stack of hard-core porno photos. They're unbelievable. It's impossible to imagine any girl we know doing those things — and enjoying it — with us. It's impossible to imagine any guys we know getting that opportunity, or knowing what to do if they did.

My best friend, David, also enjoyed suffering in cross-country but shunned my interest in porno. He called it 'vicarious'. His father was a Lutheran minister who ran a halfway house for troubled teenagers. One day, David's father ran away with one of the runaways. Obviously Dad didn't need pornography either.

I envied 'adults' in 'adult' books and guys who felt comfortable in sleazy strip clubs. If I did that, I knew it would spell disaster. I could picture it: 'We found him lying in this hotel room, officer. His wallet was missing.' 'Serves him right for going there in the first place.' What a way to go.

Growing up in the well-to-do suburbs of New England there was this pervasive feeling that anybody who was anybody preferred intellectual stimulation to 'base' sexual gratification. An older man who liked younger women simply never 'grew up'. A young woman who preferred older men had a 'father complex'. A young man who was attracted to older women had a 'mother complex'. Anyone who said they *needed* sex was 'desperate', because sexually secure people didn't need to 'prove themselves'. They were 'content' without it. No one *ever* mentioned that perhaps sexually secure people *enjoyed* seeking sexual thrills. And sexually dynamic adults had sexually dynamic fun.

Now that I'm older and possibly wiser, I want to meet the people who are living *my* fantasies. There are secret clubs for every whim, sex scandals among role models, swinger's groups filled with suburban parents, etc. There's something for everyone.

The porno people are my noble savages, those who enjoy sex without shame, who appear in magazines and perform in movies for all the world to see without concern for what anyone thinks.

Who are these people, real or fantasy, who pursue this sexual lifestyle? Do they really exist? Are they dangerous? My quest is to seek them out and find out what they're really like.

A friend yawns.

'I'll bet if you grew up around this, you wouldn't be interested in doing a book on it at all,' he says.

'You're probably right,' I answered. 'But I didn't, so I am.'

CHAPTER 3

BEVERLY HILLS BONDAGE

My other contact is a guy named EZ Rider. We met at a Las Vegas Adult Video Convention back when I didn't know a soul.

Conventions may be good for networking but me and a million other monkeys were really there to meet sexy chicks. Instead, I met this mean-looking guy with a beard and ponytail, wearing a sleeveless jeans jacket, T-shirt, key chain, flogger, etc. The rough lines on his face hinted he'd done hard time.

'A whip and a Harley,' he said. 'The chicks go crazy. It turns them on more than money and a BMW.'

EZ worked for Bon Vue, a sado-masochism production company. I couldn't meet the owner because he was inside for selling the hard stuff. While he was away, his wife, Diane, a lovely lady straight from the Mamas and the Papas

BEVERLY HILLS BONDAGE

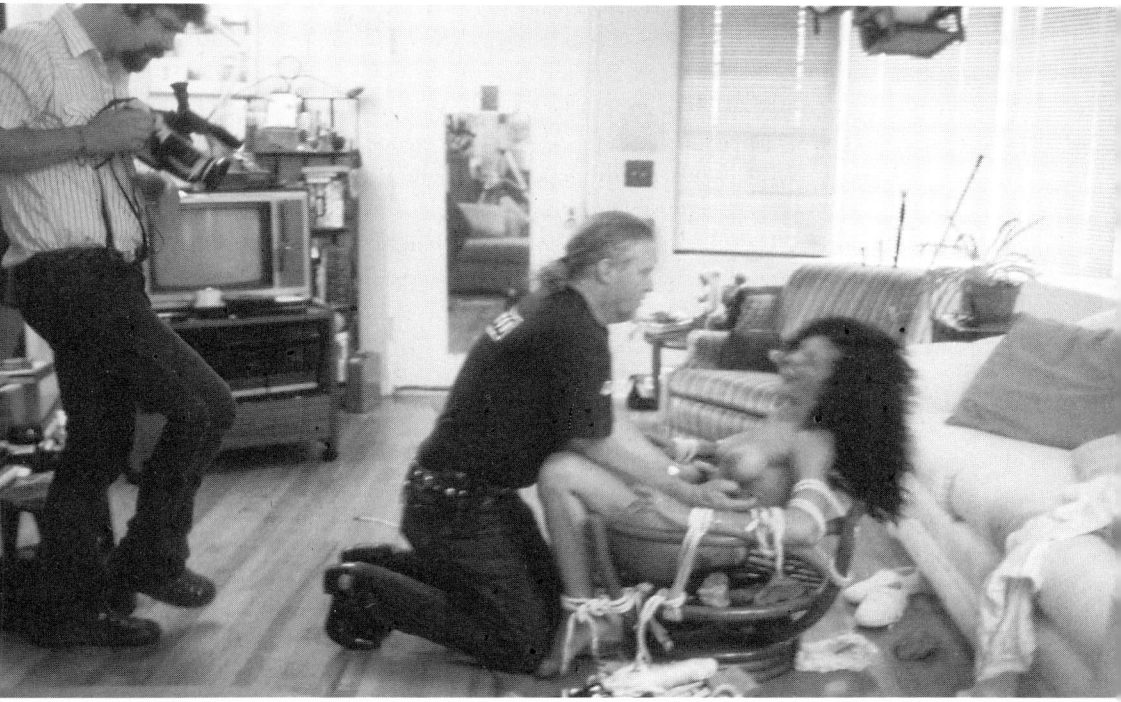

✱ Ariana shoots a video at the Beverley Hills home of EZ Rider

generation, ran the shop while her husband's 'slave' worked in production and her daughter ran the photo department. Everyone seemed pretty normal. EZ directed and performed in a series called 'Welcome to Bondage'. 'Come on over Sunday, I'm going to be tying down a beautiful woman,' EZ said.

I pull up along the tree-lined streets in Beverly Hills to EZ's building, a Harley Davidson, license plate 'EZ Rider' parked outside. A macho machine for a macho guy. Funny, a 'For Sale' sign is taped to the windshield.

His apartment wraps around the side of the building. A sign on the door reads, 'On this spot in 1897...nothing happened.' I knock. EZ opens the door to a substantial two-bedroom apartment with oakwood floors. Real classy. And a real mess. Videos and magazines piled everywhere, on the coffee table, under it, along bookshelves, under, on top and beside the television.

'Your place is a mess,' I say.

'Yeah, but it's *my* mess,' he says defiantly. I back off. I wasn't making a value judgement. I'm just there to see the girls.

The place seems too cluttered to be a film set but that's exactly what it was.

We push the television to the side, sweep the cassettes under the couch. The High-8 cameraman wears jeans and no shirt. Head shaved, front tooth missing, he looks right off the farm. We lift the glass top off the coffee table and fling the pillows away from the bamboo chair. A light is bounced off the ceiling.

A woman named Ariana arrives. She's sexy-looking, with jet black hair, intense, domineering eyes and high cheekbones. She's here with her husband, Raymond, handsome, and completely tattooed under his shirt. She stays in the living room. He goes into the kitchen.

EZ throws off her clothes while the cameraman catches it all.

'What are you doing?' she shouts. 'I didn't say you could undress me.' But it's too late. She's spread-eagled on the coffee table.

'Make yourself comfortable,' EZ sniggers while she struggles helplessly. Everything's available.

I can't bear to look and join Raymond in the kitchen where EZ has

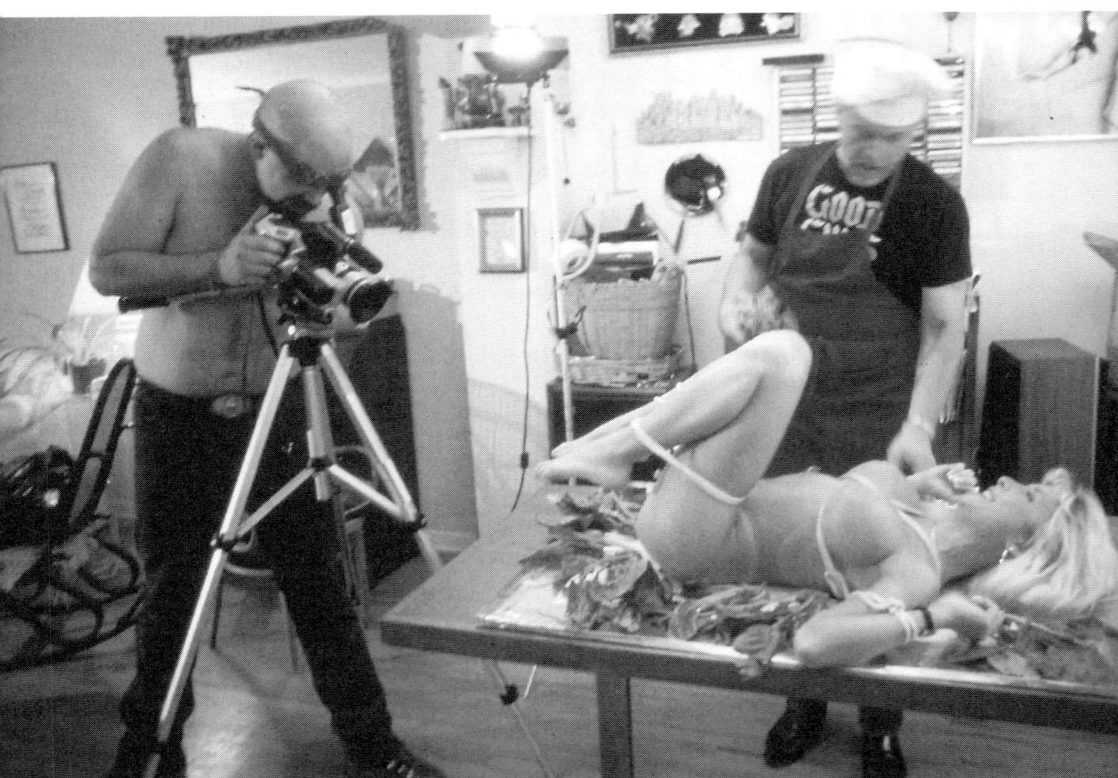

✱ Tami Monroe shoots a video with EZ Rider

prepared pots of coffee, one regular, the other decaffeinated. They both taste awful.

From the other room, we hear Ariana screaming and struggling to escape.

'I've changed my mind,' she shouts. 'I don't want to do this anymore. Untie me!'

She's frantic. EZ just laughs.

'You might want to check on your wife,' I casually mention to Raymond as he dumps his regular coffee into the sink. He seems very disturbed. He tries the decaf.

'Don't panic,' he says, cautiously taking a sip. 'She's been in this business for ten years. She's acting.'

I'm stunned. And EZ seemed so sincere when he was being so cruel. I try to hide my disappointment.

'Great coffee,' I say.

Raymond explains that Ariana is a professional performer who also runs and dances in a strip club, 'back East' in New Jersey. She also does porno flicks and all kinds of related activities.

'She is a healthy, active woman,' he says. 'On top of that, she is a loving and caring mother who is a religious Catholic and goes to church every Sunday.' He pauses, then cautions, 'Don't repeat that. We are trying to keep her image as a bitchy slut.'

Between the struggles to escape, we hear roars of laughter. EZ unties her and gets her a cup of coffee. She takes a sip.

'Mmm. Delicious,' she says.

She doesn't fool me. I know she's just acting.

CHAPTER 4

A VIVID INTRODUCTION

I remember that experience at EZ Rider's home like it was yesterday. Back then I was so naive. I wonder who he's tying up now?

I call EZ at work but the operator says he's gone. Switched jobs. Changed companies. I get his new number and reach him at a 'straight' porno company called Vivid, in the Valley.

'You got to check this place out!' he says.

A VIVID INTRODUCTION

Time for a brief geography lesson: the city of Los Angeles is divided diagonally southwest to northeast by the San Fernando Mountains. Hollywood lies to the south; the San Fernando Valley, aka 'The Valley', lies to the north. Basically, it's one huge, anonymous suburb: long straight streets, strip malls, two-storey apartments and single family homes. No monuments, no parks, no distinguishing features whatsoever.

The porno industry moved west from New York because the mainstream movie industry was here. Moonlighting mainstream professional cameramen, lighting gaffers and technicians were available as well as actors and actresses who realized they weren't going to make it big time. The porno business was a natural offshoot. First set up in Hollywood and West Los Angeles, it then migrated to the Valley because property values were much cheaper.

The San Fernando Valley's image used to be a pristine suburb where middle-class families escaped the drugs, crime and congestion found on the other side of the hill. For years, the porno business quietly flourished, undetected by locals because basically all warehouses and production studios look the same. Residents were astonished when it hit the papers in the 1980s that their middle-class 'family values' community was actually the porno capital of the world, accounting for 80 per cent of America's porno production.

I head up to the Valley, to a row of anonymous one-storey warehouses, no lavish corporate-style headquarters. Inside, the place is strictly blue-collar: windowless offices and lots of inventory. I got all dressed up for nothing.

There's EZ, chained to a desk, peering at a customer list printout, making sales calls; his ponytail's been snipped off, beard shaved, no sleeveless jean jacket, no whip. No Harley either. He's traded it for a white Kawasaki police motorcycle.

'Wait until you meet my boss,' he whispers.

In walks Dave James, fit at 50, a powerful guy with a walrus mustache, tattooed arms, barrel chest, solid chin and a fearless grin, the kind I had only seen in pirate movies. But he is no Hollywood pirate. Born in Wales, James speaks with a soft, charming brogue that whispers 'Let's do it my way.' He is a Vivid partner, chief CD-ROM salesman and ferocious would-be security guard.

James smiles at EZ, who suddenly picks up the phone and gets back to work.

'Would you like to meet everyone?' James says. He hits the intercom before I can answer. 'Jennifer darling, would you come see me whenever you have a moment?' he asks.

Jennifer comes racing into the office, panting. She's the public relations manager, meaning kid just out of college. When Dave smiles, she volunteers to spend the morning escorting me office to office so I can meet everyone. Will they give me the company line? Mainstream PR bullshit is bad enough; imagine the no-holds-barred hard-core porno snowjob I'm in for. Already I know what they'll say: It's all lovey-dovey. It's all consensual. Everyone's nice. Free Speech blah, blah, blah.

'Anything you need, just ask,' Jennifer says.

My shopping list includes studying every department, interviewing owner Steve Hirsh, visiting the sets and, of course, meeting all the girls. Jennifer says she will hook me up with someone who will *try* to arrange meeting the girls. Try? She changes the subject. What about the publicist? The creative director? Their gay division? Have I met PT, Vivid's star film director? Do I want to review any videos, CDs or interactive CDs? I get a shopping bag full of them just in case. Why can't the real world be this easy? I open up my notepad and get down to work.

In 1984, Dave James convinced Steve Hirsh they should create their own company. They were two hotshot porno salesmen who thought they knew everything. They were close enough.

From the start they had a specific plan. They would concentrate their marketing and promotional efforts around a single girl, Ginger Allen Lynn, a well-known stripper and already-established porno star. She had a huge following and Steve Hirsh knew her fans would buy her video. He signed her to an 'exclusive contract', making Ginger Lynn the first 'Vivid Girl'. When people thought of Ginger Lynn, they would think of Vivid and vice versa. Vivid was the first adult company to work the star system, like the old 1930s and 1940s Hollywood studios who 'guided' their contract girls' careers.

Hirsh hired a mainstream art director to create a glamorous look for the Vivid Girl – coordinated with a sophisticated advertising campaign and high-quality cassette packaging, he targeted first wholesale and retail buyers and then video store consumers. The results blew the market away. Vivid was off and running before Steve Hirsh turned 25 years old.

Within a decade Vivid was grossing $20 million a year. Today, Vivid is one of the biggest porno 'manufacturers' in the world. They make the movies but the key is that they handle their own distribution. In some aspects, Vivid is the industry leader; in others, it's in a market by itself.

Vivid now has 50 employees, producing 8–16 movies a month, editing with digital equipment on their own premises, making their own masters and

A VIVID INTRODUCTION

cassettes on a thousand duplicating machines. They provide 80 per cent of the Playboy Channel movies, have the soft-core market lion's share, create CD-ROMs, interactive CD-ROMs, video games and compilation videos. They aggressively sell home video, television, cable and the hotel pay-per-view international licensing rights country by country. Vivid owns bookstores and a cable station, are partners with publishers, distributors, software and hardware companies. Every possible combination of business relationship is considered.

They put out 6,000 boxes or more for many of their videos, then quickly drop prices to 'catalogue', thus reaching a mass market. They're flooding the market all by themselves. They are so backed up they have 60 movies 'in the can', meaning waiting to be promoted and released. They've signed 15 Vivid Girls, some of whom they haven't even begun to promote.

Much of their product is considered too soft for the hard-core market because they concentrate on showing cool girls instead of hot action. Their market lies where adult meets mainstream – this explains their mainstream publicist, their mainstream billboard ad overlooking Hollywood's Sunset Boulevard and possibly the red carpet they've rolled out for a mainstream journalist mug like me.

At the back of the Vivid warehouse is a row of windowless offices where I meet a guy named Michael Adams working by a computer. He has long black hair down to his waist and looks like a rock musician, the kind the chicks would really go for. To my surprise, he's a married family man, in the business because sex sells and guarantees food on the table.

'It's on our minds 24 hours a day, seven days a week,' he says.

Michael used to do hard-core, saw it all, got jaded and got out. That's why he came to Vivid. It's softer. Now, he designs animated computer games where no one actually has sex. Being on a movie set gets boring after a while, he says. It's like working in a bank: it seems great to be surrounded by money but at the end of the day, it's not yours to enjoy. Mainstream friends don't buy that. They envy him. 'Can you get me on a set?' everyone asks. Then there's the moral issue.

'I've shot a lot of girls – it's sad to see an 18-year-old girl, fresh out of home; she has a 10 o'clock call time for a double penetration with two guys she doesn't even know,' he says. 'I find that just a little on the awkward side. I find it a little disturbing sometimes. If it was my daughter or son, I would probably take her out and break her in the head then kick them out of the house. I've met a lot of nice girls over the years and I find it very sad that their main source of income is fornication. It is a form of prostitution, the only difference is that you're getting paid for doing it in front of a camera versus doing it in a hotel room. That's the only difference. It's sad.'

He's telling it straight and honest – can't you get fired for doing that? The way Adams figures it, video replaces reality for most guys. There are even several advantages. Say a dinner date costs a guy $50. What's he got to show for it? Maybe love. Maybe sex. Maybe zilch. Now, for $10, the guy takes home a video, doesn't have to shower, doesn't have to wine it or dine it. He can roll over when he's done and not get harassed for not cuddling. The performers do it all for you.

'It's a very kooky business,' he says.

'Do these performers make better lovers in real life?' I ask.

'People assume just because that you have sex for a living on camera that you're an expert at it,' he says. 'Granted, women do learn how to do a hell of a lot of things and so do guys. Physically, they could tell you how to get in different positions but mentally, that's a whole different ball game. I don't think any of these people are realistically capable or smart enough to tell people how to enjoy sex.'

'So do they do it because it's easy?' I ask.

'They do it when they want to do it,' he says. '"Don't book me until at least 12 o'clock because I can't get out of bed." It's not that they're prima donnas but they wanna do it when they wanna do it.'

'Why are you telling me all this?' I ask.

'Somebody has to tell you the real side of the business,' he says. 'Anything else? I have to get back to designing a strip-tease bowling game.'

'Can you get me on a set?' I ask.

CHAPTER 5

BEGINNER'S LUCK

'You want on a set? You got on a set,' Vivid had said. I walk into a bar in the Valley at 10 a.m., RTS (ready to shoot), for the making of *Head to Head*. I am, of course, way too early. Mainstream is always late, why should porno be any different?

This is a 'low budget' video, two days to shoot, production cost $10,000, with another $5,000 for the photos, box cover, printing, etc. Now I know porno is big business and everyone I know knows porno is big business but at that budget they could shoot a movie a week for two years before even approaching a 'low-budget' mainstream movie's cost.

The makeup artist sets up by the bar counter and works without mirrors or lights. The crew works by the day, no overtime. Performers are paid by the 'scene', whether it takes 10 minutes or 10 hours. The movie talent slowly drift in. The production manager brings them to their partners and explains their scenes.

'Hi, this is the guy you'll be having sex with today,' he tells a foxy-looking young woman with bleach-white hair.

'Hi, how ya doing?' she says.

'Great. Yourself?' he says.

'OK, enough chit chat. Let's get ready,' the production manager says. 'We got work to do.'

Paul Thomas, nicknamed PT, is the director; I ask the production manager to introduce me to PT, who checks me out before granting me an interview. PT intimidates everyone. Not because he is the tough, macho type, but because he is the opposite: educated, refined and poised.

Tall and slender, with soft, curly hair, he moves with catlike grace and aloofness and looks elegant even when wearing a sweatshirt and jeans. I suggest we sit by the counter. It's not the brightest idea because now we sit shoulder-to-shoulder facing the bar, looking at each other via the mirror.

'OK, make it interesting,' his look says.

'Who are you?' I ask. He pouts, bored already. He inhales deeply and exhales: quit college at 19, was in the original casts of *Hair* and *Evita*, had the lead on Broadway in *Jesus Christ Superstar*, turned on, dropped out, got into drugs and porno in San Francisco during the 'Love-In' days when it was very definitely a rebellious thing to do, implying, it was much wilder, much nastier, much more exciting back then than today where his production company, Cinnamon, is partners with Vivid and he directs soft-core mainstream cable movies and hard-core for Vivid Video.

He completes his one breath run-on sentence biography in 55 seconds. It's not a great interview but it's an interesting performance. He's called away. To be continued.

By 11 a.m., the six-guy crew is ready to roll. First up, Gothic sex kitten Kitty Monroe hikes up her tight mini-skirt to provoke two guys playing pool. One is Vince Voyeur, a macho type playing a sleazeball pool stud; the other is a newcomer named Ralph, with a mile-wide grin that says 'If my friends could see me now'.

PT gives Kitty a cue ball. 'Really milk it,' he says. 'OK, here we go. I'm excited. Roll sound.'

Beep! goes Vince Voyeur's beeper.

'Cut! I don't want that to happen again,' PT says sternly. 'All beepers off.'

While deciding if Kitty should break or rack, PT adjusts her skirt as the crew shoots up her dress. PT is happy. Kitty is happy. Everybody is happy except Mitchell, the newcomer who is serious about actually trying to sink his shot. He doesn't understand: this is a porno shoot, not a pool championship.

Other talent drift in, there's a dozen by now. Must be an orgy planned. It's getting more interesting. I jump when somebody taps me on the shoulder. It's PT.

'Want to be in a scene?' he asks.

Do I want to be in a scene? Do I look like I'm not interested? Of course I'm interested.

PT instructs me to stand by the bar and pretend to be talking and drinking. The action is behind me and I can't see a thing. I order a beer but am told there's no alcohol on the set. Imagine the party that inspired that rule. The guy next to me says that he's ranked fourth in the country for flamenco guitar playing. I'm impressed but he's not. It sucks, he says. He's starving: not for work, for fame.

A hand thumps on my shoulder. It's PT again.

'I said, "Pretend to talk." Don't actually talk. We're picking you up on the mike,' he says.

Sorry PT. Acting isn't as easy as it looks.

Turns out the scene is only a prelude to action later on. I didn't miss anything. I go find the production manager: I'd like to meet another performer, now, please. He brings me over to a blonde woman in a silky robe. Lovette is sitting in a tall director's chair, having her makeup done. It's very awkward for us because we're exactly eye-to-eye and face-to-face. Actually, it's awkward for me, not for her. Everytime she inhales I get distracted.

'Is it more exciting on or off the set?' I ask, fumbling for words.

'Are you speaking about sex?' she asks.

'Um, sex, yeah,' I say and turn red.

She reflects carefully. 'Sex. You seem so shy when you say that,' she says. 'It's made my outside sex life much more exciting, much more daring.'

Isn't it hot in here? 'Excuse me, I have another appointment,' I say and scoot off to the production manager who introduces me to someone else, this time a much cooler Vivid contract girl. Madeline Knight says her daddy is a banker and she's a New York table dancer out here for kicks.

'Why did you get into this?' I ask.

'Come on, to make it with the chicks,' she says. 'How else would a girl like me get to do it with someone like Janine? Women like her, you can't meet in a bar.'

Now, why was I not expecting to hear that from a woman?

Janine is Vivid's top contract girl, a big-name stripper and former Penthouse Pet. Contract girls pick their sex partners and Janine picks only other women.

'Weren't you really drugged and dragged here and forced into porno slavery against your will?' I was planning to ask Madeline but somehow she doesn't look the type. Madeline introduces me to her girlfriend and fellow performer Chelsea Blue who's sitting next to her eating an organic banana-cranberry muffin. She looks like she can take care of herself, too.

Just thinking about it makes me hungry, the muffin, I mean. I head over to the snack table laden with chips and dips, sandwiches, cold cuts, fruit, chocolate: it's a teenage boy's feast and a dieting model's nightmare. I grab some chocolate, make a sandwich and wander outside where I meet Bobby Vitale, a performer who, like Janine, only does women, too. Considering how everybody seems to prefer women here, it's strange that porno has such an anti-women image.

Before getting into the porno scene, Bobby had his own 'auto detailing' company: he travelled the city washing cars on location. Married with kids, he just had one problem: 'I was always horny.'

Every week Bobby washed and waxed a Corvette owned by an attractive older woman in the porno business. He asked for a chance. After a year of begging and pleading, washing and waxing, she referred him to a production company who gave him a chance. He came through three times in one afternoon. Soon he started a new life, sold the business, divorced his wife and remarried someone who could live with his busy schedule.

He found that practice did not make perfect: 'I used to work two times in a day and then I'd go home and make love to my wife a bunch of times and then the next day I'd have to go to work and my performance wasn't there.'

So he learned to pace himself. So did his wife.

But he wanted more out of life than just dropping his trousers. He wanted to open his mouth: 'I told them I was really great at dialogue; the truth was that I wasn't so hot at dialogue because I never did it before.'

The Hollywood teaching is 'Fake it till you make it.' Bobby did. Now he is living his dream, making love to the girls and speaking a few lines as well.

Meanwhile, Kitty Monroe is no position to say anything at all, kneeling on all fours on the pool table, giving it in front and getting it in back. When slinky Kitty is finished, she slips on a black outfit with white trim. She looks like a

Generation-X pinup girl. She has a ring in her nose and one on her beautifully pedicured toes.

'Not everybody gets so dressed up in this business,' I say to her.

'I dress up a lot because I'm naked a lot,' she answers. We sit on a step, shoulder to shoulder. When she speaks, it sounds so beautiful – gentle, sensual, soothing yet enticing.

'Your voice. It's absolutely mesmerizing,' I say. 'Are you a singer?'

'No, but I did phone sex for a year,' she answers.

We talk a while. Just think, on another day this might have cost me $2.99 a minute.

Kitty works at a strip club. Does she date sugar daddies or young, wild ones?

'It's whoever,' she says.

She was once a skinny, unpopular high school girl. But making it in the sex business changed all that: 'I have a lot more self-esteem. I base that on dancing and the movies. It's given me a lot of insight into myself and who I can be. I can be pretty-in-pink or I can be a slut. It's kind of an ego thing mainly, just being able to be happy about myself, being able to look at myself in the mirror and say, "Hey, I like who I am."'

Do I buy that? Who the hell knows.

'Why do women get into this?' I ask.

'A lot of girls have this premonition that they are going to become really big stars, adored and loved by millions of fans and they fail to realize that all we are is sex objects and sex objects can never be stars.'

'Do a lot of the women in the sex business prefer women?' I ask.

'I do it because I enjoy it. I've always had bisexual feelings,' she says. 'With women, it's more caressing and kissing, which you lose a lot with men. Sexual situations here are very cold. With women, it's very sensual, very soft. That's why we tend to cling on to women.'

So, if I understand her correctly, the more time these women spend at work with men, the less they enjoy being with them. Does that say something about something?

All this philosophizing makes me hungry again. I've heard respectable porno companies serve hearty lunches. I heard right. Picnic tables are set up in the parking lot: roasted chicken, sauteed and mashed potatoes, grilled carrots and onions, string beans, chocolate cake for dessert. Where's that production manager? I want to meet the chef. Now.

FAX
June 23, 1995

Dear Willoughby

Attached, among other things, is chapter two - which explains to the reader why I'm into this project. I had no problems writing about my past, but never would have thought of it without your suggestion.

I have not done much research as yet on fans. Each time I approached them I got nauseous and turned around. When you realize that 25% of the top porno actress's mail comes from convicted felons and the other 75% are on the streets, we're not talking about the crowd who read DH Lawrence and call it porno. At present, my idea is to put this section last.

There should be no fear on the part of the American publisher you mentioned that I won't get the necessary information. Mind sets are 25 years behind. There is no secret Mafia. These are legal, legitimate corporations, paying taxes and following all US legal obscenity guidelines. If they didn't, they would be arrested and closed down. (I have a meeting scheduled with the LAPD Vice Squad, more on this later).

My agent's hand is fully functional again. He looks forward to receiving your contract - and cheque. What do you propose to do about the clause forbidding me to include "indecent material"?

Best regards

Harris Gaffin

Harris Gaffin

CHAPTER 6
THE BUSINESS OF PORNO

Margold's office is in the Valley, on the second floor of World Model Agency, owned and operated by Jim South. It's a sparsely furnished room; on the desk sits a disused, ancient, Macintosh and modem pushed to the side. 'Even I know it's pathetic,' Margold says. There's a couch and more teddy bears. The only light comes from a window facing nowhere. South rents the room to the Free Speech Coalition who let Margold use it for a counselling service called PAWE – Protect Adult Welfare – set up after a string of performer suicides.

'I heard a couple porno stars killed themselves, Kal Jammer and Alex Jordan, over the past few years. What happened?' I ask Bill.

'Kal found out two of his friends were screwing his wife,' Bill says. He shakes his head. 'You should not take sex too seriously. In this business, it's like shaking hands. Alex started off strong but wasn't getting the recognition she felt she deserved.'

In other words, after the first year she wasn't getting any work. Instead of getting out of the business and going on to something else, she lingered too long.

Margold figures about 60,000 people have performed in porno films over the years and five have committed suicide. He's trying to prevent problems before they begin, by convincing troubled performers they need help, not just work.

Jim South is in the building; he's one of the most powerful agents in the business. He's a tall, slow-talking Texan with spit-polished black cowboy boots, a gold watch on one

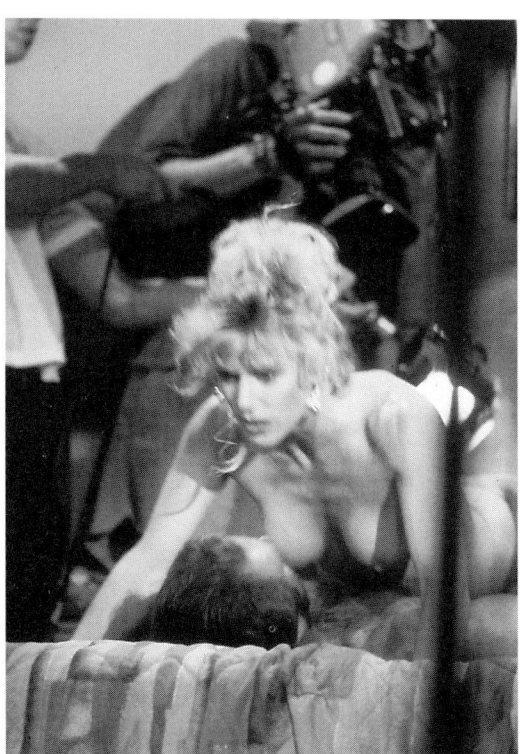

✱ Alex Jordan during a shoot

wrist, a gold bracelet on the other, a razor-cut, handsome full head of combed black hair, every strand in place and possibly sprayed to stay there. He speaks with perfect enunciation and has such a smooth methodical tone, he may have taken diction lessons. I could see him with other good old boys holding a weekly poker game, knowing when to hold and when to fold. The guy is smooth. Totally smooth. In his office, young talent anxiously wait on the casting couch, intimidated by a wall of porno star photos. South's desk sits in front of a glass door leading to a balcony. If he opens the blinds, he becomes backlit so while visitors can barely see him, he can clearly see them.

When a performer 'signs' with an agent, she states what she will and will not do and with whom. The list is pretty specific and covers masturbation, penetration, oral, anal, girl–girl and group sex, among other things. A performer can list who she will or will not work with. New performers often only want to do penetration shots with their boyfriend or husband. The information is updated as performers extend their limits.

Mainstream movie or model agents collect payment for their talent and deduct a commission on the negotiated sum. Porno agents don't. They charge a flat $60 fee per 24 hours and send two bills, the agent's fee and the performer's rate.

In theory, all scenes are negotiated beforehand. In reality, there are always last-minute changes. Performer no-shows run as high as 25 per cent so those who do show might actually end up making more than originally planned. Patient newcomers realize they are in high demand. Experience is not necessarily wanted in this job: some companies will pay a premium for first-timers.

The performer can set her own prices though standard rates keep them competitive and generally speaking performers are not in a strong negotiating position, especially newcomers. She may be booked for one thing but find herself scheduled for something else. Or she may find herself booked for one thing and find herself scheduled for two things. Sometimes it's intentional, sometimes it's a lack of organization. It helps to have negotiation know-how or a mean boyfriend who acts like he does.

The porno agent's business might not seem very lucrative but consider how many movies are being made. According to trade magazine *AVN* (*Adult Video News*), on average, about 200 new movies are made a month. Let's say they average six performers per two-day shoot. That's 2400 x 6 x 2 x $60 = $1.7 million in $60 agency fees generated per year. Subtract some for non-agency models and it's still a lucrative million-dollar business, about 15 per cent of one superstar mainstream model's income.

The agent finds talent by referrals, by networking with agents in other cities and by placing weekly ads in local 'pennysaver' newspapers. A new talent calls and stops by. The agent takes a Polaroid, usually topless, even better nude, and files it in a photo album. It's as simple as that. No portfolios. No résumés. A prospective producer can review the pictures but the regular clients simply call up and request who or what they want. Everyone accepts substitutions. If one big-busted babe can't make it, send over another.

The client and performer meet, usually exchange numbers and deal directly with each other. Believe it or not, future bookings are based on the honour system. If the client books the girl, they tell the agent. They could cut him out of the next deal but if he finds out, he takes them off his mailing list. The next time they need talent, they can pay for the ads themselves, have 200 wannabees stop by their office, spend all day looking at them, select who they want, verify they are over 18 years of age, call them back, hope they are still interested in working and then pray they will actually show up. For $60, they get a reliable performer. Meanwhile, the agent is in constant touch with the producers and can recommend new performers. In theory, this keeps everyone on their best behavior.

The porno agent negotiates for the talent but does not train them or manage their careers in the way a fashion model agency might. And a regular movie star will have an agent and a manager working on commission as well as a publicist on retainer. The porno performer's career is far more simple. The majority are 'managed' by boyfriends. The larger companies have at least one 'contract girl', paid on retainer for a year and guaranteeing them between 5 and 15 films at a rate a few times higher than other performers. During that time, the company will promote them. Performers are free to pursue all other non-video business venues. Usually, they hit the road as feature dancers at strip clubs and make far more than their video contract. In fact, most performers are already established dancers. In effect, they use their 'porno star' image to promote their dancing. Because they contracted to a limited number of films at a higher rate (they might even get royalties), a non-contract performer who hustles her own work can actually make more than a contract girl.

Mainstream movie agents negotiate for their talent and provide a sense of protection. A porno performer is on her own, just like a low-level actor or a high-level escort. The agent does not get too involved for several reasons. Performers have a high turnover rate, few career plans and soon disappear. Perhaps the most important reason, is the 'illegitimate' nature of the business. Before 1988, agents were considered 'pimps' and performers, 'prostitutes'. Most agents have faced jail at one time or another, busted back then for what is legal today.

The turning point revolved around the prosecution of film producer Harold Freeman, charged with five counts of pandering: he paid five women to have sex on a movie set for the making of *California Valley Girls Take It to the Max*. There were no obscenity charges against him but he was found guilty on all counts of 'pandering'.

On appeal, the California Supreme Court justices overturned the conviction because part of the state law's legal definition of 'pandering' and 'prostitution' requires that the sex act be 'for the purpose of sexual arousal or gratification of the customer or of the prostitute'. Both Freeman and the girls testified they did it for the *money*, not for the pleasure. By definition, Freeman was not pandering and the performers were not prostitutes.

Federal law states that *non-obscene* motion pictures are a form of artistic expression protected by the First Amendment of the Constitution. Having sex is not illegal and neither is filming it.

Justice Kaufman chastised the Attorney General for trying to avoid these citizen rights, writing 'The self-evident purpose of the prosecuting authority in bringing these charges was to prevent profiteering in pornography without the necessity of proving obscenity.'

Harold Freeman won the case but lost $300,000 in lawyers' fees and soon died of ill health.

From that day on making non-obscene pornography for profit was legal and a new tax-paying industry was officially born in Los Angeles. Most future court battles would be fought over what constitutes 'obscene' which each community can legally decide for themselves.

Nowadays it's OK to make adult films in Los Angeles, just get a shooting permit like everyone else. Simply visit or call the film office. Pay the $385 fee plus $85 for a fire marshal spot check of two locations. The permit is valid for 14 days and up to 10 locations. Getting the permit requires proof of $1 million of general liability insurance which covers performers, crew, equipment, automobile and property damage. Cost averages $1,500 per year. Professional rental studios already have permits and insurance.

The 'Freeman Decision' was a landmark case and the porno industry lionized the defendant as a freedom fighter. Margold worked with the guy and thought otherwise.

'He fought to stay out of jail,' Margold says. 'He was a lecherous, talentless man of non-creative ability making $100,000 with 10 cents of imagination. He chased the women and was the exact stereotype of the pornographer that people want to hate, a fat, sweaty, vulgar, misanthropic, misogynist creep who thumbed his nose at the vice cops.'

But then, Margold has always felt money soils pornography's dirty reputation.

CHAPTER 7
CASTING CALL: THE GANG'S ALL HERE

Big casting call at Jim South's agency. The place is packed: directors, producers, manufacturers, distributors, performers, all mingling and posing.

There's voluptuous Lovette, naked as the day she was born. She's done 60 movies and 30 'box covers' since she arrived from South Bend, Indiana six months ago. Her first day in porno, she recalls, was pretty rough. She did both 'A' (anal) and 'DP' (double penetration) scenes. I cringe.

'Could you handle it?' I ask. She seems so easygoing.

'It was kind of a fantasy for me so it was all fine and dandy,' she says. 'I'm a workaholic anyway but I was really, really sore.'

Performers line up along the walls, waiting to be interviewed by directors sitting at tables in the various rooms. There's EZ Rider admiring the new talent. He's not working at Vivid anymore. He's working at *AVN* in 'the morgue'. Instead of asking how it ended, I ask how he got started.

EZ's real name is Peter Gallant. Once upon a time he was doing just fine working in New York's garment district. Then his company went broke. He lost his job, his wife left him. He tried selling drugs – his first client was an undercover FBI agent. With a little finagling and a lot of cooperation, he got his 15-year sentence reduced to six months. When he returned to society, he had no friends and, of course, no job: 'Everybody stayed away from me like I had bubonic plague.'

Finally he landed a job as a sales director, remarried, redivorced, moved to California, married wife number three named Lisa. Through work he met a wealthy distributor of porno.

'I'd like to do that!' Lisa blurted out.

'If you would, I would,' Peter said.

It doesn't work that way, the distributor explained. A girl is one thing, a guy is another. If she gets in, she can choose her partner and the guy might get a shot.

Lisa did two films before they even let Peter watch and that was on condition he keep his mouth shut, did not interrupt the scene or freak out when other guys did his old lady.

'If she's happy, I'm happy,' he said.

So, at 51, Peter became the rising star known as 'EZ Rider'. But what goes up must come down, followed by thoughts of 'What if I can't do it again?' which only made things worse. By the third film, EZ was told to pull up his trousers and consider mainstream acting.

Most guys would have thrown in the towel but EZ threw on his Levis and sleeveless jeans jacket, bought a whip and a Harley, and created his macho bondage-master look. It worked. In 1995, he won *AVN*'s 'Best Non-Sexual Actor in the Industry Award'. The chicks still adore him.

As we are talking, one starlet jumps into his arms. He pulls off her shirt. She loves it. He loves it. I love it. Even the discreet gentleman standing next to me loves it. Gentleman? In this place?

The guy's wearing a suit, a necktie and the crispest white shirt I have ever seen. He definitely doesn't look the porno type. His name is Peter Davy, owner of a new company called Nitro. Peter's from London, migrated to LA to start a Rolls Royce dealership, one thing led to another and now he sells 'adult erotic thrillers'. He still drives a Rolls Royce. He got it wholesale. He promises to put me in touch with Rodney Moore, a successful director with his own product line, and Nitro contract girl Houston. Just call his office. Easy as that. Whatever you say, Mac.

Funny. I expected a young, dating scene-type atmosphere. But there's a lot of older men here looking less the sleaze-ball type and more the pay-the-agent-fee-on-time type.

I meet Larry Ross, fifty-something, speaking with a heavy Brooklyn accent. He's tall, bald with a trimmed beard that gives him an Amish-Yiddish look. Larry doesn't look the porno type, either, but says he's been at it for 30 years, specializing in enemas and fetishes with a client list of 100,000 happy customers. He doesn't want to brag but brings to my attention an *AVN* feature on him entitled 'From Enemas to Empire'.

'Does fetish make good business?' I ask.

'People are very loyal, and tend to stay with you as long as you produce good product for them,' he says. 'They don't bounce checks hardly at all because they want to stay on the mailing list. They're very serious about what they do. It's their way of life. We try to listen to all their letters and that's how we learn what the people like.'

'Such as?' I ask.

'Take foot worship, for instance. When I started, all I thought about was a man kissing a woman's feet,' he says. 'But that's not the way it works. There are so many nuances. There's people who want bare feet, people who want stockings on, people who have black stockings, brown stockings, people in sweat socks, feet that smell, feet that don't smell, long toenails, no long nails, painted toenails, etc. High arch is important to many people. Showing the top of your feet and not the bottom of the feet causes a lot of anguish. It's very difficult to satisfy everyone every single time. They get very frustrated. We're in a way helping. We are giving them what they want. It's harmless. No sex is involved in fetish but we do get strange requests.'

'Do you enjoy your work?'

'If I didn't, I would not be here.'

Just then a woman walks by wearing a T-shirt with the message 'As a matter of fact, I do fuck on the first date.' Her girlfriend's reads 'Total Slut'. I smile. Larry smiles.

Lovette is still naked in the corner, effectively promoting herself on a less-than-shoestring budget. Her uncle owns a pyrotechnical company and she lets off steam by blowing things up, a skill she's incorporated into her strip-tease act.

Lovette is pretty laid back but trouble always seems to find her. After she recovered from her heavy intro to porno, she was shipped off to shoot in Amsterdam with Max Hardcore, a cowboy whose reputation lives up to his name. They went from canal boat to canal boat doing open-air sex scenes. The Hardcore brothers got into a fight and one of them threw the day's shooting cassette into the canal. The other brother broke open Lovette's new suitcase and used her fishnet stockings to dredge the waters and recover the tapes. She tells tales of stalkers, threats at strip clubs, confrontations with fans in the supermarket. She gained 15 stress-related pounds and was in dire straits, when she met Greg Dark, a director who thrives on a performer's misery and anxiety. Dark was impressed with her distress and starred her in *Sex Freaks*.

'It was the turning point in my career,' Lovette says.

In it, she did three sex scenes, one with four girls, one with six guys and her ultimate fantasy, eating while having sex. She was in porno heaven.

'I like weird porn,' she says. 'Normal boy–girl is just kind of boring.'

Here's another regular-looking guy, named Dick James, in his mid-50s, silver hair, chino pants, V-neck sweater. He owns a direct mail company, DOM. 'Direct Order Marketing,' he says, then whispers, 'It really stands for "Dirty Old Man".'

'There sure are some good-looking women here,' I say.

'Yup, the quality keeps going up,' he says. 'There are some girls in this business that you look at them and they almost take your breath away they are so beautiful. When I got started, the pretty ones were few and far between. Now, some are just naturally spectacular. Some girls are so pretty that they make your jaw ache.'

Dick came from a very religious family in Iowa. Since he's been out here, he's gone from religious to atheist, sexually repressed to sexually libertine.

'Some of the girls are rebelling that way, too,' he says. 'Others are just looking for an easier way to make more money.'

'Do you date them?' I ask.

'A guy like me doesn't have a lot of flash,' he says. 'I'm interested in them, but they're not interested in me. These women want the guy with long hair that looks like he's a member of a rock band: then he may live off her earnings. "Why don't you leave him?" I ask them. "I can't," they say. "I'm in love."'

'How do you know what will sell?' I ask.

'I've been in the business a long time and my interest in sex is very similar to the average American guy. All you have to do is look at what they spend their money on. Go pick up a copy of *Playboy* or *Penthouse* and look at the women in there. This is what the average guy wants. He says he wants somebody with intellectual substance, someone more mature and all this kind of stuff. Naw, what he really wants is some 19-year-old hardbody girl that is sexually fun and won't give him the encumbering baggage.'

'Do you ever send unsolicited sexual material to people?' I ask. He laughs. That's not how it works.

'I love it when the wife finds it in the mail before he does. Naturally, he claims it's something that somebody sent to him without his permission by someone renting the Kiwanis Club list. She wants to believe him, so she writes "Take my husband off your list. He does not like to receive this obnoxious, terrible, sinful material."'

'You don't think people just get bored by all this?'

'Sexual titillation is kind of like pizza, you eat all the pizza you can possibly eat in one sitting and you're so full you don't want anymore. You know you're not going to want more of it for about six months. About ten days later you think "You know, I could really use a pepperoni pizza..."'

Margold's office is packed. A shapely, short, brunette is sitting on the couch holding hands with a thin, tall young man with waist-length combed red hair. Rayveness and Red Boan are married, and just flown in from a small North Carolina town.

Rayveness has been busy all week, doing advertising photos for cinnamon-tasting 'Candy Ass - Hot Oil Rub', a new dildo-line box cover; this afternoon, she was cast in plaster of Paris to mold a plastic doll in her image.

'It has a vagina, an ass, hair, face, lips,' Red says. 'These things are fucking awesome. I was really surprised at the realism.'

'Are you concerned that they won't have to see you anymore if they can buy the doll?' I ask.

'No, they'll be watching one of my movies while doing my doll,' Rayveness answers.

The doll's sponsor, Adam & Eve, is also from North Carolina, one of America's most conservative states. Hollywood pornography's biggest mail-order catalogue distributor is based 2,000 miles away near Rayveness's hometown in North Carolina where the stuff is illegal to sell.

Rayveness was raised by a strict Dad who made sure she never had any fun. At puberty, she ran away and latched on to the first good-looking guy she met. At 15, *she* proposed marriage and had a baby by 16, the rural American norm.

While fulfilling her husband's wildest dream of two girls at once, she realized she liked girls. So the guest was invited to stay for a year. They made hot home videos for fun but after winning a television competition, they wondered how they could continue to make fun, easy money. She started sewing outfits for strippers but when she realized how much feature dancers were making, Cinderella the seamstress became Rayveness the stripper. She hit the road promoting her name, selling her Polaroids and knick-knack's, posing in magazines and coming to California from time to time to do porno flicks.

When not modelling box covers, doing oil ads, lying in plaster-of-Paris molds, stripping, performing in X videos or posing for pretty-girl magazine layouts, Rayveness fills in fan club orders, answers letters and is a volunteer firefighter in her hometown.

Rayveness and Red wander off into another room. I look around. A French woman is sitting topless on Margold's desk, seriously distracting him from guiding and counselling. Others are sitting on the couch, some are standing, undressing, dressing, posing for Polaroids. Margold seems particularly impressed by the woman on his desk. She crosses her legs provocatively. A photographer asks her for a nude pose; she objects, not because she's shy but because it would take 20 minutes to unlace her knee-high boots. She convinces the photographer to just shoot her topless. When I ask her, she tells me her name is Carol Rouge. Actually, she's Swiss. Her hobbies include tattoos, dungeons and witchcraft. What no yodelling?

CHAPTER 8
A MAN WHO HAS FOUND TRUE JOB SATISFACTION

Peter Davy has done exactly what he said he would do, and he's set me up with his 'contract girl', Houston, and Rodney Moore, a successful director with his own series.

I invite Rodney to my place because I just got a heavy-duty commerial kick-ass espresso machine. Actually, I would expect a big-name director to pick a fancy café but he seems happy to come over.

Rodney arrives, looking smart, in the head, that is. His sense of style is non-existent, poor college-student mode, worn jeans, cheap, zip-up sweatshirt and sneakers. He's tall, thin, with curly hair and thick glasses. He looks shy and speaks very softly and slouches slightly. Have an espresso, Rodney.

He sits at the dining-room table while I stand in the kitchen. My 'group handle' holds a double shot and I pack it down. I may have put in too much because it drips out too slowly.

Rodney doesn't actually direct a crew. He works alone. And he wasn't actually trained in film. I serve him a double shot. It's a little too strong. Actually, it's a lot too strong. I'll try again, later. Rodney's style is simple. He holds the camera while screwing the girl. Or vice versa. Call it gonzo porno.

What about lighting? Sound? Props? Casting? Minimal – it's all done in his apartment. He bypasses the cameraman, gaffer, boom operator,and everyone else and goes straight for the girl. This meek-looking guy calls the shots and decides what, when, where, how and who he gets to do it with. Inspired by *I Love Lucy*, Rodney does everything in his apartment, shooting in the living room with a few scenes in the kitchen or the bedroom. He works it on a closed set - alone. This guy has really beat the system.

Naturally, it's not as easy as it looks. The espresso that is. Try this one, Rodney, though I may have used too little coffee this time. Start from the beginning.

Rodney was a shy adolescent and kept to himself. Whenever his parents went away for the weekend, he and a buddy took out the 8mm projector and watched the porno films his parents hid in the library.

He moved to LA to make it big as a commercial musician, but didn't make it at all. He ended up in a telemarketing job, renting porno tapes after work. He preferred the reality and freshness of the emerging amateur movies to the

A MAN WHO HAS FOUND TRUE JOB SATISFACTION

slick, polished films with unapproachably beautiful models. His hero was 'Buttman', a very successful series about a guy who travels all over the world meeting sexy girls. The viewer becomes the camera and the film is shot in a well-planned, wandering, spontaneous style. You *become* Buttman. (I make a note: 'Meet this Buttman.')

Rodney spent so much money renting tapes he eventually figured he could do them too. He placed an ad in the *LA Express*, a sex ad newspaper. People responded and he taped a couple in a hotel room.

He had no idea what he was doing and he didn't have as much fun as he expected because he had to concentrate on running the camera. Fortunately, the couple knew more about making porno than he did: the guy gave him pointers about shooting still photos for the box cover and getting proof-of-age documentation.

When Rodney went to sell the video to a porno shop, the owner roared with laughter: 'This is the worst video I've ever seen!'

It was so bad, the guy bought it just to have a good laugh with his friends.

But for Rodney, it was one try, one sale. He had launched a new career. He did a few more before he realized something was missing: 'I wanted to get laid,' he says. So he held on to the camera while actually having sex. 'There's no way you can hold a camera steady but it has an intense look to it, a sort of documentary feel,' he says. 'The girls always had fun and there is just something thrilling about knowing that some girl is going to come over my house, walk into my dining room and just take off her clothes and I get to have sex with her.' Of course, you have to pay her.

Rodney was having a ball. Women answered his ads on a regular basis: young ones, old ones, thin ones, fat ones, women came over who wanted to get into show business, women who desperately needed money, women who just wanted to have fun. Some wanted too much money, others, none at all.

How can he be sure he's hired the right person for the job? Quite a dilemma, he admits. After all, when a singer applies for a job in a nightclub, she has to show she can sing. So, when a performer applies for a job in a porno movie, she should show she can, you know, do her thing. And once cast, don't forget the practice 'scene'.

'I won't deny that a handful of times, they either volunteered or just started to do it,' he says trying to conceal a grin. 'Usually, I'll have them come over and "test" them.' Girls who pass the test are paid $250 for half a day but if she's exceptional, she gets $300 - $350. Some girls get his day rate of $400. An oral scene pays $150.

For a while, the system worked great. But Rodney wanted more. After all, he was a successful director now and wanted recognition. So he started to feature himself in the movies and on the box covers and promoted his 'unique act'. Mother Nature, he realized, had endowed him with copious ejaculations: these became his trademark. The 'King of Cream' released a hit series, 'Creme de la Face'.

Each cassette is two hours long consisting of four or five scenes. Rodney shoots High-8 and edits on Beta-Cam. He photographs the box cover, duplicates the master and sells them to the distributor in a straight buyout, relinquishing all rights. Rodney has made about 200 boxes, which means he has had sex with between 300–400 girls, not bad for an average Joe Blow. For the soft-core market he shoots 'guerilla'-style: in a series called 'Fabulous Flasher' he shoots isolated scenes where a girl walks through a grocery store and pulls off her top, flashes some guy and walks out the door.

Despite having found his ideal lifestyle, he leaves Hollywood every year, just to get a breather. From the air, not the girls. Every summer he vacations in Seattle, America's coffee capital. He places his ads there while enjoying the cool air by Puget Sound. Rodney tests, rehearses, performs and films a holiday series called 'Pussy Fest of the Northwest', though he doesn't get nearly the variety of women up there, mostly strippers.

Most people I interview over a coffee relax as they get to know me but Rodney seems to be getting more shaky. Maybe another espresso will calm him down. Here's one for the road.

CHAPTER 9

KEEPING UP APPEARANCES: HOUSTON

Contract girl Houston has a sophisticated image. In her publicity photo, she wears a full-length mink in front of a white Rolls Royce. She probably has a Beverly Hills mansion, a banker for a sugar daddy and an Italian bodyguard for a paramour. *I* know how it works, though I've never really met anyone who really works it.

I pull up to an ordinary apartment in the Valley, pass the ordinary swimming pool and knock on an ordinary door. Houston's wearing a white jogging suit covering a not-ordinary body.

'I just ran four miles,' she says, walking into the kitchen. 'Do you mind if I

✳ Houston relaxes at home

smoke?'

'I figured you would be "kept" in Beverly Hills,' I say.

'Yeah, right,' she answers, grabbing a gallon Tupperware bowl filled with watermelon, cantaloupe and honeydew fruit salad. She hands me a tall orange juice.

The place is normal. Too normal. The dining room is a dining room. The living room is a living room, green and maroon couches color-coordinated with no-statement paintings. Nothing indicates wealth or exudes sex, except of course, Houston. The kitchen is full-size Americana, stocked cupboards, full fridge and packed freezer. Family pictures hang on the walls and the ground-floor terrace is filled with kids' bicycles. I peek in the bedroom. There's a four-poster bed: no ropes, pulleys or mirrors, just a mountainous pile of laundry.

'Everything's so normal,' I say, a little disappointed.

'Yeah, we were discussing that,' she says. 'We thought maybe it would be better for our image if we were screwing in the bedroom when you arrived.'

Houston lives with her daughter and has a live-in boyfriend, a porno performer named Brandon. He's clean-cut, handsome, healthy-looking. He could do normal mainstream, if he could act. Brandon grabs some quarters and goes off to do the laundry.

Houston was born Kimberly Halsey. She's a California blonde, 5'7", bops around the house to Madonna's *Material Girl*.

She dropped out in 11th grade, waitressed at Coco's, bought a car, hung out at the Red Onion. At 15, she took first prize at the Wednesday night bikini contest and came home with $500: 'Mom! I won!'

She eventually got her diploma, worked and saved and at 18 bought herself silicone implants and a new car. Her twin brother was an outgoing, 6'4" party animal jock who's now a cop.

After a bad marriage, she went home to Mother, had a baby daughter and started stripping at bachelor parties again and mud-wrestled at the Tropicana.

She met Daniel, a wealthy wine merchant, fell in love, flew off to Paris, learned how to shop in French: Chanel, Hermes, Dior. She lost her love, but kept the clothes, and became a personal secretary, making the boss look good at two-hour lunches and Friday afternoon parties. Still living with Mom, still bored as hell, she answered a personal ad promising 'money, travel and adventure.' She got a rich boyfriend and a three-karat diamond ring, lost the boyfriend but sold the ring

'I know how to work it,' she says with a wink.

She sank the money into a car and her current apartment. After a few 'B' movies, and waitressing in a bikini, she was introduced to Jim South who sent her to Nitro who booked her that day.

'I wasn't nervous at all,' she says. 'I was meant to do this.'

She's worked the gig into an annual contract, and become the sophisticated lady.

'Do your neighbors know what you do?' I ask.

'Not really,' she says. 'We're Mr and Mrs Smith. Outside of work, we keep extra discreet.'

She met Brandon on the set and chooses him when the director approves. But the porno market is down and dirty: if Houston wants to maintain her normal middle-class lifestyle, she must get less normal, more nasty and bring up her image.

'Bring up your image?' I ask.

'Yeah, everybody thinks that I am passé,' Houston says. 'My scenes are boring because I'm not passionate and I'm not shouting "Oh, fuck me harder!" But now I am saying stuff like that to bring up my image.'

Brandon's back from the laundry. 'The whole point is to get her name recognized and get her big,' he says. 'It's not that she wants to be this superslut whore, but it's gotta sell out there.'

'So now I'm getting raunchier,' she says cheerfully.

Houston started later than most performers so she has a more mature outlook making her less susceptible to parties and drugs.

'Whatever the usual problems, I don't have them,' she says. 'Mentally, I was prepared for this industry. It wasn't, "Oh my God, what am I doing?"'

And the money?

'I'll start saving again, once I get on the road, I will.' she says.

She'll be traveling two weeks a month as a 'Triple X Feature Dancer'. Dancing at a club, celebrity porno stars earn a minimum of $7,000 a week guaranteed plus thousands more in tips, 'lap dances' by the $20s, $50s, $100s per three-minute song, then they sell Polaroids, posters and T-Shirts autographed with a kiss and videos they buy at manufacturer's cost and sell at retail. They make at least ten times more than the local house dancer. A smart cookie can touch $15,000–$25,000 per week on the road.

'She saves all her money,' says Brandon, almost convincingly. 'She's buying certificates of deposit, investing it wisely and preparing for her child's future.'

Because women make more than men per scene, men have to work more gigs. That can lead to more conflicts in a relationship and is more stressful than people realize. Porno stars have more opportunity for jealousy, the same kind mortals worry about.

'Sometimes it was awkward, only because set sex is totally different from bedroom sex.'

How so?

'Emotions. If you're not loving, you can't get nastier, you can't do things you would do at home,' she says. 'It's easier to get nasty at home than on the set.'

'You can't get nastier on set?' I ask.

'You can, but it's hard to describe,' she says. 'You are at work and you're told to perform instead of performing when we want to. You can't be as passionate and say the things you want to say. You just don't want people to know that you're that way.'

What about home movies?

CHAPTER 10

TOTAL QUALITY CONTROL: STEVE HIRSH

It's Saturday and I'm waiting outside the locked Vivid warehouse for a noon appointment with Vivid owner Steve Hirsh. I want to find out what makes his world go round. Hirsh chose Saturday so we could meet without distraction. Who says Californians are lazy?

At 11:50, the door is still locked. I start to get fidgety. Is it the right day? The right time? I hate waiting.

At 11:58, a black Ferrari convertable purrs up the driveway. Steve Hirsh, the porno industry leader, grossing $20 million a year before the age of 35 gets out of the car.

'We still have time, right?' he says as he unlocks the door, picks up the newspaper and glances up at the wall clock, 11:59.

'Want something to drink?' he asks. Without waiting for a response, he goes to the mini-refrigerator in the back, pulls out two Perriers, slides one towards me, twists open his bottle, takes a swig, stretches his legs on the desk and leans back with time to spare. Twelve noon, precisely.

'I'm all yours,' he says.

Is this guy smooth or what? He's wearing a gray T-shirt, gym shorts and sneakers and is built like a wiry college wrestler. He has eyes like a hawk's. Behind him is a framed photo of his wife and two kids. His desk is completely clear.

Here is the mastermind behind the Vivid strategy. From Cleveland, where, it's said, the Hollywood porno distribution system began and still has deep roots. Steve's dad was in the 8mm stag film business and was one of the first to jump into video. Steve started up Vivid just as film was going out and video was coming in.

He's got both feet on the ground and plays it straight. He obviously likes his work and trusts his employees. I've been free to wander his premises.

'How come you're so trusting?' I say. I wouldn't even let an assistant touch my color slides.

'You will not be a successful company running a one-man show,' he says in a clear, smooth, methodical voice. 'You've got to let other people feel that they have a part of it. If I've made the decision to bring them in, then I believe that they are good at what they do. If I believe that, then it's better for me to step back and let them do their thing. That lets me run the company and look at

* Steve Hirsch at work on a Saturday

each company division to be sure it's profitable.'

From the start he wanted Vivid to have a glamorous high-quality look. He hired the best-known dancers and commissioned porno's most polished advertising campaign. The girls are fantasy figures – dreamlike and unapproachable.

'What is Vivid's niche?' I ask.

'Ultimately quality sells in movies and that works worldwide,' he says. 'If you look at any successful company in the general release market, they're successful because they are quality-oriented. As people reduce their movie budgets, we're increasing ours. Then our distribution network should be stronger because we have no competition with that type of quality. A conscious decision was how to best market and promote our company: when people thought of Vivid, they thought of the best girls, the best quality and the best packaging. That was always the goal.'

Vivid is known as one of the most respectable companies. They get the necessary permits, rent the necessary equipment, have insurance, have workman's compensation, the contract girls all have health insurance. All the shortcuts the small companies cut to survive, Vivid can afford to pay. They are in it for the long haul. As other companies jump on the bandwagon of fancy box covers, heavy advertising and contract girls, Vivid continues to refine its approach. For example, Vivid Girls can give input into the product: 'They have script, editing, and box cover input, as much as they'd like to give we want because happy girls make good movies. Good movies sell well. Movies that sell well generate revenue. Revenue allows us to produce better and better movies.'

But in this business, trouble is never too far away. In the 1980s, the US government tried to drive all the porno makers out of business. Virtually every company was fined and the owners threatened with jail. Almost everyone plea-bargained so they could get back to work. Vivid paid a million-dollar fine and softened up their material to avoid future trouble.

'From the beginning of time, sex has been considered taboo,' says Hirsh. 'It always will and there will be a certain segment of the population who does not agree with it. They have their right to believe that. We also have our right to believe that anyone over the age of 18 has the right to watch what they want in the privacy of their own home. Nobody is God out there and can tell somebody else what is morally proper. We'll always have to deal with that. This industry has been around for a long, long time. There are peaks and there are valleys and you have to be able to deal with that if you want to be in this business. There's always somebody who's going to say "What you are doing is wrong and I will take it upon myself to stop you from doing that." That's the way it is.'

We've talked for a good two hours without the slightest interruption. He hasn't moved except to swig his Perrier.

'What really motivates you?' I ask as we head out the door.

'I don't know,' he says mulling over his words. 'I've always been interested in maximizing my financial potential and this seemed like a good avenue to pursue that endeavour.'

As I'm loading my equipment into the trunk, the purring black Ferrari rolls away. Funny, I always thought love made the world go round.

CHAPTER 11
THE IVERSON RANCH BOYS

Vivid has invited me to meet their performers and cover their big-budget production, *Bobby Sox*. They fax a map and confirm it by telephone. They confirm the meeting with the production set manager, then reconfirm with me that it's confirmed with him. Everything's confirmed with everyone.

I head up beyond Porno Valley. Evening rush-hour commuters return home heading north on 405; a 15-minute ride turns into a two-hour nightmare. When it rains, it gets even worse. I arrive late, past shadowy rock formations and tall pine trees.

Iverson Ranch was once a sprawling place where great Hollywood films were shot throughout this century – the original *Tarzan*, *Ben Hur*, the entire 'Lone Ranger' series, Westerns with stars such as Gary Cooper, John Wayne and Ronald Reagan. But over the years, land values rose and the city encroached. Now a chain-link fence cages in the ranch from its suburban neighbours, the property a mere shadow of its earlier grandeur. On this very spot, where Charlton Heston once defied the Roman Empire in *Ben Hur*, Nikki Tyler now wrestles a green swamp monster in the porno flick *Bobby Sox*.

The place is quiet. While some of the crew prepare a shot, others are playing ping pong. In the garage, there's a table laden with potato chips and cookies, coffee and a cool-box of Cokes and juice.

'We've been expecting you,' says the production manager.

'Take me to your talent,' I chuckle. He doesn't laugh.

Vivid was the first porno company to sign guys to an annual contract. Steven St Croix and Jon Dough are proven reliable performers who represent a new generation that grew up with adult videos in the home. Making porno movies is no longer the symbol of rebellion that it used to be. Since porno's become legal, it has increasingly become a viable career option. As 'adult' becomes more commonplace, I don't see why their media exposure can't bring them untold opportunities including 'B' movies, foreign film productions, cable television films and, if they have the talent, maybe mainstream movie parts. And all the while, they date the sexiest chicks in the entertainment business. Even rock stars envy them. The reward is not the good life, it's the great life.

I'm betting these two guys have media savvy and will enthusiastically greet me because they'll know the importance of a good press. I'm in ideal circumstances because I'm the only journalist there. Hopefully we'll have time to talk after they've finished with their sex scenes.

I spot them lounging on a couch, watching a cowboy movie. I flip open my notebook, click my pen, clear my throat. Nobody looks up. I introduce myself. Nothing. I greet Jon Dough. He won't budge. I greet St Croix. He's even worse. I return to Dough. 'Me again,' I smile through my teeth.

'OK, what do you want to know?' he asks while staring at the TV.

'Let's go elsewhere,' I say.

'Is this really necessary?' he frowns.

We go into a hall made to look like a tacky hunting lodge with fake antelope heads mounted on the walls. We drag over two cinder blocks for chairs.

Jon namedrops a couple of European cities he visited on a shoot. Go ahead, say them again. He does.

'Wow! Prague! You get to travel! How lucky! It must have been great!' I say, feigning fawning. Suddenly, I'm back in Prague, when the Wall came crumbling down, downing Becherovkas at Karlovy Vary with a recently liberated maiden named Tereza. What do these porno stars know about adventure? Then I'm back at the ranch, and the fake hunting lodge. I hold my tongue – if I burst his bubble, I blow my interview.

Eventually, he lightens up, the prick.

'I'm not a big working stiff,' he says. He's lazy and lacks ambition, otherwise he'd be doing something else. I soon realize this Jon Dough is not pretentious and doesn't take himself seriously at all. Maybe he's not a prick after all.

Jon's not motivated by movie making, has no dreams of glamour. He's not rebelling against a strict upbringing. He didn't run away. He's not making a social statement. No wonder he avoids interviews. In fact, he's not even an exhibitionist, can't stand most directors or guys watching him perform.

'Why, can a director affect a guy's performance?' I ask.

'And how. The best part about working for PT is that he never gets in the way,' he says. 'He knows when to *not* direct. And he keeps the crew to a minimum. Some directors invite their friends so it's like putting on a theater performance,' he says. 'You know, "Come on, pull up a chair and watch the monkeys mate."'

Before porno, Jon worked as a bartender at night. By day he took acting lessons.

'But *that* shows ambition' I say.

'Come on. I just went to meet chicks,' he says. 'Working in a bar. Working in porno. Same thing.'

There's no reason to bother with mainstream. Mainstream values only bring trouble, especially with girlfriends. Few women want their man going with others. Fewer want everyone to know it. Jon was sure his girlfriend would never approve. He wanted to keep her and his lifestyle, especially since he clearly had porno potential. What could he do?

He lied.

'Where did you go?' she'd ask.

'A modelling job,' he'd answer.

When they passed an adult video store, she wanted to rent a porno tape. 'Can we watch one together?' she giggled. 'I never watch those videos,' said Jon. 'No porno in our house, man. Are you kidding me?' He pushed her along before she noticed him on the box cover.

Then, one night, between tokes on a joint and swigs from a big bottle of wine, Jon was preparing a romantic dinner for two, when Annabel entered with something behind her back.

She slammed a magazine on the table and opened it up to a full-page picture of him, his big dick sticking out, a girl on her knees at the end of it. What a prick.

'I can explain everything,' Jon said. 'Now *look*. If you look at these pictures...'

She looked at the pictures.

'Imagine the nerve of them using such an old picture of me,' he said. Big mistake.

'That shirt I bought for you,' she cried.

'Look at these pictures,' he said. Once more she looked. 'Now, the girl never *touches* my dick. Never touches my dick. Do you see any penetration, ever?' Jon was impressed with his own performance. Who says porno guys can't act?

'No, but your dick is so hard," she sobbed. "How did your dick get so hard?'

Fighting hard not to laugh, he said he used some special lubrication. She didn't buy it.

'Look, it was just a soft-core layout,' he explained. 'It's not like I *liked* her or *talked* to her or anything.'

They got through the evening but things went from bad to worse. Finally Jon ended it.

'We split up' he said. 'I said it was all my fault.'

'And then you left?' I ask.

'Hell no. It was my place so she was the one who had to pack her things.'

Gentleman Jon learned his lesson and stuck with pretty porno stars, like Mona Demoan. Before signing a contract with Vivid he worked up to 25 days a month, a different girl each day. He didn't have very much free time. Now that his workload has eased, he can do other things.

'I really should be using this time to develop other projects,' Jon says. Right. 'But I got to tell you, man. It's great. Come on. What a fucking ego boost. It's every guy's fantasy.'

I've read various explanations for why guys get into porno work: to prove adequacy, a need for approval, a social death wish, a decline in hometown jobs forcing them to the big cities to find work. Yeh, yeh, yeh. In truth, there's only one reason. They do it to date the girls. They tolerate the work for the party afterwards. Hot action with sexy chicks. A bunch of lucky pricks.

We head back to St Croix, who's shifted to a different couch, and is now ensconced in Walkman headphones. He's wearing a black leather motorcycle jacket and has a look that says 'Stay away.' I do.

In the other room, there's PT. In porno, PT's revered, the only successful mainstream performer to actually prefer porn by choice. He's worked *out there*. A black sheep in the family, he is rumoured to be heir to one of the wealthiest trust funds in America, rumoured to be a classical pianist, rumoured to be a fine-tuned pervert, the only trisexual in the business. He'll try anything. Everyone in the industry looks on him with awe.

There he is, sprawled out on a love seat, one arm over the back, one leg over the armrest. He looks like he's either waiting for his close-up or for someone to peel him a grape.

'This is blue-collar work,' he says. 'They're certainly not actors really, or artists. And if you go in expecting to make movie magic that day, you might be disappointed. But if you go in with the attitude that you're a blue-collar worker and you're coming to do your job, period, sometimes you're pleasantly surprised. It is amazingly like making movies.'

'Can the director affect the guy's performance?' I ask.

'They're what we call "welders". And a true welder, or "woodsman", won't be deterred by the style of the director, whether the director is presentational or representational, the difference being where the director gets his hands on everything and stops and starts and stops and starts and he wants exactly what he has in mind or where the director is more into the Zen of film making and just says "Show me what you've got." The pussyass actors who you probably talked to, who said they were affected by the style of the director, are exactly that. They are not true welders. A true welder, they don't give a *fuck* about the director or his style...'

'Or the journalist,' I add.

'Or the journalist. Fuck the journalist. It's that "fuck you" attitude that serves them well. A true woodsman doesn't give a *fuck* about the director's style. He does good work.'

He's still sprawled like a starfish.

I run into the guy in charge of editing who asks to be called, 'Evan Daniels'. Who would have thought that an invisible, behind-the-scenes editor-type would use a stage name?

College-educated Evan has a wife and kid. He's a straight kind of guy but mainstream was just too straight. Too regimented, he says. Call him a refugee from the 9 to 5. He's not into porno but here he can breathe. He credits Steve Hirsh, says his boss knows how to cut workers slack. Evan's a big fish in a little pond and likes it that way. He can make suggestions and they get implemented. For example, when he arrived, master tapes had working titles which were usually changed. Good luck finding them. Evan instituted a numbering code so every video can now be easily found. He started as a director's assistant, now he runs the editing department. He used to edit films of couples going up the aisle for $50 a day. Now, he edits Nikki Tyler going downtown for $150 a day.

'So what makes these guys so special?' I ask.

'We have people like Jon Dough and Steven St Croix because they can chew gum, walk at the same time and get it up in front of a crew of 25 people. That's the end of their credentials.'

Come again?

'Don't misunderstand,' Evan says. 'I have a profound respect for the guys. Not just anybody can do this. It's a rare breed that can pop on cue. We have to get the camera guy, the sound guy, the lighting guy and the props together in one room all at one time, ready to go. We can't be sitting there, "waiting for wood", as we call it in the industry. It doesn't matter if he can't talk. If he can't talk, don't give him any lines.'

Was that once called the strong, silent type?

'Let me relate this to golf,' Evan says. 'Some of your best golfers are the people that don't think that much. They just get up there and hit the hell out of the ball and they get it in the hole. I think some of your best porno actors, they just get up there, bam! It's not too complicated for them. If you have a guy who's the sensitive, intelligent type, they would be like, "Wow, all these people are around me and they're counting on me to do it." Instant wilt. I think if you're a little bit off up here, you're right on down there.'

Meanwhile, the crew and performers have moved outside, only to watch a complicated rig mounted on the side of a red Cadillac convertible take more time than anticipated.

'You know, for the price of renting this Cadillac, we could have shot three anal scenes,' PT says. 'Which do you think the audience would prefer?'

CHAPTER 12
A DAY OUT AT TRACK TECH

The following morning the drive up to the Valley is a breeze. Going against traffic, I'm headed for Track Tech Studio. As soon as I open the door, there's St Croix. Before I can say 'Not you again', he greets me with a sincere smile and a hearty handshake.

Wearing glasses, a maroon long-sleeved shirt, chino pants and loafers, today he's playing an intellectual drunk returning home to a sexually demanding wife, played by Anna Malle, renowned for being '100% hot, 100% of the time'. They're working with a new production manager, planning sexual positions and discussing the script.

'She's supposed to dominate you,' he says. 'I want her to slap you around.'

'Listen, I'm acting and directing and I got to get slapped around?' St Croix protests. 'I can't handle it today. How about verbal abuse?'

'We can go with that,' the manager says and off they go.

The studio has a number of sets so several companies can shoot simultaneously. Vivid 'pretty girl'-style performers in Barbie-doll curls mix with inner-city street-style girls in oversized, colorful sweats; a single guy with a high-8 camera chases a Scandinavian blonde with incredibly long legs and an incredibly short skirt in one door and out the other.

Track Tech is happening, the most professional studio in town. Every porno company that can afford it shoots here. It has fully air-conditioned sound studios and a large prop warehouse. Everything is pristine clean.

Upstairs there's a hallway with couches, a snack table, a counter with bar stools, a make-up room with a wall of properly lit mirrors, showers, TV lounge, full kitchen, a well-stocked linen closet. Everyone mingles freely. I make myself at home and meet this big happy family. Vince Voyeur is watching

A DAY OUT AT TRACK TECH

television. Bobby Vitale uses the pay phone: 'Hi honey, I won't be home for dinner. We have to work late tonight.'

More of the regulars are here: Wicked Pictures owner Steve Orenstein, Metro general manager Tony Cleary, talent manager Lucky Smith, international rights negotiator Todd Blatt, porno starlets galore of various shapes in various stages of dress and undress. Here it is, Ground Zero, Pornoville, USA. Track Tech Studio is owned by VCA, porno's largest company, owned by Russ Hampshire, reported to be the most powerful guy in the porno world.

Outside on the sunny patio, Tony Cleary introduces me to his contract girl, a voluptuous brunette with sad eyes.

'My name is Shayla Foxxx,' she says.(Can you hear those extra Xs?) 'I was born "Anutza Herling". I am an adult entertainer and I'm very good at it. I had a killer body at 13 and after that it all went downhill.' She still looks good to me. Sitting opposite me, she's wearing a tight button-down shirt with open cleavage and seems very warm and sensual.

A Puerto Rican raised in Chicago in a very religious strict family, Shayla was not allowed to go out, or have her own friends. Life was no fun.

Trouble really began around the time Mother Nature endowed 13-year-old Shayla with her killer body and nowhere to prey.

Mom caught Shayla using a phone-sex line, on her knees in the dining room playing with herself. Mom shipped Shayla off, now 14, to live with her grandparents in Puerto Rico. She skipped school, got herself a 'loser' boyfriend. A 'loser' is a guy any sexy girl falls for. 'Why?' I ask.

'Well, they have more time to spend with you,' she says. 'Men with responsibilities don't have time to give you the attention you need. I need attention."

Of course, losers aren't called losers for nothing. When she broke it up, trouble followed. Dad sent her a plane ticket home.

'What are you doing here?' were Mom's first words.

Shayla got pregnant, had a kid, went on welfare; after three months she gave the baby up for adoption. 'It's a lot more than I could have done for him at 17,' she says sadly.

After a few stints as a dancer, she got a sugar daddy named Louie, who owned a string of chicken restaurants. What Louie didn't spend on her she bought for herself.

'The money I went through was ridiculous when I was young. Ridiculous,' she says. Everyone told me, "Put it away. Save it." But I didn't know any better. It was a good time.'

A DAY OUT AT TRACK TECH

Eventually she made her way to California where she found this Metro porno contract.

'What did I just do?' Shayla worried after her first scene. 'What am I going to tell people when they find out? What will my family say?' She was always the family's black sheep. They knew she danced but never discussed it. Now, Shayla's adventures are coming soon to a video shop near them and she lives with a sense of shame, but just a little sense of shame.

'*I love my job*, okay?' she says. 'I like it when there's all these people around and they watch. That's what does it for me. It's a taboo I'm breaking and I *like* being a bad girl. Anything you're not supposed to do is where I have the most fun.'

'By the way, how is sex on the job?' I ask.

'When you're at work you can't be intimate, you can't touch and hug and stuff. On the set, the crew will say, "Let's get finished, so we can have lunch,"' she says. 'When you're at home, you do whatever you want.'

Todd Blatt is a sophisticated guy. I can tell by his colourful Italian shirt, expensive pleated trousers and the right Italian shoes. The package says, 'Showbiz American at Cannes'. The gold chain resting on his hairy chest matches his gold-framed glasses and his gold Rolex watch. He looks older and more savvy than his 27 years. With black hair, Todd Blatt looks Italian macho but he is Valley Jewish.

Todd is second generation in the business – his dad was a porno publisher and distributor. Todd's one-man company, Antigua, specializes in selling international video, cable television and hotel-chain movie rights. While most producers shy away from international business, he thrives on it.

His office is located on the premises of VCA, his largest client. He likes to work and loves to make money. His Ferrari indicates he loves to spend it as well. Despite his evident cosmopolitan flair and international business savvy, his vocabulary is pure blue-collar construction worker.

We're standing in the hall when the leggy, mini-skirted blonde comes running by again laughing, being chased by the same guy with the high-8 camera. That's Todd's brother. For years, Todd has been providing porno companies with marketing reports on foreign buyer's needs. They want new faces, the more the better. For years his clients had ignored his advice. Finally, Todd and his brother set up Snatch Productions, and produced a series called 'Pussyman Auditions' specializing in new faces, and new bodies.

Todd's mainstream film contacts ask so often about the porno girls that he's convinced they have mainstream potential. The problem is the performers.

They sell themselves short and create their own problems. 'They're so beautiful,' he says. 'They carry themselves well. They walk nice. Yet, if you talk to them they act like they're ugly, fat, nobody likes them. You look at them and go "You're fucking crazy. Look at you." But they don't see the same person that you or I see."

'Do their boyfriends all "manage" their careers?' I ask.

'I see them when they come to the sets,' he says. 'You make the checks out to them. The girl's out in the back humping and they're collecting the check. A lot of times you make the deal with the guy. A lot of pretty girls, too, that don't need to be doing this.'

Years ago, it was common for the man to work all week and hand over his paycheck to the wife who managed the household finances and gave him an allowance. The typical porno relationship, it could be argued, advocates similar family values, only in reverse. The woman works all week and hands over her paycheck to the man who manages the household and gives her a small allowance, etc.

Women in this business are notorious for spending all the money they earn, but a closer look at a man's household finance management habits in sunny Southern California will note that the save-for-a-rainy-day policy has been replaced by a live-for-today mentality. Therein lies a key difference between yesterday's mainstream world and today's porno community.

'It's not a negative,' Todd says. 'Any time you speak to any of the girls they're very happy with their situation. None of the girls walk in and say, "Oh, my fucking husband's taking my check." Every one of the girls is very happy. Nobody's putting a gun to their heads. Let them do what they like. For them and their life, that's a great scenario. For me and my wife, it wouldn't work like that. It's not a negative situation in the business and I've been around it since I was a kid.'

'Something happens here,' he says. 'If all day long people are fucking, then it's gotta to be okay. These girls all think that they are "actress-models". If the card said "Cocksucking Whore" it would mean the same thing. That's the bottom line. There's not a girl back there right now, if you offered her $1,000 to suck your dick wouldn't line up to do it. I don't care who walks in. If they are in this fucking studio, they'll suck your dick for $1,000. I don't care if it's the girl serving food who says she doesn't do it. If she's in this building and watching sex, something happens in their minds which makes them feel it's okay. Look at my brother. He has a successful company. He drives a brand new Mercedes. He has money in the bank. He has a house. Right now, if we go downstairs, I betcha he's fucking the girl in the video. He's single, why not?

He's living the American dream.'

That reminds him. Todd has to run downstairs to make sure his brother is working the American dream, not just living it.

In the kitchen, there's a pretty, coffee-coloured woman wearing a Fat Albert T-shirt and crunching on a green apple. She's wearing no makeup and her hair's done up in curlers. She's tall and slender and built more like a fashion model than a porno performer.

'What do you do?' I ask.

'Fuck,' she explains.

A woman of few words. Her stage name is Jasmine Pendavis.

'Has this work affected your outside life?' I ask.

'Now that times have changed, it's getting more acceptable,' she says. 'But it's a strain on my personal relationships. I'm lying to someone right now, saying I'm not working when I am because he couldn't handle it. I told him, "I'm going on a shoot. I did all the sex in the videos already. I just have to do the box covers."'

She gives a big, naughty, fun-loving laugh. Jasmine has her alibi down pat. She tells them that all the films released in the future were shot in the past. She's given it all up for you, whatever your name might be.

'Why do you have to lie?' I ask.

'They all want a freaky girl, but they can't handle the repercussions of it. Every guy's fantasy is to find a woman, that will do everything he wants 'em to do. When they actually find somebody like that, they get freaked out and scared because they don't know how to handle it. It's like, "Great! It's everything in one package! I like her too much! But I can't like that kind of girl! I want to marry her but I can't marry that kind of girl!" Guys get really sprung when you're in the industry.' Nevertheless, she says she's dating an entertainment lawyer.

'Hey, aren't you supposed to be dating a creep that takes all your money?' I ask.

'Who me? Fuck no, man. You must be crazy. A lot of girls do that, but I want lots of money and fame and fortune and I don't need no jackass pretty boy on my coat tails unless he's got just as much money as me, you know what I mean? All the people in this business go to after hours parties and I don't understand it. Why would you want to fuck somebody for free that you can get paid to fuck later on? It doesn't make sense to me. I don't want to fuck these guys off the set. To me, it's work.'

'How much does work bother you?' I ask.

'Sometimes I think, "Girl, what the fuck is wrong with you? Why do you do that stupid shit?" You know what I'm saying? And the other side is not caring too much. Doesn't care at all. I separate work and home.'

'Which is better?'

'At home. I like to have my windows open. I'm an exhibitionist. I enjoy being watched. It excites me.'

'Can you tell me when your next performance at home is scheduled?' I ask.

'Every night! Go to 1800 Cherokee and look up at the window right facing the front building!' she says.

I notice that Jasmine has a pierced tongue. Does she have anything else pierced hidden somewhere? And 'does it work?' I ask.

'There is no stimulation that goes on while you're walking or any of that stuff,' she says. 'In fact, when you masturbate it can be kind of annoying. It gets in the way of the vibrator. It's ornamental, a great visual aphrodisiac. Other than that, man, the clitoral ring is nothing. But for guys, they dig that.'

She laughs. 'This is a fun conversation,' she says. 'Because it's not about blow jobs.'

Before heading downstairs to the studio area, Jasmine and I make plans to meet the following evening, to watch her perform on location. On the set there is a break in the action. Director Mr Marcus, wearing a clean new sweatshirt and baseball cap, smells a journalist and makes himself available.

I'd read an article saying more guys go into porno who might have stayed in their hometown factory jobs had the jobs stayed there. 'Tell me, did you get into porno because there were no jobs available?' I ask Marcus. He doesn't know what I'm talking about. Mr Marcus was a truck driver hungry for porno-chick nookie.

"I would go into these bookstores, pick up a magazine and I'm saying "The bitch look good. She's fine." I get these thoughts in my head. I'm looking at these pictures and thinking, "How do I get into this?" I mean, find some phone number, find some people. I want to see them. I want to be a part of this.'

One set is the inner-city sex scene. Before filming begins, we press photographers get to shoot the models, who'll pose for us. While we're waiting for our chance to take pictures, I meet a guy named Floyd Hardwick, a regular on the porno beat. Floyd attends as many shoots as possible, working with two beat-up cameras, one of them held together with Scotch tape. He publishes a low-brow niche magazine called *Skin Trade* combining porno sex and rock stars. Of course, Floyd hopes to get involved somewhere along the line.

'I photograph all the women,' he says. 'I try to get them to pose for me for as little as possible, if I have to lie to them, whatever.'

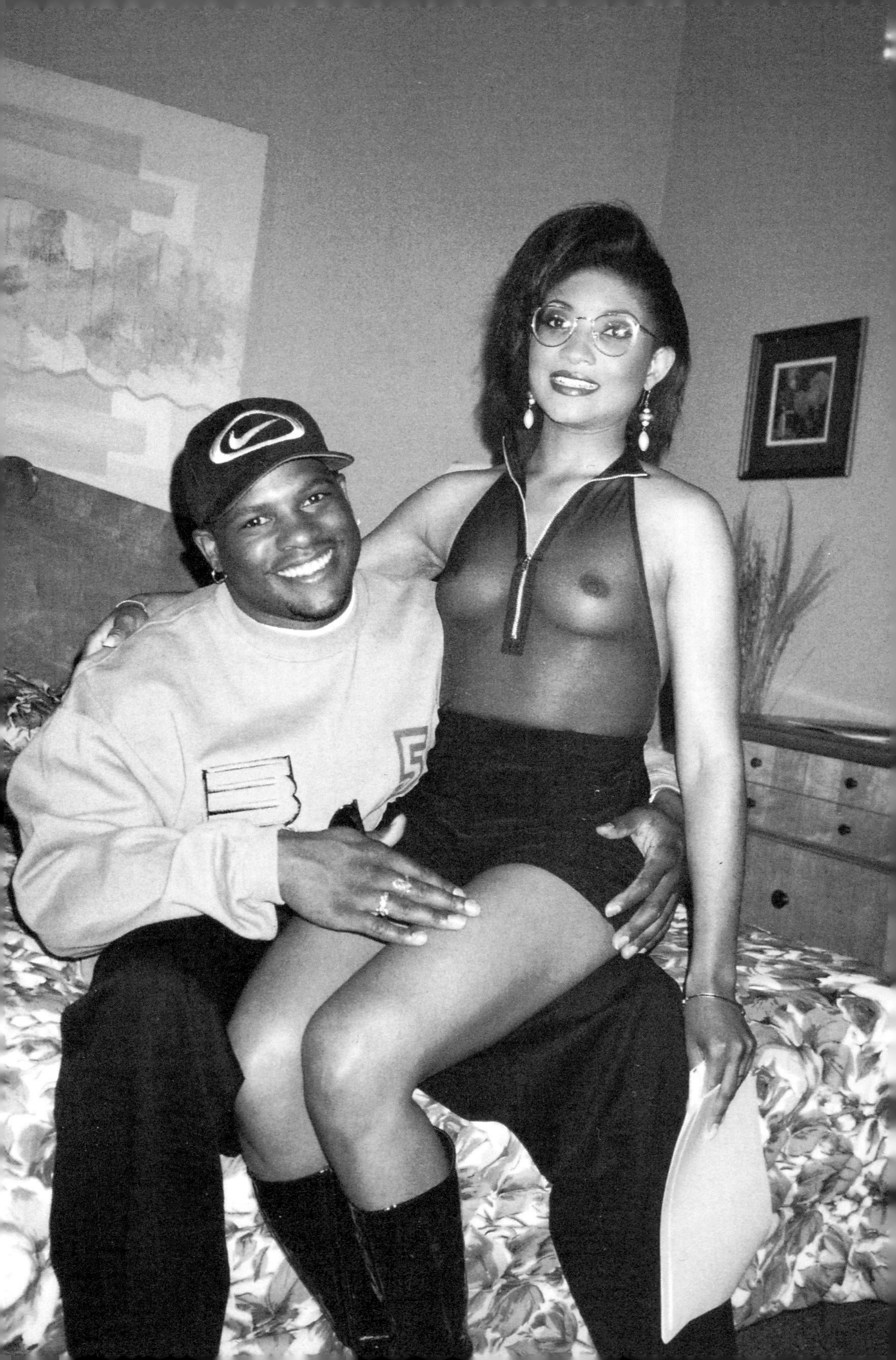

A DAY OUT AT TRACK TECH

✱ Mr Marcus and Jasmine

'What's a lie?' I ask.

'I tell them I'll pay them,' he says.

Floyd does everything in-house, shooting girls in the living room, processing in the bathroom and hopefully developing something in the bedroom. Floyd's not picky, any babe will do. *Skin Trade* offers tips about high living on a low budget, such as a recent article entitled 'How to Get Laid with Very Little Money'.

At lunchtime I meet St Croix. We go outside on the patio where it's supposed to be private but he's constantly interrupted by staff asking questions.

He asks a production assistant to bring him lunch. The assistant returns with a chicken burrito, refried beans, fried rice, salad and soft drink. Nobody offers me nothing. St Croix digs right in. I'm about to start the interview when St Croix sinks into his burrito.

St Croix gulps down the refried beans.

He wolfs down the fried rice.

He's obviously concerned only with his lunch. I check my watch. I'm out of here.

CHAPTER 13

MY WAY OR THE HIGHWAY

Performer/director Ron Hightower is king of the 'black' porno market. He lives in the Hollywood foothills (finally I interview someone who actually lives in Hollywood!) and I've an appointment to meet him.

A football player-sized guy lets me into an apartment filled with things that single guys buy: a wall-size home entertainment center, large-screen television, video tapedecks, a stereo with lots of lights, speakers sufficient for a rock concert and a pool table in place of a dining table. A young man is practicing on a keyboard in what is normally a bedroom.

The big guy flops down on the couch, watching a porno flick on the large-screen television. I ask to see Ron's video list. Without saying a word or taking his eyes off the on-screen action, he gets up, picks up a couple of huge albums, dumps them on the floor in front of me and flops back down on the couch. Each album is filled with scores of flattened box covers.

Is Ron here by any chance?

After a while, the phone rings. It's Ron checking his messages. The big guy tells him there's someone here who says he has an appointment. I'm handed the phone.

'Oops, sorry man. I forgot,' Ron says. He's on his way.

Generally speaking, the porno-making community is not too comfortable with outsiders, mainstream, other races, foreign accents and things like that. Black productions are sponsored and distributed by white companies but there are virtually no integrated sex scenes. In fact, some states might prosecute them as obscene, consensual lovey-dovey relationships or not. So, usually, black does black and white does white.

Ron arrives. He's a big guy too, with a shaved head. He's known as a ladies' man but his place is more like a clubhouse than a bachelor pad. He gets me a Heineken and himself a Coke. We go out on to the balcony, which is littered with barbell weights the size of manhole covers. He straddles the bench. I grab a chair.

'Do you have a personal philosophy?' I ask.

'It's my way or the highway,' he says. I believe him.

Hightower came from the mean streets of New York. Upon relocating to Hollywood, he became one of the industry's star studs and within eight months started directing low-budget but successful films. The manufacturer pays him a lump sum, in advance, thank you, and Ron delivers the product. The end. Ain't no such thing as production-cost overruns like mainstream Hollywood. He keeps whatever he saves and loses whatever he spends. That's how it works. He stars himself, finds the talent and coordinates the shoot, gets no royalties and relinquishes all rights upon delivery. The sponsor absorbs the cost of the box cover artwork, as well as printing and advertising costs which can run as high as making the movie.

'Do you remember your first video?' I ask.

'I try to forget!' he says.

After Ron shot his first scene, he prepared for the next but left the camera running by mistake. When they were ready to roll again, he pressed the button, which shut off the camera. He then directed the entire sex scene without a break. The guys delivered the money shot. Everyone was spent, smoking a cigarette, relaxing and ready for a nap when Ron realized he only shot the floor. Ron recalls rebooking, reshooting, repaying the performers to return the following day. He never made that mistake again.

'Being a director is like being a baby-sitter. Everybody's got a problem,' he says. 'Everybody comes into the business thinking sex is easy. Girls on the set change their mind, have flashbacks of home. They miss their mother. Assistants are unreliable. Guys talk rude to the girls, then can't perform.'

'I tend to be hard on the guys because they come in here with no respect for the industry. They talk all this crap and the minute the lights go on, "Oh, hold on! Hold on! I'm not ready yet. See, yo man, I'm, I gotta go now? Let me go last, man. Let me go last. You know what I'm saying? The floor is green. You see, my floors is brown. It's fucking with my head,"' he says, mimicking his performers.

'It's hard for a lot of guys, especially for black males.' It goes without saying that Ron is the rare exception. 'Black males have more "pride" about themselves, more of an ego. Bottom line is "you gotta be cool." You know what I'm saying? You can't be cool when it comes to sex. Sex to me is one of our animal instincts. And you can't tame what was meant to be wild. It's just not natural.'

'Believe it or not, a lot of these performers are lousy behind closed doors,' he says. Again, there are exceptions. Hightower's performers have real sex, study no scripts and memorize no lines. He tells the girl to yell louder if he needs a bigger orgasm. No problem. Hightower finds performers who are not self-conscious, not afraid of looking stupid. And while they enjoy themselves and entertain their audience, society scorns them, the porno industry, too, I might add.

'I started writing scripts but then I threw them away because nobody can act in this goddamn industry anyway. It's pathetic. It's a heart attack,' he says. He doesn't watch porno for the dialogue. He fast-forwards that stuff. So do most people. So he cuts that part out. 'A lot of people appreciate that,' he says. Hightower sticks to normal scenes the viewers can imagine doing at home. Forget *101 Sex Positions*, he's strictly a couch and bed man.

Hightower gets calls from celebrities and professional athletes wanting to talk in person, not over the phone. They take him to lunch and want it kept private. Some prefer talking to a performer rather than to a therapist. They want to enjoy things, not discuss their subconscious motivations. They know a porno star has already done it and won't be condescending.

He believes that being a porno star involves a lot of stress for a woman. Guys take it lightly because it's easy for them. But not necessarily women, despite earning double or triple men's pay. Few in the industry seem willing to recognize this. As macho as Hightower appears, he is one of the few guys sensitive to this issue.

'You got to remember, no matter how big the star is, it's really somebody who wants to be involved in doing other things,' he says. A big-name performer with a larger-than-life reputation goes into clubs, gets noticed and recognized. She feels on top of the world. Tomorrow, she's back on her hands and knees paying for the groceries.

Everyone thinks they make good money. Say a respected performer made $5,000 for a week's effort. Not bad. At that rate, a porno star would have to work 50 weeks a year for 40 years to make Demi Moore's cut for six weeks of revealing nothing topless dancing in the mainstream box-office bomb *Strip Tease*.

'It gets depressing. I've seen girls freak out,' Ron says. 'They go through so many head trips.' Added to that, most don't save a dime.

Yet, porno stars are looked upon as the icons of sex; the viewer sees them as godlike creatures because they seem so free sexually and live out the viewers' wildest fantasies.

'It's funny how fantasy, porno, distorts reality,' he says. 'A girl screws in the parking lot, she's wild. Put a camera on her, she becomes a larger-than-life sex goddess, all because it was videotaped.

'Do you think this attention affects them?' I ask.

'These people have obviously never been captain of their own tag team when they were children,' he says. 'You know what I'm saying? They were never the ones who were chosen first to play basketball. And now, all of a sudden, they're seen all over the world. Now, they're patted on the back. These are people who let it go to their heads and it's obvious to see why.'

'You got to remember, this whole industry is built on low self-esteem. This whole business is built on people who thought they couldn't make it in the real acting world, who thought they could never make it as models, who thought they would never become film directors. It's so open and opportune. They did the first thing they could to get famous. That's why they're doing it. If anybody says they're doing it for the money, trust me, there are other ways of making money. They let the money be the excuse. Everybody wants a piece of fame. They want a piece of what it's like to be somebody. Porn is the vehicle for that.'

FAX

March 19, 1996

Dear Willoughby,

I've sent you about 50 pages of work today with some artwork. Can you read Macintosh format? Do you have a Fedex account number?
In addition I've got about another 50 pages that my secretary will deliver to me today. I'll send this on to you once I've whipped it into shape.

Last week I was watching some television violence to take my mind off the sex business. The news report said that the LA Police Department has the largest air-borne law enforcement agency in the world. It's called ASTRO – Air Support to Regular Operations – and has 15 helicopters. The best are French-made, the six-seater Aerospatial A Star Model AS350B, top speed 270 kph, maximum ceiling 5 kilometres, and equipped with FLIR – a heat-reading Forward Looking Infrared device. At night police can see people hiding in the bushes or hopping over fences. They've got gyro-stabilized 10x50 binoculars which enable them to read a license plate at a thousand feet, and a 'Night Sun', a 30,000,000-candle-power flashlight. ASTRO doesn't land or shoot from the air: once the suspect is spotted, police cars surround the area, then send in the canine unit or shoot suspects with the 'bean bag', a shotgun that fires a non-lethal round powerful enough to knock anyone out of a tree. After last night, I can confirm it's all true...

Hope all's well with you>

Best regards,

[signature: Harris Goffin]

Harris

CHAPTER 14
DOWN IN THE ALLEY

The night after meeting Hightower, I go up to Jasmine's place. Several intimidating-looking black guys are sprawled out on the couch; they don't look like they are waiting for someone to peel them some grapes. Then I realize it's the same guys I met at Track Tech, including the director, Mr Marcus.

I Love Lucy is playing on two televisions in two rooms. The place is a mess.

'Damn, girl, how do you get your place so clean?' Mr Marcus asks Jasmine.

'Shut up,' she snaps.

Finally, after waiting an hour for Jasmine to get ready, we head out in convoy over the Hollywood Hills.

The story we'll be filming tonight is about two detectives having sex with a hooker in an alley.

One of the performers, Edward, is a regular Joe who works days as an hospital EKG technician.

'Can you separate the two, your day job and porno moonlighting?' I ask.

'Of course, I can,' he says. 'Otherwise, I'd lose my job.'

We take the 101 from the San Fernando Valley into Little Tokyo in downtown Los Angeles, ducking into an alley in an industrial area. The guys roll a dumpster into the middle of the alley to discourage any curious patrol cars. There's a guard dog playing with a torn ball on one side of the alley. On the other side, a chain-link fence surrounds a scrap metal junkyard and a small warehouse. A pick-up truck down the lane bothers the cameraman. He wants it cleared but who's going to knock on the warehouse door at midnight and ask them to move it? A group of black guys might look intimidating. They want to send Jasmine but I suggest her miniskirt and knee-high boots might also send the wrong message. They want to send me because I'm white but since we're in Little Tokyo, I suggest the owner might not be. We agree the pick-up truck can stay and I'll be look-out.

'Leave your keys in the car in case we have to peel out quickly,' one of them says. Good idea, run from armed police, probably equipped with a canine unit. Except for the amateur high-8 video camera, this might look like a drug deal or a rape – they might shoot first and ask questions later.

Suddenly, overhead police helicopters in the sky turn on their spotlights. It's the Aerospatial! Everyone ducks for cover except me.

'Don't bother, they have FLIR and can see you hiding,' I say. On second thought, I duck behind the car too. We wait until it's gone.

Already Jasmine is in a bad mood and we haven't even started. 'Personally, I'm tired of this shit,' she says. 'I just want to do a normal fucking in front of the camera.' She goes into the BMW and turns on the heat while the guys plan the scene.

'Hey, if the police pull up, my bail comes first before anybody,' says the cameraman.

'I ain't jumping no fences. Ain't climbing no walls,' Edward says.

Julian, the other lead performer, is sure that if the police come, they'll assume the black guys are mugging the white boy.

'That's OK officer, they're with me,' I promise to say. 'These guys? Never saw them before in my life' is more like it.

The cameraman finally finds his blank tape buried deep in the trunk.

Meanwhile, Jasmine shivers by the dumpster in a sleeveless vest and miniskirt. They won't give her a jacket because they're about to shoot. 'I'm not gonna freeze,' Jasmine protests. 'I got sick the last time and I still haven't recovered.'

'That's a real problem when girls have an attitude,' Julian says.

'Come on, I'm not in the fucking mood,' she says.

'Then why are you in the fucking business?' Julian mutters.

Action!

Detective 1: We're police. Hey, you a hooker?
Hooker: Are you police? Let me see your badge.
Detective 1: We don't need to show you no badge, bitch.

We keep rolling despite the guard dog snarling and dragging around the torn ball in the background. Jasmine is doing two guys. I'm watching two alleys. And Jasmine. The helicopter returns and hovers overhead. Right overhead. Cut! The guys shove their tools into their trousers. Everyone scatters until it buzzes off.

'All clear!' I shout.

They start again. Edward gets on his knees and lifts Jasmine's skirt, Jasmine starts on Julian.

'I ain't never did it for anybody in an alley, not even for myself,' she says.

'Come on join the action,' Julian calls to a black homeless drunk staggering down the alley.

'Hello, can we joke later and get this done with?' Jasmine says while continuing with Julian.

'Smoke him like a cigar,' says Mr Marcus.

Julian bites his knuckle not to laugh and loses his close-up. The cameraman zooms in on Jasmine.

'Somebody's coming!' I shout. Everybody picks up their trousers and scatters again. My mistake. It's just the homeless guy coming over to watch. 'How y'all doing?' he asks.

'Come on! I want to get this fucking thing over with,' says the cameraman. 'My batteries are low.'

Edward continues under Jasmine's skirt. She smiles with her eyes closed. Before they worried about the homeless man watching. Now they're worried about him stealing one of the cars.

'Me personally, I would go for Mr Marcus's black BMW,' Julian jokes. Everyone laughs except Mr Marcus.

Next scene, Jasmine turns around. Action!

Hooker: Fuck me in the ass, you dirty pig cop. I may be a slut and a whore but you're a pig!

Years ago, the government passed laws making it illegal to show non-consensual sex. Now, every sex scene shows willing participants no matter how precarious the situation. The anti-porn people are just as disgruntled by these 'consenting' situations as die-hard porno fans.

'Alright, everyone get their dick hard so we can do some hard-core,' Mr Marcus instructs.

Problems.

'Nobody's hard,' Jasmine says. She's unhappy again. Big delay. Mr Marcus grabs two porno magazines from the trunk and gives them to the guys for inspiration. Jasmine and I head into the warm car and leave them in the cold to deal with their predicament.

'That's all we need, two brothers jerking off in the alley,' says the cameraman.

Ed is bragging outside: 'She likes me. She said I suck pussy just like a girl.'

'Come on, help me out,' Julian calls to Jasmine. Fat chance.

The homeless guy wanders by again. The two guys face the wall and keep trying while pretending to pee.

Meanwhile, Jasmine is complaining inside: 'His hands are cold and covered with gravel from touching the cement and I don't want him touching me any more.' She starts crying. 'I'm just better than this fucking in an alley. And that guy had bad breath.'

What do I say, 'DP one for the Gipper'? Or 'Don't screw the guys. Screw the film and the 1,000 bucks'? I take her hand and shut my mouth. We start laughing watching the guys. The cameraman is secretly filming them playing with themselves to show at the next party. Everyone's getting bored waiting. Mr Marcus starts playing with the guard dog who is wagging his tail. Some guard dog.

At last the guys are ready.

'Jasmine, where do you want it?' they ask.

'Ain't got no napkin. I don't want it on my clothes so do it in my mouth so I can spit it out,' Jasmine says. 'That's what a hooker would do.'

How would she know?

Final scene: Action! Jasmine gets them off. They arrest her for spitting, then they all leave together down the alley like the Scarecrow, the Tin Man and Dorothy in *The Wizard of Oz*. The Aerospatial A Star buzzes overhead, flashing 30,000,000 light candles of 'Night Sun'. We pile into the cars. Mr Marcus settles up with Jasmine, who doesn't get the DP rate but earns enough to pay her entire month's rent and then some.

CHAPTER 15
CULTURAL EXCHANGE: REBECCA LORD

French performer Rebecca Lord looks like a fashion model but she is not too tall and has just enough meat on her healthy bones to make her just right for taking to bed. That's what I like about this business. Those thoughts are treated like a compliment. Which they are. The women don't panic. They smile. 'I'd love to do a scene with you someday' is polite porno chit-chat.

Rebecca lives in a simple house in the Valley.

She opens her door and looks at me. I look at her. She's wearing a single string of pearls and a simple one-piece, revealing her slender, well-shaped legs. Her face and jet-black hair hint at Mediterranean origins.

I know what she's thinking. She knows what I'm thinking but hesitates.

'Would you like something to drink?' she finally says. Her eyes say 'Don't ask.'

'With pleasure,' I say. It's too late. My mouth has already gone dry. That often happens in this business. She reluctantly goes into the kitchen. I follow. She opens a cupboard. It's empty. She opens the fridge. It's empty, too.

'Is instant decaf OK?' she asks.

'With pleasure,' I say again. Why did I say that again?

Rebecca may look fresh, but the coffee definitely does not. It looks like dust. She puts too much into a cup. I watch her stir it and know it will taste like mud. We go into the dining room.

'Is always the journalists ask the same questions,' she says. '"Who do you like to do it with and what are your favorite positions?' Funny, I was just going to ask you that.

I was right. The coffee tastes like mud.

Rebecca's career really took off when she came to America. Though she struggled in France, it was not until she was published here that the French magazines and video companies offered her work. *C'est toujours comme ça.*

'In France I didn't work out so well,' she says. 'Is mostly amateur so they don't have things, like money, or towels. And they treat the girl like she is a piece of meat.'

In a culture famous for fine dining, I guess that's a compliment. It must be. It certainly sounds better than treating her like skin and bones.

'As a kid, you were the troublemaker?' I ask.

CULTURAL EXCHANGE: REBECCA LORD

*Rebecca Lord and friend

'Yes, exactly!' she squeals with delight.

'Did you run away from home?'

'No, I walk, then take the bus,' she says.

Three big dogs are fighting in the living room. She rushes to stop them. Now's my chance. I go into the kitchen and pour some of the coffee in the sink. I pretend to take a sip just as she enters the kitchen.

We return to the dining room. One day she answered an amateur film newspaper ad. 'I'm going to be an actress!' she joked. 'It was for the curiosity. And the money. I went. I try. I like it.'

Eventually, she made her way to Hollywood where she works on a regular basis, rents a nice home with a tiny unfiltered swimming pool. That's the good side of the business. But making friends has not been so easy.

'When I get friends, I like to talk about everything, movies, the theatre, the travel,' she says. 'But the people are too involved into the business so discussion is *always*, *always* sex or business. Is true for actor. Not producer, they just make the money. In France, they do that because they have a problem, a sexual problem. Is like fantasy. Is like because he cannot do that at home.'

'Is your head OK?' I ask.

'I really feel to do the business, is not going to be in my favour,' she says. 'It won't be good for me. Everybody does that because they got a small problem. Everybody. Some people is big problem. I talk about everybody. No one would be normal, if there is a normal, to do that for a living. I know some girls in the business, they were raped when they were very young. Is a big problem. My family was very Catholic. Is not an excuse. Is just I'm looking for a reason and sex was a shame. They didn't talk to me. Never. They always keep me at home. Never could go to the parties with friends. I think it can be from that.'

'And the others?' I ask.

'An actor, a very famous guy, he's very sad right now. He's getting old and never had a private life. Never could have one because he always have to be in good health to be in the movies because actors they are working every day. You can't have fun at night. To kill the private life for the business you really have to want it. I think is pretty sad.'

Americans are like that.

'For the men, the penis is like, everything. It seems to me, there is nothing else in life for them. It's ego, selfish. When the guy cannot have a hard-on, is always the girl's fault. Always. Always. It cannot be them.'

'Some girls also, there is a lot of lesbians. It is very sad. They will not tell you that but it's very sad. I don't understand why, so don't ask me why. Is OK for some girls, is for me a big question. Seventy per cent of the girls, her husband is like pimp. Some girls are pretty, they are not stupid and they pick a loser. A real one. He doesn't work. He take the money and he buy a Corvette. I don't know how those girls can stand that. The kind of people who do this business, they like to get their money right away. Is quick money.'

'If it's so bad, why don't you quit and take a regular job?' I ask, knowing it is not French to not complain.

'I like the business because I hate to wake up at 8 a.m.,' she answers. Her eyes light up. and she flashes a big smile. Porno may not always attract happy people, but a good night's sleep keeps Rebecca cheerful.

CHAPTER 16

GREG, PRINCE OF DARKNESS

Director Greg Dark opens his downtown Los Angeles apartment door; he's dripping wet, holding a towel around his waist, a cigarette butt hanging from his mouth. He lets me in without saying a word.

It's not like I was expecting a bearskin rug in front of a roaring fire. But the entire living room is actually an editing room, filled with monitors and tape decks. A beefy editor, his T-shirt creeping up his back and his jeans creeping down his buttocks, is working away on one of the machines.

People in the porno industry call Greg Dark 'weird'. He's a professionally trained director and has had a number of very successful porno titles. Ten-year-old *New Wave Hookers* is *still* popular. He even directs mainstream HBO cable-television movies. But he doesn't toe the porno propaganda line. He's not involved in the porno 'family'. In fact, he berates it, pointing out that a pimp and hookers call themselves a 'family', as do heroin addicts who hang out together. These aren't supportive, nurturing families. They only isolate people from society and rationalize negative behavior. Dark prefers to remain an outsider and doesn't participate in the industry functions.

'I don't see it as a big happy family where everybody hugs each other,' he says. 'I'm a cold imagist who uses pornography to explore types of emotional imagery. Pornography provides a ground for my creative explorations. My problem is to show the disintegration of the humanism of the female, or the male, and show the pure animal nature which is pornography. Sex is animalistic. I want to see a beautiful woman, maybe a young woman who doesn't look like she's going to do that and then she goes to the other end of her mind.'

Dark dons a pair of gym shorts and basketball sneakers. As we cut across the manicured lawn, he pulls on an old black T-shirt. We jump into his blood-coloured, dirty, Corvette. His tattooed forearms look like Popeye's, veins bulging from the martial arts he's been practicing all his life. He's wearing black wraparound shades, a Rolex watch, three earrings and a perpetual snarl which either expresses contempt for society or, more likely, is the result of a kick-boxing match he lost in Thailand.

'Do I look like a pimp?' he asks.

Dark once ran an escort service and almost got run out of town. He rented the same office which Margold now uses in Jim South's office; he secretly pimped out the porno chicks. The police closed down his 'family'.

'I'm a law-abiding citizen and a good reformed criminal because of it,' he says as his snarl turns to a grin. An outlaw among outlaws, his hard-core pornography is distributed by John Stagliano's Evil Angel production and distribution company.

The Buzz Coffee Shop sits across the street from the Etz Jacob Torah Center on Beverly. I get a double cappuccino sprinkled with cinnamon. Dark picks up a granola cup with fresh strawberries, studies it, puts it down, takes another filled closer to the top, pours in non-fat milk and picks up our tab. We grab an outside table, next to an attractive single young woman. He takes the

✱ Harris flanked by Greg Dark (left) and John Stagliano (right)

seat furthest from her so he can talk to me and watch her at the same time. He flicks his cigarette butt 20 feet into the street. It catches her eye. She glances at him and doesn't smile. He returns the non-smile.

Dark's work is like an X-rated version of *Pygmalion*. Women start out looking sweet and innocent and become wild and untamed. He calls that 'maximizing a performer's potential'. Dark portrays men as anonymous sex objects; it's the women he likes to provoke.

'You think you're a whore, don't you?' he challenges them. 'I generally try to make them feel bad about what they're doing because then they give interesting, real emotional responses and you can watch them squirm if they try to cover it up,' he says. 'The porno girl will often let you see part of the manufactured personality that they believe the public wants to see. They want to be the persona of that which they've created and there really is nothing else but that persona. There's no depth to most of these people. They're not able to become intimate and close. There's a fear of intimacy, of closeness. There's a fear of being real. They were that way when they went into it. Pornography is the great flypaper for these people. Their intellectual depth is "Do you find me desirable?" That's the bottom line. They need to express their desirability, their feeling of well-being through the act of sex. This is how they relate to the world. They hide behind their sexual persona,' Dark says behind his Foster Grants.

'These girls think they're "conceptual", erotic performers,' he says. 'Ninety-eight per cent of them turn tricks on the side. And the other two per cent just do girl-girl stuff. I have not heard of one of them that doesn't. They "flatbed it" for a living. I don't dignify them with the word "actor".'

Don't take it personally, Dark doesn't dignify most directors as directors since most of them let the cameraman direct. He doesn't dignify producers as producers, either. They pretend they are mainstream film studios and try to deny they are pornographers. 'They're such hypocrites,' he says. 'They always want beautiful wholesome girls to defile.'

If Dark is such a hot-shot director, why does he stay in a field filled with phony producers, unskilled directors and talent that can't act?

His snarl turns to a grin again: 'I have various foibles in my personality.'

CHAPTER 17

WHERE EVERYONE'S A WINNER: THE FOXE AWARDS

It is the evening of the FOXE Awards – Friends of X Entertainment – an annual event set up by Bill Margold in 1989 hoping to create a happy porno family of fans and performers. Fans vote for their favorite male and female performers, and there's also an award for 'Fan of the Year'. Performers mingle freely among the fans. The event is taking place in a nondescript nightclub on Sunset Boulevard. I get there early. So does everybody else.

Most of the time, fans won't talk to interviewers. Certainly not in dirty bookshops. They don't want anybody to know. At conventions, thousands of guys are roaming around, waiting in line for autographs and they don't want anybody to know either. Their wives might get upset. Or their boss. Or their neighbour. Or their pastor.

'What stuff do you like?' I ask.

'Why do you want to know?' they counter.

But Bill Margold's contacts aren't ashamed. For example, the Wilson family are the First Family of porno fans. Trophy and plaque engravers by trade, Ray and Paul Wilson are known throughout the industry as OK guys. They get to go on sets, sometimes play extras in movies. When that happens, they bring a grab-bag of sex toys, which is always appreciated. Performers invite them to the club where they are dancing. It's always nice to see a friendly face in the crowd. A dozen or so performers have accepted their home-cooked dinner invitations, the house specialty being iron-packed liver and onions. Ray's wife watches videos when she's in the mood. Sometimes in the evening, they get a pizza and watch a video with their cats. Ray will watch a video while he's getting ready for work. Fans this involved have a personal interest. They know the players. It's like watching pro wrestling or rooting for the home team.

At the entrance, a buxom woman wearing just a leather waistcoat comes over to the sales counter to look at the merchandise.

'Can you flash?' asks the clerk behind the register.

Without hesitation, she snaps open her waistcoat. Ask a simple question...

Master of Ceremonies Bill Margold is wearing his usual short-sleeved shirt open over a coloured T-shirt, jeans and sneakers. Bill is Bill. He never changes. Except his socks and underwear. I hope.

'Hey Bill, is Mike Albo coming?' someone asks. Albo writes for *Hustler*. Definitely not. Margold banned him for calling the fans 'geeks and creeps'. Freedom of speech is one thing. Ridiculing fans is another.

The evening includes strip shows and choreographed events. Fans have the chance to meet their favorite performers who roam the dance floor, posing for pictures and giving out autographs.

Fans who watch the videos at home and imagine they are actually getting into bed with one of these women come to see these girls and they're real, not on tape anymore. They've seen these girls naked, and taking it every which way conceivable. And now here they are. 'Boy oh boy, maybe it can happen to me,' the fans think. That's the whole fantasy of it.

For most fans, but not all of us.

In the VIP lounge, I recognize a number of people. EZ Rider, Rayveness, among others. A rotund guy named James Sullivan, wearing an orange toga with a wreath decorating his head, reclines on a sofa. He has a lapful of chocolate-covered donuts, potato chips, brownies and grapes. 'I live life in the fat lane,' he says. A couple of years ago, he was voted 'Porno Fan of the Year' and ever since he's felt part of the industry. Now, he's no longer just a fan, he's talent, too. While he may not be good-looking enough to get booked for boy–girl straight-sex scenes, he meets both requirements to participate in sado-masochism videos: he enjoys abuse and will work for free. Recently he played a filthy, lecherous old doctor who abuses nurses then gets his due.

It's not lost on him that the Vivid girls have never attended this event: 'The sad thing about them is they see fans as lecherous, pud-pounding, raincoaters. It would be nice if they saw there were fans who made them feel comfortable. They're birds in a gilded cage. If it weren't for the fans, they would be doing something else.'

James saw his first X-rated film at 15 and has since seen over 5,000 movies. He works as a compiler for a film company and is responsible for the record-keeping required by federal law. He's a scholar of porno film history, circa 1974–1986, what he considers the golden years, before terms like 'politically correct' and 'sexism' took hold, and before video recorders. Back then, scripts were written anonymously by English teachers and college professors and movies were shot on film.

'Now, it's as dull as dishwater,' he says. 'Things are so bad that some distributors won't allow voyeurism because they are concerned about being arrested for "unspecified obscenities".'

All this censorship makes him mad because, in theory it's protected by the US Constitution. 'Religious groups should have no political power whatsoever,' he says. 'They pay no taxes and should not be entitled to more power than a Chinese restaurant.'

Right on. The industry gets attacked because it won't band together. 'Nothing is ever destroyed from outside until it destroys itself from within,' he says as he methodically devours a chocolate-covered donut.

Lovette's here. She's not naked this time, just discreetly topless. She's here to mingle with her fans. And perpetuate some myths: 'It's every man's fantasy to believe that you are the whore of the earth. 'So let it be their fantasy, even though it's not true.'

But fans have their aggravating side as well. 'I can never get out of the gas station,' she says. She dreads meeting a fan in a grocery store because they follow her up and down the aisles. 'It's like, I appreciate that you watch the movies and that you like it and everything, but scram. Then they try to proposition you for sex, and say really dirty, disgusting things. Hey, if you want to talk this kind of thing, come see me at the strip club. But this is my time, thank you.'

WHERE EVERYONE'S A WINNER: THE FOXE AWARDS

Once a fan followed her out from the checkout line, leaving his groceries behind. She warned him to leave her alone. He waited in the parking lot, got in his car and followed her. 'I was scared,' she says. 'I mean, this is LA, not Indiana. People are really crazy about me, but just because I enjoy sex and I get off doing it in front of a bunch of people, doesn't mean that I'm a prostitute and that I want people to stalk me.'

She used to do private dancing for a customer, 'a butt and leg and foot kind of guy'. He spent a lot of money, about a hundred bucks a pop. Then he started writing letters to her: 'I'm not attractive and no women want me. The only time women pay attention to me is when I spend a lot of money.'

'This fellow was 50 pounds overweight and bald and had a big lump on his head and didn't dress the best,' she says. 'His breath stunk and he smelled bad. He was kind of weird.'

He followed her. She warned him to stop. He did. Then he got weirder. One thing led to another and he pulled out a knife during her show. 'I didn't know if he was going to kill himself or me,' she says. She called the police; they arrested him and found a loaded Uzi in his vehicle with a couple dozen pictures of her, and newspaper clippings of her club schedules. He'd been following her around a three-state area. 'That was kind of freaky but otherwise business is cool,' she says.

Naive newcomers are the most vulnerable. They get in for the attention and overlook the danger. Lovette has a girlfriend who got a knock on her hotel door from a fan who said he wanted an autograph. She opened. He entered with three buddies who helped themselves to non-consensual sex for twelve hours.

Onstage, the rock band has stopped and the show is about to begin.

'I'm Bill Margold, but you're the important ones,' he shouts over the microphone. As he gives out the FOXE awards, each recipient mumbles something, quickly, before the crowd gets too restless.

The Wilsons provide the 'FOXE blocks', engraved Lucite awards which, they note with pride, are the highest quality in the adult business and retail for $120.

The natives are getting restless. Bill better introduce more girls. Quick.

'How many believe sex gets better with age?' Bill shouts into the microphone. 'How many believe the more you practice, the better you get? Let's bring on the Silver Foxes!'

Seven women, ranging from ages 40 to 60, wearing old-fashioned lingerie,

✱ Lovette at the FOXE Awards

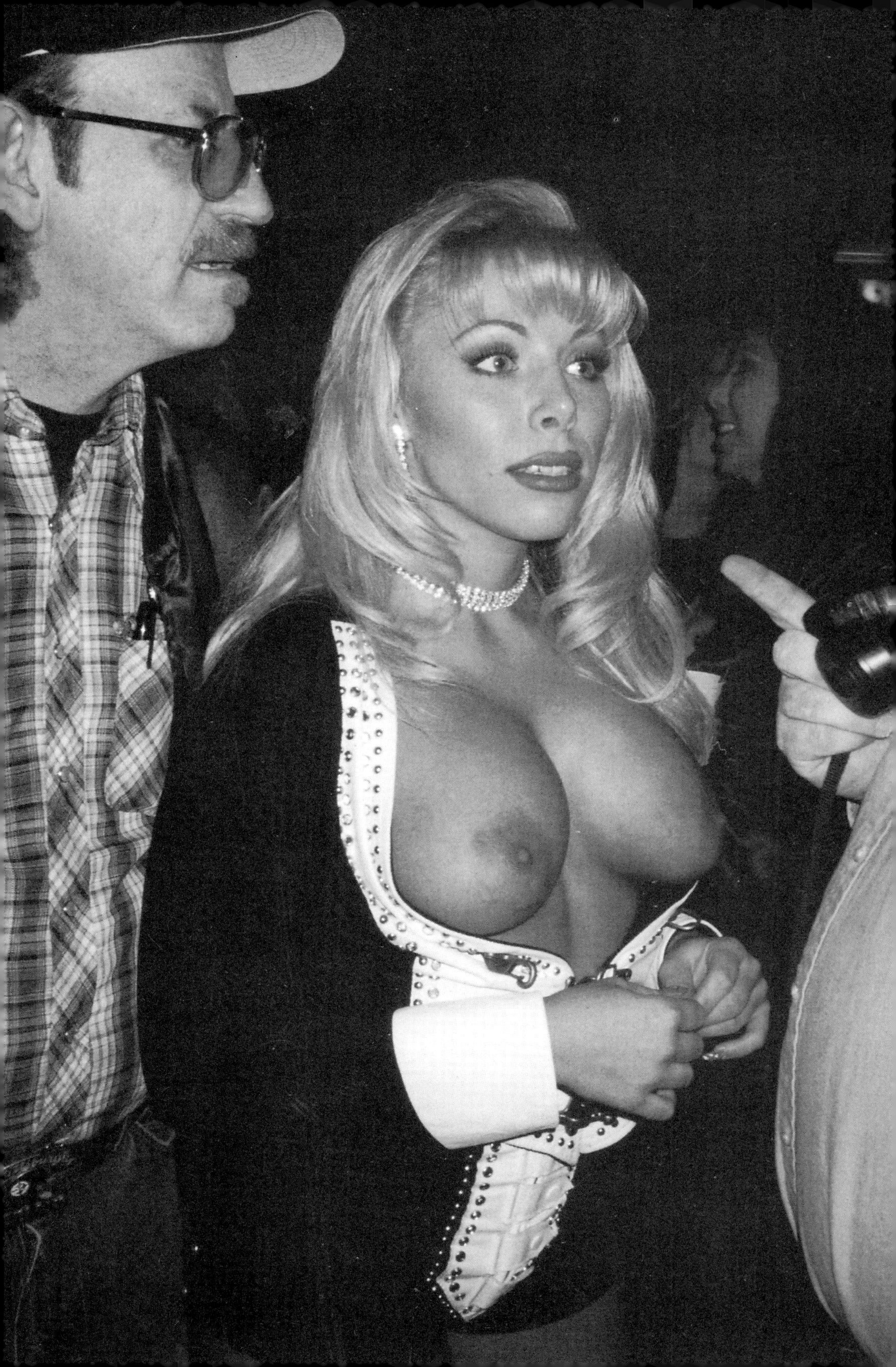

do a choreographed strip show, including solo acts. The women are loving every minute of it and so are the fans, who know some of the Foxes from the 'Totally Tasteless' video series.

Kitty Foxx represents a new market niche, porno stars over 50. Kitty has been happily married for 30 years and is old enough to be mother for most of the performers. She used to be a hairstylist. Now she publishes *Over 50*, a porno magazine. She keeps fit by working out an hour a day and by getting it on at the weekend at the Red Rooster Swinger's Club, where she's a lifelong member.

She got her start in 1990 at a lifestyles convention when she was approached by a film production company. Shucks, it wasn't nothing getting into porno. Las Vegas is a resort area and attracts lots of swingers. Kitty already had lots of experience.

'Most of our friends are either swingers or in the porn business,' she says. 'And after two drinks, you know, straight people get pretty boring.'

'Do you find the photo shoots arousing?' I ask.

✶ Harris and Kitty Foxx

WHERE EVERYONE'S A WINNER: THE FOXE AWARDS

'Oh yeah. Definitely. *Definitely*,' she says. Forget the photo shoot. She's getting aroused just answering the question. 'The gals over 40 who are in the business are doing it because they want to and they like it. Most of them have had professions all their lives and their husbands are well situated. They don't need it for the money.'

Ironically, being a porno performer has opened doors, not closed them. She's done television and radio talk shows because she is considered an authority on sex and swinging. 'I don't know that I'm an authority on it but I know more than a lot of people do based on some of the letters I get,' she says.

'How is it different doing it later in life?' I ask.

'My theory is you don't get your shit together until your body's worn out anyway,' she says. 'It takes a lot of years to really get your head right, to be secure in your own way of thinking and to have a lot of self-confidence. The attitude of a 40-year-old is they think it's an honour to be chosen to be in a men's magazine. Sometimes, a 20 or 30-year-old thinks it would be degrading. At this point in my life, what anybody thinks about what I do doesn't affect me in the least, financially or emotionally,' she says.

Another woman, older than most but younger than some, stops by. Corky Alexander is the publisher of *Over 40* magazine. She too is a happily married woman, highly experienced in the swinger scene.

'Did you feel like an adult before you started "adult"?' I ask.

'You know what, I didn't. I feel more like an adult now because I love what I'm doing. I've always been a bit of exhibitionist.'

That shouldn't be surprising. She and her husband have been nudists for 25 years. When they vacationed in the south of France, she became recognized as the lady who dressed up in restaurants and then undressed on the table.

'Give her another beer, she'll take her clothes off,' someone said when they recognized her. 'I don't need another beer to take my clothes off,' she answered back.

Scarlett is another Silver Fox, a good-looking red-head with a no-nonsense, 'I know what I want' stare that would scare the pants off any young man.

Tell me about yourself.

'No husband, no kids, no dogs, over 40 and insatiable,' she says.

'What were you like in your twenties and thirties?' I ask.

'Married, fat, a wallflower, an introvert, ugly, no friends,' she says. Now she's making up for lost time. She accepts a dance from a fan while waiting for her partner, a handsome 27-year-old aspiring porno performer. Ponce de Leon would have been amazed.

CHAPTER 18

JUST HOW MUCH IS YOUR NAME WORTH?

Phone rings: 'Janine and team will be promoting their on-line fan club and signing autographs at the Green Apple, a comic book store on Melrose Ave. This could be your chance to meet her.' Click.

I'm on my way out the door but then remember I should first phone Green Apple's owner so that I'll get in without hassle. He wants to see ID plus proof of this and proof of that. After all, *everyone* wants to meet these girls.

When I get to the shop, I show the boss my ID, clips, press card, the whole bit. He's not impressed. Maybe it's all fake. He's not a bad guy. I'm just in the way. I can watch for free and stay clear but no pictures and no interview. Thanks but no thanks. I'm out of there.

Outside, there's a block-long line of hormonally turbo-charged teenagers, ready to fork over the $20 cash entry fee to meet the four porno stars selling autographed videos, Polaroids, posters, playing cards, and promoting their $20-a-month on-line fan club service.

When I was a teenager, my idols were sports heroes. Every September, Eric Steven's in Boston, the local young men's clothing shop, sponsored several of the world champion Boston Celtics, the greatest team that ever played basketball. John Havlecek gave me a personalized autograph with a smile. I idolized him. I remember it well. He was my hero and never charged me $20 to meet him.

I go back to my car, pull off the $30 parking ticket stuck to my windshield, and peel out.

FAX
April 30, 1996

Dear Willoughby,

30,000 words went out to you yesterday. Obviously, in the long run, lots will be edited out, but I leave it for you to review before making too many cuts. My agent is glad that the pictures arrived safely. There is a separate fee for these??? Let me know when you've decided which ones to use.

I mentioned in my coverage of the autograph-signing experience that I'd never had to pay for an autograph when I was a kid. It turns out that on *60 Minutes* the other night they had a feature on autograph selling, not porno stars but sports heroes. What they used to give away they now sell. And it's big business. There was Boston Red Sox great Ted Williams making $50,000 on a weekend and the New York Yankees' Joe DiMaggio making $150,000 for signing a thousand autographs *in a day*. They say 70% of all sold or traded autographs are fake, including those with a $5 'authenticity certificate'. And way back when, the report said, the free autographs were all signed by the bat boy. The only way to guarantee getting the real thing was and apparently still is to get it yourself. So in a lot of ways role-model porno stars are really just like role-model baseball players.

I guess Herbert Hoover was right. The business of America is business.

Tomorrow I'm off to meet Vivid's publicist and I've an appointment with a bondage expert later this week. Never a dull moment...

Best regards,

Harris Gaffin

Harris

CHAPTER 19
A FRESH APPROACH: SUSAN YANETTI

Vivid has saturated the adult market, now they are broadening their base by reaching for borderline consumers. They've taken out a billboard ad on Sunset Strip and advertise in mainstream publications. They've also hired a new publicist, Susan Yanetti, who'd only been working in mainstream a couple of years when this offer came along. 'Let's do lunch,' she says. It can't just be anywhere. She picks the classy Bel-Age Hotel. Vivid must be springing for it. Public relations people eat well.

I wait in the lobby. She's late. That's OK, it's her tab. But it's like a blind date: I don't know what she looks like. Do I ask every single woman in waiting in the lobby, 'Excuse me, are you Susan, a mainstream publicist for a porno company?' Just kidding. Think I'd risk a free lunch?

Susan arrives, rushed but cheerful. A hefty woman with a beautiful face and hair falling all over itself, she reminds me of Georgie Girl. I can tell by her enthusiasm, she's not jaded. She's going to do this and she's going to do that. You can't do this and you can't do that, I try to explain. She won't listen. Mainstream America is going to love these beautiful young Vivid women if they are just given a chance. She has so many ideas I shut off the tape recorder.

Susan's overall strategy is to make the Vivid stars spokespeople for the company. When people meet them, they'll think 'My goodness, this woman is no different than my girlfriend. This is not a sleazy person that's been drugged up and coerced into something against her will.' Who would think that?

Susan has plans to give these women exposure around college spring-break vacation areas. Let them attend charity fundraisers, model lingerie, put them in an art gallery, create a 'Team Vivid', have them attend stock car rallies and open football and basketball games. When the camera searches for sexy close-ups, Team Vivid will get free national advertising. Market them as 21st-century feminists, involve them with mainstream Hollywood, associate them with adult-friendly movie stars and get them invited to parties where they will be hotter than any mainstream actress. Encourage media profiles. Let the press meet Vivid women on a one-to-one basis. (Isn't that what I've been trying to do?) Get them on TV and radio talkshows.

Get them on talkshows?

'They're great people. They're loving, kind, wonderful people,' she says. 'When people see them it will change them. They will say, "Maybe I should check this out. Maybe I should open my mind. Maybe these people aren't so bad after all."'

'Have you met them yet?' I ask.

'Not yet, but I've only been here two months,' she says.

Only two months? Even me who knows nothing about public relations knows you meet your client on the first day. 'Are you sure they're not trying to avoid you?' I ask.

She's undeterred. She's on a mission. Besides, she doesn't have to meet them to love them. A lot of people are just in porno for the money. But a lot are true believers, driven by a libertarian philosophy. Susan's obviously committed. For some reason. She comes to the table with more enthusiasm than anyone I've met in the industry thus far. Except Margold. What is her private agenda? Does she think the porno-star glamour will rub off on her? Maybe by associating with porno, she is mildly rebelling without crossing the point of no return.

Susan's unstoppable. She doesn't have any of the gloom or doom influence. I don't say a word. When a steamroller heads my way, I don't try to stop progress.

CHAPTER 20

THIS GIRL SCOUT ISN'T SELLING COOKIES: KRISTINE IMBOCH

In the porno world, there are many niche markets. Kristine Imboch, for example, specializes in girl–girl bondage videos. I attended one of her seminars where she demonstrated her expertise in rope and knots to a hard-core group of sado-masochism leather enthusiasts. Kristine herself never wears leather: at this particular seminar, she wore a Girl Scout uniform, complete with green kneesocks and penny loafers.

Tonight I am covering her shoot. She was reluctant to let me watch but I promised to make myself useful by being her assistant or carrying things, whatever she needed. She finally agreed.

I meet Kristine in a gay neighborhood in West Hollywood after office hours. In front of a small office building on Santa Monica Boulevard I help her scrawny male assistant unload the trunk, which is filled with sacks of equipment. The office upstairs is floor-to-ceiling, wall-to-wall gay porno production, crammed with desks, equipment, rows and rows of shelves in every room. I've seen more free space in the back of a Chinese laundry. One room is for inventory and shipping: brown envelopes registered 'wedding gift', all headed overseas, stacked next to a kick-ass meter-long Pitney-Bowes postage machine. One room is full of master tapes. Dirty, beat-up PCs on every desk. Somebody's keeping overhead tight. After we unload all the bags and equipment, she gives her assistant, Jan, a big kiss on the mouth.

Kristine may look meek and mild but she directs, models, lectures and demonstrates bondage. Rope, tape, torn sheets – she likes to tie and be tied. She is one of the foremost specialists in the bondage world. Tonight, this office is her set. She's wearing a white shirt and a drab, calf-length skirt. She flips off her shoes and slips on fluffy big bunny-rabbit bedroom slippers.

The coffee area has become the make-up room for model Morgan Knight, a full-figured, wholesome-looking woman who lives on a horse ranch and drives a pick-up truck into town whenever there's a bondage gig. Kristine gives her her lines and her direction, she'll improvise the rest.

The first scene takes place in the inventory room. Morgan is bound and sitting on the floor comfortably. Her nose is itchy – Kristine has to stop to scratch it for her. Next scene, Kristine selects a roll of tape and teaches me how to roll it around Morgan whose shirt is fully opened. We play the bad guys who tie up the secretary. Quick, think of something to say.

Action!

Innocent (but consensual) secretary: What are you doing here?

Thug one (me): Hey, Joe look what we got here. We just want to tie you up, lady.

I start taping Morgan.

Cut!

What did I do wrong?

'You're not supposed to put tape across her breasts,' Kristine explains patiently. 'The company has a policy of doing non-sexual bondage. Besides how can the viewer see her breasts if you cover them over with tape? Tape over them. Tape under them. But don't tape on them.'

Sorry. Rolling tape, take two. Action! I get it right, I think. There's a disruptive sound. Cut!

The Mexican cleaning guys arrive with vacuums and cleaning gear but don't seem surprised to see Morgan gagged, breasts exposed, writhing around the floor. They go to vacuum around her. Kristine asks them to return later and

THIS GIRL SCOUT ISN'T SELLING COOKIES: KRISTINE IMBOCH

they oblige. Thanks guys.

The final scene: Morgan is tied to a chair. 'Chair ties are great for giving a model a break,' Kristine says. 'There's not much for her to do.'

Once bound, Morgan sits, rocks and squirms as Kristine shoots both video and stills.

Kristine was the first of three kids her parents raised in Michigan. As a kid, she loved to be tucked in bed with five layers of blankets, she just liked to feel things pressing on her. She even took extra pillows and stacked them on top of her. She liked her St Bernard dogs to lie on her legs when she was sleeping as well. She just loved pressure. 'I like the feeling of somebody rolling on top of me,' she says. She likes the pressing of wrestling. 'To me, bondage is a hug,' she says. 'Physiologically, people like to be hugged, that feeling of squeezing and the pressure. I just love all the different aspects of the hug sensation. That for me is a basic pleasure.'

When she turned 18, a male friend escorted her into an adult bookstore. 'I was shocked,' she says. 'I thought that I was the only girl that was into bondage and that these magazines were all for men who were actually rapists.' She wasn't into being raped so why did she have the same interest as them?

'I felt like I was mentally ill,' she says. If she told a regular guy he felt disgusted and offended. Finally, she bought an on-sale three-pack but she was still in the bondage closet.

Bondage Life magazine made it clear that not only could fantasies be played out but others could play, too. However, the poor bondage quality bothered her.

Her next boyfriend was a control freak who found her bondage magazines hidden under the bed. He thought he could 'cure' her through aversion therapy and wrote 'Disgusting slut!' all over her

✱ Kristine (a.k.a. Lorelei) photographs a video box cover

magazines.

'That was the turning point,' she says. 'Instead of feeling more guilty, his over-the-top rage and hysteria made me think 'Hey, I'm the normal one.' He was the insane and irrational one.'

She returned to her earlier boyfriend. This time it was different. 'This is my thing,' she told him. Together they went through her magazines page by page, girl by girl, position by position. She practiced on herself for a few months. He tied her hands so she could escape if she was panicking. Eventually, he did elaborate bondage. After all, he *was* a sailor. 'It was precision work,' she says. 'I liked the feeling of the rope work being perfect.'

'Do you sail?' I ask.

'Everybody thinks that all the knots have a lot to do with bondage, but I use the square knot almost exclusively. The most famous bondage artists only uses a square knot.'

They started taking pictures, made a photo album and showed them at parties. She was a big hit.

'More than half of the women wanted me to tie them up and take pictures,' Kristine says. 'Generally, women were more responsive and looked at the book longer.'

She sent photos and letters to bondage magazines. The publisher of *Bondage Life* invited her to a shooting in LA. 'It was very strange tying up someone who was just receiving money instead of doing it for fun,' Kristine says but she decided to stay. 'It was my hobby, my sport, my art, then it became my job.'

'I have a physiological reaction to bondage that isn't related to anything else,' she says. 'Physically, I love the feeling of bondage on me. There are some bondage fanatics for whom the physical is not the issue. It's the mental idea of helplessness. They really don't care that they're helpless.'

They also like the attention. Their fantasy is to be helpless, vulnerable and at the center of attention. They get past the trust thing because they crave that kind of attention, that unconditional positive regard.

Now Kristine is a bondage community celebrity. She is one of perhaps ten big names in the business but customers notice her more because she is female. She produces two videos a month.

'When you get into fantasy and role playing, whatever personality you have most of the time is submerged and you want to bring out some other part of you,' Kristine says. 'But there are also others, called "naturals", who are submissive all of the time. But I think of myself as a "balancer". Most of the people I know are balancers, very quiet and unassuming, stay in the

THIS GIRL SCOUT ISN'T SELLING COOKIES: KRISTINE IMBOCH

background. But in terms of the bedroom, very dominant.'

Bondage is usually associated with S & M but the two do not necessarily go hand-in-hand. 'To me, the S & M is a side-dish,' Kristine says. 'I could do without any spankings or stuff like that. But I couldn't do without bondage. That's my hobby and that's that. If I kneel in front of someone and I am not bound, then I'm not even kneeling. There's nothing in my mind. But if I'm tied up and I'm kneeling then suddenly it has all this meaning to me.'

Kristine likes the way her outfits defy stereotyping. She never wears *de rigeur* black to parties and people ask her why. 'I would say that 95 per cent of the time I consciously wear a bright color or white,' she says. 'People who want to be nonconformist will desperately conform within their group. Very strange, yet very human. But there are plenty of people who come to me and say, "Oh, I love to see what you're going to wear at every party. You always dress so weird."'

✱ Kristine's videos and personal handiwork

CHAPTER 21

GIRLS ON TOP

Janice Rainer is a New Yorker staying in a nice normal suburban LA neighborhood. Over the past generation, she has built up a female-domination magazine and video mini-empire, Star Maker. It's is a family business. Janice's brother, Conrad, handles the sales and daughter Christi designs the art work. They have rented a house for a shoot.

Female domination is not to be confused with S & M, sado-masochism, or B & D, bondage and discipline. Anti-pornography feminists who rail against man's exploitation and degradation of women, never seem to mention the big demand guys have for female domination videos. In fact, even pro-porn people have a negative view of it too but for their own reasons. I wonder why?

'They're not going to interpret female domination in terms of mother, nurturer and other ways that I perceive it,' Janice says. 'A domineering mother does not mean that she's not a nurturing woman. Women have been dominating men in the household and in the kitchen for centuries. And in the bedroom. It doesn't make it any less of a need in both of them. I try to project that real need. It is a luxury to some men to acquiesce in the bedroom. It doesn't make them lesser men. It just means it gets them aroused to be treated that way by a woman. Let's get into a little reality: man is the dominant species that has conquered and dominated this earth. Society is still governed by men.'

The Rainer family is congregated in the kitchen. I arrive ready-to-shoot, but they even haven't started breakfast or gotten dressed. The performers and the crew haven't arrived yet either.

Janice's friend Noelle is making scrambled eggs with ham and cheese. I pull up a chair. Nobody is dressed in black. Nobody has an attitude. It really is a happy family. And I was expecting a page out of a porno book. Janice is a motherly woman in her 50s, wearing a T-shirt and slacks. Because the atmosphere is so comfy, Christi says, performers often get homesick and start crying. They see a mother and daughter working together and wish their family was close like that, too.

Janice wants to talk privately with Noelle so kicks me out of the kitchen. Out back by the fake waterfall and real swimming pool, Christi and Penny are taking topless photos of each other and tell me to scram, too. No guys allowed. I wanted female domination. I got female domination.

I go into the living room. In walks tanned and athletic-looking Sharon

Mitchell, director of today's shoot, wearing pink jeans, black patterned sneakers, a white T-shirt with pink trim. Her handshake practically crushes my hand. A porno legend, she was a star back when films were shot in New York on 35mm and played in regular theatres.

The crew wanders in. I swear half the guys have to walk through the doorway sideways. Suddenly the place is crowded. 'Mitch' lights up her first cigarette, takes a mug of coffee, tosses a toy into the pool and barks her first orders to the crew.

'Tony, shoot the fucking duck in the pool for five minutes to make sure the video's working,' she says.

Next Mitch orders a sound check. Where are the fucking headphones? Conrad looks everywhere. He finds them in Christi's bedroom attached to her Walkman.

'Because editors are fucking stupid you do the opening and pull back,' Mitch says and addresses the rolling camera. 'Hi Rick, this is Mitch. This is your master shot,' she says then explains fully how to edit the scene.

Meanwhile, inside the house Noelle sets up bowls of snacks: chocolates, tortilla chips, salsa, fresh tomatoes, watermelon, blueberry and walnut-banana muffins.

Two silicone-implanted young women – the performers - arrive in gay spirits, hair and make-up already done. They usually work together and have a choreographed and scripted female-domination routine so this job will be a piece of cake. There's virtually nothing to direct. Today's production is called *A Picnic of Pain*. All the cameraman has to do is shoot it and call it a movie. Even Mitch is surprised to find her job will be easier than planned as well. We've got lots of time to sit around the kitchen while Mitch tells us stories.

Mitch grew up 'back east' in New Jersey where her rebel streak didn't develop until her adolescence. Her first sexual experience was with her girlfriend. Then came her girlfriend's brothers. She was a high-school cheerleader but got thrown off the team for asking another cheerleader for a date. At 16, she modelled lingerie for catalogues, studied dance with Martha Graham and took professional acting classes.

Through her theatrical and artsy friends in New York came porno opportunities. 'I was a recovering Catholic,' she says. 'I wanted to put on a uniform and pull up my skirt. And then people told me I would be paid to have sex. Not bad!'

And definitely more exciting than going to secretarial school.

In 1976, Mitch was dancing at the Show World Theater on 42nd St when the police arrived for her noon performance. Mitch was still on stage, dressed as Roy Rogers in white chaps with toy guns and dancing to 'Don't Fence Me In' by Gene Autry when suddenly the music stopped.

'Everybody out!' the police said. 'Off the stage, smart ass. We're going for a ride downtown.' A detective followed her into the dressing room. What the fuck! Mitch turned her back to him. How could the arresting officer testify if he could not describe her? Mitch has tomboy features and to confuse him further, she went into the urinal, pulled down her trousers and peed just like a boy, a trick she's learned as a contortionist. At the trial, the detective didn't know if Mitch was a boy or a girl and the case was thrown out.

The rebel in her caused a scene in Boston: after the release of *The Nun's Bad Habit*, she got stoned. With rocks. In front of a church, just like in the New Testament.

But Mitch recalls fondly the 'good old days' when she was on the big screen. 'My pussy was 16 feet high like it was supposed to be with $350,000 budgets with premiers,' she says. 'You saw people jacking off to you.' Once she got into porno, she realized that very few others were as well prepared considering she had acting, theater and dance training. 'I found this industry to be more than a piece of cake,' she says.

Not quite. There was a heavy emotional price to pay.

'You're performing an act of intimacy without the intimacy,' she says. 'That's the main thing that's fucked me up all these years.'

Since she entered the scene in 1970, she's pretty much done everything, including heroin addiction and turning off from guys for a number of years. She survived. But she had to fight.

'I've been with guys that have said "I don't care. I really don't care if you're uncomfortable on your hands and knees right now because you're ovulating." They got four other scenes in the movie, they could get somebody else to go on their hands and knees. It's no big deal. At that point, what I would do is make sure he had just enough footage so that he couldn't fucking hire anybody else and I'd turn around and say, "Now, I don't care. What are you going to do, hire somebody else? I know you don't have enough money to do that. Now, I don't care, motherfucker."'

Mitch went to school and learned film directing; few today possess her technical training.

'These cocksuckers don't have an idea about what the fuck they are doing,' she says. 'I don't validate 98 per cent of the directors in this industry as any kind of fucking directors at all. They're out for the quick buck. They're insulting the intelligence of the general public and it hurts me because I've been in the industry for 21 years where I've truly tried to bring the public the best that I could. To be part of something for so long and then see it fall on its ass with a bunch of cheapskate cut-throats, it's a drag.'

Casting is the key.

'Directing a scene requires finding out what the young lady does. Can she handle this part? Find out what she's done, not how much money she needs and what she's willing to do for it.' If you really care about what you do, the casting is everything.

'The word "director" means that you're able to do absolutely everything on the shoot – if something goes wrong you must know how to fix it whatever the problem. Being a director means covering your angles and making sure you go into the editing room with the proper amount of footage with your soft-core version and your hard-core version and a beginning, a middle and an end to a story – call me crazy, but I'm an "old school" film maker.'

She'd always considered herself a feminist until she got into porn and they turned on her. 'All of a sudden, I'm getting shit from feminists,' she says. 'Feminism goes beyond what you do for a living.'

She's also had to deal with abusive men on the set. She recalls 'Porshe Lynn, Nina Hartley and myself were on a set and a young, obviously inexperienced, woman came up to us and said, "I just came from Jim's office and I had to give him a blow job, and I need money right now so he's sent me down here to do a 'DP'. A friend of mine in the movies said I have to suck off the director of photography." We just reached in our pockets, paid her and told her to leave the set. Those are the kind of things that scare me, what women are willing to do for so little with the pimp/manager, the boyfriend/manager, the pimp/asshole that comes in with this poor woman as if she can't speak for herself.'

It's a business with a high turnover. Get in and get out, make as much as possible before becoming

✱ Harris meets Sharon Mitchell

'over-exposed'. Experience doesn't count for much. 'This is not the fashion industry and it's not the legitimate industry,' she says.

The old pros lament the good old days.

'We all took care of each other. We were a family. That's the most disturbing thing. I feel like I have nothing in common with the new performers. When a pretty girl comes up to me and says "Can we get this over with, please", it hurts me.'

Now, she's fit, tan, in surprisingly good shape considering all she's been through. She now specializes in transsexual movies, a growing field with its own niche markets – transsexual straight, S & M, Hispanic.

She is not married. Could she ever settle down and have a close personal relationship?

'Intimacy? I have no idea what the fuck intimacy is,' she says. Challenging men in a 'man's' job can take its toll: 'I can't tell you the stress of being in a business and all the guys only look at you wondering what you look like with a dick in your mouth. As long as *I'm* in control of the dick, I'm OK. But now I need a fucking cigarette.'

Outside by the pool, the two performers are ready and waiting for the easy shoot. One gets on her hands and knees, offering her back as a table for the other, who eats a sushi lunch with chopsticks.

'I love eating sushi this way,' she says. 'I should give you a good switching.'

'If you have to.'

To keep her table from complaining, she shoves an apple in her mouth then gives her a few well-paid switches. She doesn't leave any marks. They have another gig tomorrow.

CHAPTER 22

AT THE ADULTDEX CONVENTION

Porno software has always been on the cutting edge of technology. They were the first ones into Beta, then VHS, then transferring movies for computer geeks as well as creating high-tech adult video games. The breaking big porno frontier is CD-ROM.

I'm heading out to Las Vegas for a week of 'Comdex', the world's largest

AT THE ADULTDEX CONVENTION

computer show. As late as 1994, the adult CD-ROM section was welcome at Comdex. But the porno makers became fruitful and multiplied and brought in porno stars first wearing bathing suits, then Brazilian-thongs and negligees, then see-through negligees, and before you knew it, a lot of the 250,000 Comdex attendees were spending more time in the adult CD-ROM booths when they should have been browsing memory chips, cable wires, modem boxes and other computer turn-ons. In short, adult took too much attention away from too many corporate sponsors who finally said 'If they stay, we go.' So, when porno was evicted from Comdex at the Hilton, 'Adultdex' in the Sahara Hotel was born.

I arrive a day early and wander the convention hall where carpenters clank, bang and screw booths together. I admire a pin-up poster on the wall.

'Wow! Who's that?' I ask a blue-ribbon official carrying a clip board.

'She doesn't really exist,' he says. The original shoot came out lousy so with Photoshop, they took the body of one girl and put it on another, then took half of her face and flipped it. One face is actually two halves.

'Isn't that a complicated way to make porno?' I ask.

'Don't think of it as porno,' he says. 'Think of it as a showcase for the cutting edge of technology.'

A chick that doesn't exist, what will they think of next. There's Bill Margold, in his usual old T-shirt, sweatpants and sneakers. Hammer in hand, he's building his own booth. He's here to raise funds for the Free Speech Coalition, selling T-shirts, hats, calendars, and porno star merchandise.

The stand installed, Margold wants to pay his respects to porn bigwig Ray Pistol. I tag along. It might get interesting here. We're off to meet a money guy.

We pull up to a regular suburban house on the edge of town. No security gate. No body guards. A perfect decoy. The front door is wide open.

Inside, it's all business, even though it's a Sunday night. The living and dining rooms have been turned into offices, filled with desks, files, stacks of videos and magazines. A white-haired old lady cheerfully works the computer in one corner next to a printer which never stops.

Sitting at a very dishevelled desk is Ray Pistol, in his mid-40s, slender, with dirty blond hair needing a trim, and wearing a sweatsuit top, blue jeans and white socks without shoes. His feet are propped up on his desk as he casually puffs on a pipe. Over his shoulder, a little bird named Bib wanders out of its cage. A framed copy of the Declaration of Independence is on the wall.

In walks Treasure, Pistol's foxy-looking girlfriend, wearing a Vivienne Westwood tartan skirt under a very noticeable, firm, bosom. 'Pistol bought them for her,' Margold whispers. She throws back her shoulders, thrusting out her present for all to see, including Bib the bird who takes off and lands on Treasure's chest. The bookkeeper comes over and drops another pile of print-outs on Pistol's desk and smiles affectionately.

'And the image of us porno dealers is that we would sell our mothers,' Pistol says.

Mom and he get along fine, he says, except when he loans money to his strippers short on cash or puts them up after their unemployed boyfriends smack them around. Those things drive Mom up the wall. She don't want him involved.

Pistol works with his mom but he is no mama's boy. Born in 1947 and raised in Bible-belt Texas, he served in Vietnam, First Battalion, Fifth Marines, the platoon that inspired the movie, *Full-Metal Jacket*, taking a bullet in the arm. While recuperating in Okinawa, he impersonated a military policeman and became a local brothel's 'security advisor'; perks included steak dinners, Asian babes and a chauffeured yellow Mustang convertible. A disgruntled superior officer arranged Pistol's discharge for 'service unbecoming of a Marine'. Imagine that.

In college, Pistol minored in journalism and majored in girls, then failed as a Hollywood screenwriter and got run out of town by Orange County for selling smut. Relocating to Vegas, he set up the Talk of the Town porno shop, Showgirls strip club and the Slightly Sinful lingerie boutique, in that order, and has been rolling in dough ever since. Now he wants more. Pistol's got big plans, going to build an Internet empire linking up his strip shows for worldwide viewing, have girls take one-on-one video telephone calls and sell downloadable movies.

'What Ted Turner did for news, I want to do for pornography,' he says. Dream on.

Pistol calls Brittany O'Connell, tonight's 'feature' dancer, and invites all of us for dinner.

We head for a real meat-and-potatoes place, the House of Lords in the Sahara Hotel.

'I'm not dressed for this,' Margold says. If Margold's worried about appearances, Pistol must be important.

'Tuck in your shirt,' I suggest.

'What and cover my Lions T-shirt?' he answers. Maybe Pistol's not that important. Margold stuffs his shirt into his sweatpants but leaves it unbuttoned so everyone can see he's a football fan. Some people never grow up.

In the restaurant, Pistol snuggles between Treasure and Brittany. He's in a celebrating mood.

'I'll have some of that Pouilly-Fuissé stuff,' he says, lighting up his pipe in perhaps the only non non-smoking city in the free world. Brittany lights up her cigarette. She reaches across the table and grabs a roll from the bread basket. Please pass it to others, darling.

The waiter opens the bottle and pours a sample for Ray to taste.

'Did you sniff the cork, sir?' the waiter asks Ray while gawking at the girls.

'I was going to gargle first,' Ray answers. He swishes the wine around the glass to see how fast he can make it spin without spilling. 'It tastes like spoiled apples. Is that good?' he says nodding his approval. 'To life, liberty and horniness.'

My meal includes 26 ounces of brisket, a six-inch baked potato and a 'small' Caesar salad large enough fill an army helmet. Dinner conversation covers great anal video scenes, why women pee more than men and should strippers do their first girl-girl 69 on or offstage. Meanwhile, Britanny's cigarette smoke hangs over my plate and Margold is licking the meat sauce off his fingers. Miss Manners' hope for humanity would end among porno people.

After the meal, I'm so stuffed I can hardly move. And now Brittany has to dance all night. This is a tough business for women.

At the Adultdex Hall, there's a pretty girl ready to sign autographs at every booth. Unfortunately, they are wearing pretty tame bikinis. Tame for porno anyway. After a slow start, Comdex patrons trickle, then pour in. I'm wandering around from booth to booth when I see the pin-up poster girl. She's much prettier in real life. Next time, just take a better picture and skip the body-changing and face-flipping.

I note that Vivid and VCA have their own booths and have by far the largest presence in the hall except for a distributor called GVA – General Video of America – from Cleveland. Each booth has young women available to sign autographs. They're all discreetly dressed. I guess the word got out: tone it down to be accepted by mainstream.

I meet a stripper Morgan the Morman, from Utah. She wants to give porno a shot and is waiting for her first opportunity. It goes without saying she's in great shape. She has a gentle, intelligent look on her face and a nasty barbed-wire tattoo around her arm. She is staying at Bill's while visiting out here.

'I get the impression, a lot of women go into stripping hoping to be admired by men, but end up turned off by them,' I say.

'A lot of strippers are attracted to glamour,' she says. 'But you get up there, bare everything that you have. You work your butt off and all you see is some fat slob, a balding toothless 40 year-old asshole in a stained T-shirt that makes it seem like he's doing you a really big favour by giving you a buck.'

Suddenly, she has a change of heart. After all, they pay her rent.

'I kind of feel sorry for your average straight white middle-class American male because a lot of women are just not taught to fully enjoy their sexuality and their own bodies. There's that element of guilt there.'

"Do strippers make better lovers?' I ask.

'Some of these girls will just absolutely screw the hell out of you,' she says. 'They will suck the chrome off a trailer hitch. That does not mean that they are going to want to do it all the time because sex is what they have to deal with every day on their job.'

By late afternoon, thousands of fans are crammed into the hall, getting porno star's autographs. Guards are posted at the door directing traffic. Most booths are staffed by only one or two people. The Vivid booth must have a half dozen performers to sign autographs and another half dozen staff to discuss sales.

A skinny guy with thick glasses, in a business suit and a baseball hat, wanders around the floor like an undernourished Godfather, holding conferences with various figures before meeting with Margold. He's Jeffrey Douglas, a lawyer and board member of the Free Speech Coalition.

Douglas doesn't look he has sex on his mind. He never turns when a woman walks past despite porno protocol. He doesn't look the money type either. In fact, he must be the only person in the porno industry who actually looks like a rocket scientist. Margold suggests I hear him speak.

Inside the hall, Douglas is on the podium, as well as Ray Pistol, who smokes his pipe until a hotel guard makes him extinguish it. Jim South's up there, too . So are two women with larger-than-life reputations in the porno world, Nina Hartley and Ona Zee.

Douglas is leading a legal symposium, exhorting the adult industry to organize and stop getting pushed around by politicians who pass laws without even consulting the industry they are regulating.

'The amount of material that's rented increases grossly every year,' he says. 'The amount of material that's purchased is unimaginable. That demand for material is obsessive and infinite.'

'There is a contradiction in our culture,' he says. 'You're voyeuristic. You love to watch it. But you don't want anyone to know you're doing it. You want your exhibitionism and your voyeurism in private. I understand that's paradoxical, but that's the truth.'

On the way out, I pass a booth of sexy women calling out to every guy who passes, promoting a swinger's club and escort and call-girl service. Basically, they are available to anyone who wants their exhibitionism, voyeurism or fantasy available in private. Discretion assured.

Any parties? I figured Margold would be the one to hang out with. No parties. We'll go get some dinner. Margold wants ribs. I recommend Gate's, famous in Kansas City. The original one, I explain, is in the soul-food part of town where white boys don't generally go. They even have an armed guard at the door.

'Sounds great,' Margold says.

In Las Vegas, Gate's is in a good part of town. Not a good sign. At least I get a chance to learn more about Margold, the rebel. He's the right age but to my surprise, he was not into Woodstock.

He was born in 1943 in Washington DC. His father was Nathan Ross Margold, a Harvard University graduate, and a judge. As part of Roosevelt's New Deal Era, he was Assistant Secretary of the Interior, and became a civil rights and NAACP activist who was almost nominated for the Supreme Court.

His mother was very bright also, raised in the Brownsville slums in Brooklyn. When her husband died, she became mentally unstable. Bill did well at school but as the situation at home got worse, he was sent to a series of military academies. At the age of nine, he ran away. He left in such a rush that he was already out in public before he realized he'd forgotten to put on his trousers. He hid in a nearby trash can but was apprehended, charged with incorrigibility and sent to Central Juvenile Hall. While locked up, he saw a kid at breakfast, sitting all alone, talking to his food. Bill kept him company. An officer noticed.

'You paid attention to him,' he said. 'That was a very nice thing you did.'

Bill earned the supervisor's respect and liked Juvenile Hall's stability. When he got out, he wanted to be a Marine, but this was 1960, pre-Vietnam draft, and the Marines wouldn't train an 'incorrigible'.

So he job-hopped. At 18, he worked graveyard shift in the post office, and at the Szabo buffet food service. He became a door-to-door salesman for Consolidated Pet Foods.

'I became the best dog-food salesman in the world,' he says. Making 15,000 sales in five years. It consisted of hard boiled eggs, garlic, pure ground beef and by-products, cottage cheese, alfalfa, wheat germ, soy beans and cereal. 'It tasted OK with mustard,' he says.

In 1963, aged 20, he had no social life, knew nothing about girls or porno. He was still a virgin. He went to college, studied journalism. He worked at the *Santa Monica Evening Outlook* but got fired asking for a ten-cent raise. So he became a probation officer in Juvenile Hall in June 1969, 13 years after being imprisoned there. He worked with the ENF youth, the toughest kids with hardened criminal records, aged 17-18. He was never threatened. The kids loved him. Margold bent the rules whenever he could. He made them 'mixed drinks': he mixed whiskey, gin, vodka, vermouth and rum, shook and served the concoction, thinking that's how it's done. Everyone got sick. 'Mixed Drink Margold' got fired in 1971.

Bill next sold sex-club advertisements in the *Sexual Freedom Alliance* magazine. One day Reb Sawitz, who owned Reb's Rent-a-Chick Service, came in to complain that he'd paid for an ad that didn't run. Margold went over to rewrite the ad and while there saw a woman strip right in the office, right in front of his virgin eyes.

In those days, porno films were soft-core 'Nudie-Cuties'. Bill got cast as an extra for *God's Daughter*. He was so proud, he took a girlfriend to see it at the Pussycat Theater. He never appeared and vehemently complained to an unapologetic manager who admitted the projectionist skipped two reels. 'Nobody cares about the plot,' the manager said. Poor Bill.

Margold got such a kick out of being around the sexy scene that he offered to run Reb's office for free in exchange for first choice of all work that came in. Reb was an accident-prone Hell's Angel's biker and after another debilitating accident, agreed. Over a nine-year period Margold wrote scripts, directed and performed: he did 500 sex scenes, appeared in 300 titles and learned an awful lot about the business.

Bill's story is interesting, but the meal is a bummer. 'This is the worst barbeque I've ever eaten,' he complains. 'A good sauce should stick around your fingernails and take days to clean off. Look, I can lick the sauce right off my fingers.'

Just my luck he turns out to be a ribs connoisseur.

CHAPTER 23

SEXUAL HEALING: NINA HARTLEY

For more than a decade, Nina Hartley has been one of the most popular touring strippers in the country, as well as giving public lectures and teaching one-on-one informally. Nina's pretty assertive looking and at first I wasn't sure if she would give me the time of day but Margold gave me the go-ahead: 'Nina, she's great,' he said. 'She's even nicer than me.' So I've invited her for coffee and she's picked Jackie's in Marina Del Rey.

We have a Monday 10 a.m. appointment. I arrive ten minutes early and wait outside. Will she give me attitude? The point of meeting casually is to find out what she is really like, not the sexy stage persona. Three minutes to go. How will I recognize her if she's not wearing the only thing I've ever seen her in – man-eating black? She wouldn't be dressed like that on a Monday morning, would she? One minute to go. I enter the restaurant. There's one solitary woman, buried in a newspaper and wearing a pink jogging suit and sneakers, her legs comfortably extended on another chair. She looks well settled in. On the hour I sit down.

'I'm all yours,' I say. She looks at me funny. She has already finished a large coffee. 'Have you been here for a while?' I ask. Exactly an hour. 'Did you remember to turn your clock back over the weekend?' she asks.

She doesn't even look angry. She's like an angel, totally calm, totally forgiving. I hate that. The next time someone is an hour late for me, I won't be able to yell at them. I get up to get something. She touches my hand and gives me a motherly look. 'Don't get the espresso,' she says. 'The regular coffee is strong enough.' I think I'm in love. It's easy to see why.

'I am on a mission from Aphrodite,' she announces with a smile.

Nina is a registered nurse and for her, porno has medical value because people can live out sexual fantasies not available to them. It also educates, however crudely. Porno films are the first time many men see a woman's genitals. It's not the perfect medium but fulfils a natural curiosity albeit inadequately. So no one is misled, she would like to see it come with a disclaimer 'This is fantasy material.'

'It's sad to think that in our culture, sex education has been left to an entertainment entity instead of an educational entity,' she says. 'For me, the study of sexuality, and being able to explore mine, became paramount. To explore this through this industry has been so beneficial to my own personal happiness, that I feel an obligation as a nurse to help other people through that jungle. I remember what it was like to be scared and uptight and all the things that stop people from having sexual experiences.'

Everyone is comfortable around Nina. She once got a letter from a tired, pregnant woman with three kids who wrote, 'Thanks for keeping my husband happy.'

'That's a very wise wife to realize that he's not transferring his affections to these two-dimensional creatures, but he needs more than his exhausted wife in bed to get aroused,' she says. 'I have guys who feel very, very close to me. They had that orgasm with me. Contrary to popular opinion, men do pay attention to nuances and the little details. There are guys that look for signs of humanness – authenticity and compassion and real personalness on the part of the performers.'

She's convinced women can enjoy porno just like men: 'Women need to know their own bodies to tell the guy how to steer,' she says. She advises guys to get the girl a vibrator, bring home half a dozen tapes of various kinds and leave her alone for a few hours. A lot of women want to watch movies, but they want to have their first reactions alone without worrying about what he wants, what does he expect, what's he going to think.

Once women get over the initial shock of seeing things they never expected to see, they can get into it: 'A lot of women still don't know what pleases them and they're still waiting for the guy to make the first move. That puts a tremendous burden on the male.'

Nina is an unapologetic feminist. 'I believe in my right to make pornography,' she says. 'It's my right to control my body.' That's my kind of feminist.

As compassionate as she is, don't expect sympathy from sad stories of exploitation and feelings of degradation. You get what you project, she says. She never projected victim and she was never treated like one in the two hundred films she's done since she's been in the business.

'A hard-nosed businesswoman can do very well for herself in this industry,' she says.

As far as exploitation of the sexes, Nina feels it's the men who carry the burden. 'The men in the business are required to get and maintain an erection and cum on cue regardless of whether or not they're in the mood,' she says. 'They are not allowed to be human. They can't have a bad day. If you do that often enough, it really kills a part of you. This is an assembly-line business and we are assembly-line workers. Nobody asks you or cares how you feel. That's why I try to do everything I can to make sure the guy has a good time.'

I tell her she should do a sex education series. Too late. She's already done that, commissioned by America's largest mail-order company, Adam & Eve. In *her* instruction tapes, the teacher gets it. She's as comfortable with medical jargon as she is with slang, getting naked and demonstrating. She's certainly not the stand-offish, white-coat clinical type. Definitely my kind of teacher.

✱ Harris and the legendary Nina Hartley

ADAM & EVE

CHAPTER 24

ADAM & EVE: NORTH CAROLINA'S FORBIDDEN FRUIT

Hollywood porno's largest catalogue company, with a mailing list of one million, is distributed from, of all places, North Carolina. And the $90 million-a-year company is owned by one guy, Phil Harvey. There's no information about him in LA. So I've called him.

Phil Harvey was in the military before the Vietnam War and then worked for CARE in India's school feeding programme: 'It became particularly clear that family planning was an important programme,' Phil says. 'Just transferring massive amounts of food was not helping.'

He returned to the US in 1969 and entered a Masters program at the University of North Carolina in Chapel Hill. As part of his thesis work, he wrote about the effects of planned parenthood and contraception on the population.

Next he tried selling condoms by mail order. However, there was still a law from 1873 making illegal the mailing of any sexual material. Consulting with lawyers and the Post Office, he learned that enforcing this law was not a high police priority but, because it was clearly illegal, no one else was doing it. He started advertising condoms in local college newspapers. The response was fabulous.

Phil and his partner Tom Black rented a room above the Chapel Hill Bank, raised $10,000 in capital and bought Julian Simon's book *How to Start and Operate a Mail-Order Business*. Tom Black went to Africa to start the overseas operations.

They tried selling digital watches, ship-building kits, jewellery, leather goods, handbags, belts, books – 'It was all a big yawn,' Phil says.

They tried contraceptives, sex guides and sex aids. All the erotic material went off the charts. 'It became fairly clear, fairly quick that people who wanted condoms wanted sexual content material,' he says. They built a catalogue page by page, adding lingerie, sex toys, vibrators, oils, gels and creams. Then came video.

'VCR clearly became America's way to watch sexually explicit material,' Phil says. It was compact, mailable and customers could enjoy it in the privacy of their own home. Video has become their single biggest category. They now screen 150–200 videos a month.

The review process is the key to their business. First, they screen out illegal material. They send anything borderline to two outside sex therapists. They review all material before it is released and make sure sex is depicted cheerfully between consenting adults. The therapists then sign a paper stating that they find the material useful to improve communications between couples. 'This seal of approval is good legally and good for ourselves in that what we sell is useful to people,' Phil says. One of their bestselling titles is *Ordinary Couples, Extraordinary Sex*.

Adam & Eve buys video titles by the thousands at catalogue prices, $3 per box compared to $15 per box retail. Six times a year, they revise their catalogue. Lotions and other goods, produced to Adam & Eve specifications, are sold only in the United States.

They are just warming up: in recent years they have begun sponsoring videos and were partners with VCA in cable. Everyone works with Adam & Eve, a company owned by one guy in one of the most sexually conservative states in the US.

In the 1980s the US government went after all the big pornographers. With the government prosecuting companies in several states simultaneously, most defendants would not have the resources to fight back and would be driven out of business.

The government's guns were pointed at Adam & Eve and a three-pronged attack was launched from the State of Utah, the State of North Carolina and, locally, Alleman's County where the sheriff's office joined the raid of the premises. The government likes to prosecute in virulently anti-sex Utah where they have a better chance of conviction. Adam & Eve was not selling in Alleman County so government officials had to buy the material elsewhere and bring it in.

Thirty-five undercover agents and sheriffs, armed with shotguns and two machine guns, raided Adam & Eve's offices. They sealed the doors, separated the workers from the supervisor and photographed and interviewed each employee one by one. They didn't abuse anyone physically but made it difficult for anyone to consult a lawyer. They sent everyone home and told them, 'Don't come back today' to intimidate the employees into quitting.

'We were afraid the workers would never return,' says Phil Harvey. 'But they returned the following day, mad as hell.'

In March, 1987 the government case went to trial. In the first round, the judge was obviously very disturbed that the government was putting people out of business by threats. He chastised the officers for their excessive behaviour.

Other companies including Vivid and VCA had been raided as well, but they agreed to plea-bargain. Vivid paid a heavy fine and got out of mail order. VCA's Rush Hampshire, facing indictments of his wife and employees, basically fell on the grenade, and took a nine-month minimum-security prison sentence as well as paying a heavy fine. Harvey, whose company was by now far larger than Vivid and VCA combined refused to plea-bargain and instead, countered with a civil suit against the government. The fight lasted for 18 months and took place in courts in Utah, Denver and Washington DC.

The minister who brought the indictment was a key government witness. Upon cross examination, it became obvious that what he described as 'community values' was something he arranged with the district attorney, not concerned members of the community. The minister said anybody who worked for Adam & Eve was unfit as a neighbour. The jury smelled a politically motivated attack. Then it was brought out that the material would not be here if it had not been imported into the state by the government. That's not an illegal tactic but juries don't like it.

'He was a bad, bad witness for them,' Phil says. 'The government's attitude was "We'll break you. You'll go broke and we get you."'

Instead, a jury acquitted Adam & Eve in less than ten minutes.

Then Adam & Eve sued, challenging the constitutionality of efforts to put legitimate freedom of speech out of business just because it was sexual material. 'To the government, it became clearer and clearer, as well as for the Feds, that this was a bad case to prosecute and continue. We would win our civil suit against them,' Phil says.

In 1993 they reached a settlement. There was a new attorney in Utah who didn't want the case and it was dropped. Adam & Eve agreed to drop their civil suit and the government agreed that all prosecution for activities from 1986-93 would be null and void.

The government spent millions of dollars on the case: fifty federal attorneys worked full time for almost two years as well as state attorneys from Utah, Alabama, Kentucky, North Carolina and other states. Adam & Eve spent $3 million in lawyers' fees and in return got a lot of free publicity while the government decimated their competition for them. Since the lawsuit there have been no further multiple prosecution cases.

Since then, Rob Showers, who led the charge, was fired for irregularities in his travel expenditures and using taxpayer's money for his personal business. The commission fell into disrepute and changed its name to NOEU – National Obscenity Enforcement Union – so that it could continue to get taxpayer funding. Patrick Truman left the Justice Department and joined Donald

Wildman's pro-censorship organization, apparently using his Justice Department position to pursue his own anti-pornography agenda.

'They think they're doing the Lord's work,' Phil says.

CHAPTER 25

RON JEREMY: THE FIRM FAVOURITE

Ron Jeremy is the most recognizable face in the porno industry. He could go to a small town in Poland, sit down in a restaurant, and someone would say 'Oh look, it's porno star Ron Jeremy.' He's appeared in about a thousand films: *Debi Does Dallas, The Devil in Miss Jones, For Your Thighs Only*. He's done some mainstream and has done a great job promoting himself around town for almost a quarter of century. Ron is the one that makes every guy say 'If he can do it, so can I.'

A guy like Ron deserves a nice meal on a Friday night so I've offered him a steak dinner at the Rainbow, a heavy metal hangout on Sunset Boulevard. Ron is famous for eating, almost as much as he is for other carnal delights.

Around midnight I arrive at the Rainbow. We would have met earlier but Ron has to 'work'. How he does it, I don't know. I would be exhausted. The walls by the entrance are covered with hundreds of celebrity photo snapshots. Sure enough, there's Ron Jeremy with Heidi Fleiss, the famous Hollywood madam.

Mario, the Rainbow's owner, is standing outside. A handsome Italian man with a full head of beautiful white hair, he still looks the same, just as feisty, still surrounded by pretty chicks and long-haired rock stars as he was years ago. Mario signals the gatekeeper to let me pass.

Ron strolls in wearing a green T-shirt that reads 'Extra Large', slacks torn at both knees and sneakers. 'This was the style a couple years ago,' he says. 'I worked very hard to get them like that.' Unpretentious is an understatement.

'Ron!' shouts the maitre d', holding out both arms to give him a hug. He then looks at me: 'Why didn't you tell me you were waiting for Ron! I would have brought you a glass of Champagne.'

Ron works the crowd. He can schmooze with the best of them, like a campaigning politician, shaking one hand over the other. They recognize him at each table. Young guys pat him on the back and ask for an autograph, ask

RON JEREMY: THE FIRM FAVOURITE

※ Ron Jeremy and Harris compare sizes

to be an assistant, ask to get on set.

We head for the kitchen, Rainbow's VIP section. It's too crowded. Pick another place, Ron baby, this is your night.

We take his car, an old Ford Escort with a cracked windshield, no radio. Who said everyone in Hollywood is status conscious? Ron is considered the most frugal person in the industry. Rumour has it he's saved every penny he ever made in this business, something unheard of for a performer.

Everyone in Hollywood knows Ron is the porno connection to mainstream and vice versa. 'Celebrities know that I'm the guy to approach,' he says. 'I'm like the liaison between porn and mainstream.'

This week Ron was invited to speak before executives at Paramount Pictures and Columbia Tri Star on the theme 'Why can the porno industry can spin out films for $50,000 in three days and make big profits while the major studios spend $40,000,000 in six months and can't?' After dinner, Ron got up and spoke. 'Low overhead,' he explained in two hours over lunch.

We get a booth over at Jerry's Famous Deli, packed with a young fashion crowd as opposed to an old garment crowd. Ron whispers who's who sitting at the other tables while they whisper about us, or about him.

Ron is better-looking than his meatball image. He has beautiful blue eyes and dark eyebrows. Sure, he's pudgy and nicknamed 'Hedgehog'. He started off skinny. He just gained a couple of pounds for every one of the 25 years he's been performing.

'Hey, Ron,' calls a young man on his way out, handing him his card. 'I'm a photographer. Give me a call if you need someone.'

'Thank you. Sure. Will do. That's nice of you. I appreciate it,' Ron says and takes the card. He pretends to put it in his back pocket then stuffs it down the back of his chair. 'I get about five of these things a day,' he says. 'You didn't want it did you?'

No thanks.

I study the menu. He doesn't. Sex icon Ron Jeremy is a deli aficionado – he orders creamed herring for an appetizer, sweet and sour cabbage soup, half a pastrami sandwich with a side of mayo. Somebody really should tell him to use mustard, not mayonnaise. 'All in all, way less than a filet mignon would have cost at the Rainbow,' he says.

Still, Ron can't shake the glutton image. Actually, it's only part of his image and everyone likes to make fun of him. His long-time friend, New York publisher Al Goldstein, called Ron a beached whale. Ron loves it. 'He said my Mom filed for retroactive abortion when she found out what I looked like,' Ron says. 'He said that if it weren't for a director yelling "Action", Ron Jeremy would never get laid at all.'

Paunchy Ron Jeremy, pushing 50, is still going strong, still a more reliable performer than most guys half his age. One person who doesn't make fun of him is porno legend Sharon Mitchell. She won't ever forget the time she was down and out, strung out, and thrown in jail in New York, back when strip shows were raided for obscenity and performers were busted as prostitutes. Few know that Ron paid her bail as a professional courtesy though the two had never met.

Sometimes, performers get more respect off the set than on. 'We're basically props,' Ron says. 'Fans put themselves in our shoes and become us. That's why I get a lot of work. I am not a gorgeous guy and regular guys can relate to me. They say "There's my buddy. There's Ron with another girl. Way to go, Ron."'

Ron is a professional comedian with stand-up comic experience. He is a toastmaster as well. He can 'fuck in character'. When he played a nerd in *Fascination*, he asked, 'Is this okay? Am I going too deep? How am I doing?' While the girl was screaming 'Come on and fuck me', Ron never shut up, asking, 'Are you sure? You don't mind? Are your parents coming home soon?'

Ron is a college-educated performer – he has a BA in theater studies and is a licensed schoolteacher. Such a nice man. Shouldn't he have a sweetheart and settle down?

'The only thing I miss is romance,' he says. 'We know that romance is romance and sex is sex. This is such a cold business. It's a choice I've made. I will have it after I leave this business,' which, at the rate he's going, might be a while.

Ron is the porno version of a *mensch*. Normally, I don't talk about myself but I feel very comfortable with him. 'You know, I'm well-travelled and live quite an adventurous life myself,' I say while studying the menu. I look up. Ron is sound asleep. Snoring. Loudly.

I don't take it personally. I researched Ron on the Internet before our meeting. He fell asleep during an interview with a *Los Angeles Times* journalist in 1991. And Bill Margold confirmed he once fell asleep in the middle of a scene. Ron amazed everyone by screwing in his sleep.

The waiter comes by. 'If you guys aren't buying any more food, pay up and get out,' he says. Classy guy. I try to wake Ron up. His fans are watching. A hard day's work can do that to a guy, although most don't call it work.

An attractive young woman walks by. As her perfume reaches us, Ron suddenly wakes with a jolt.

'Yvonne!' Ron calls. She comes to join us. He puts his arm around her. 'You're not wearing a bra,' he says looking into her shirt. She smiles and likes the attention. Obviously she's in the business. 'Have something to eat,' Ron says.

'I can't. My boyfriend's waiting,' she says, blushing. 'He's straight.'

The Hedgehog bristles.

As we are leaving a young man comes running after us, calling our attention. Ron looks at me and rolls his eyes, takes out his pen and gets ready to sign another autograph.

'Are you famous?' he asks.

'Yeah, that's me,' Ron cuts him off.

'No. I meant the other guy,' the young man says looking at me. 'I was a student at Bill Margold's lecture and I saw you in the audience taking notes. Are you like some famous journalist?'

I roll my eyes at Ron Jeremy, take out my pen and sign an autograph. The young man hands me his card and leaves.

'You want it?' I ask Ron. 'I get about five of these things a day.'

✱ Ron Jeremy proudly displays his 'Lifetime Achievement Award'

FAX
June 12, 1996

Dear Willoughby,

Here's a progress report. I've got about another 30,000 words and am polishing up interviews at the rate of 2-3 a day.

Last week I was with porno icon Ron Jeremy until sunrise. He was on the cover of *TV Guide UK* during Valentine's week. Tomorrow I'm taking Al Goldstein to lunch. I'm still waiting to hear from the LA vice squad. I've been promised at some point to go on set for a 'how to do spanking' video.

The one truly amazing thing I keep hearing is that for many sex is simply not taboo. It's hard to fathom. They treat it like eating watermelon. There are guys screwing a different girl every single day of the week, all year long. There are people actually living the type of fantasy that a psychiatrist would tell you 'Don't even bother thinking about it, it doesn't exist.'

I'll call you next week for a general review of where we stand so far.

Best regards,

Harris Goffin

Harris

CHAPTER 26
SEAWEED SALAD WITH AL

The (in)famous New York publisher Al Goldstein is in town and I want to get his perspective on the business.

At 12:25, a shiny red Pontiac convertible, licence plate 'Lucifer', pulls up in front of Chaya Brasserie, a classy Japanese restaurant in Beverly Hills. Al emerges, smoking a big cigar. He's not quite as big as I remember, but still big enough, wearing shorts and a golden Florida tan.

Aya from Chaya, the maitre d', escorts us to a table in the back so we can talk quietly, and obscenely, without disturbing anyone. So far so good. I hope he approves of the low-calorie menu.

'Hmm,' Al says. It's a hmm of approval. He looks at the menu.

'Hmm. Not over-priced,' he says. 'And low calorie. I've lost 50 pounds. And I still have 100 pounds more to lose.'

He orders a grilled red snapper. I get the poached salmon and a seaweed salad.

'Seaweed salad?' he says. 'Look at you. You must be a 27-inch waist and you're getting a seaweed salad? You little fuck. I hate guys like you. From now on, that's your nickname. I'm going to call you "Little Fuck". Waiter! Put extra butter on his fish. I see people like you in the emergency room all the time. With your tennis wounds. Fuck you. I never got hurt on a buffet line.'

Al Goldstein is one of the original modern-day pornographers. He started in 1968 as a patron of the arts, paying for hookers, getting blow-jobs in men's rooms and going to porno films, actually nude volleyball films. He started a consumer magazine called *Screw*, which rated everything in the New York sex scene. 'I am the Ralph Nader of the business,' he says. Since then, he has added two of the most popular adult cable networks, the soft-core Midnight Blue, and hard-core Ecstasy Channel. The money he gets from his hooker ads and *Screw* permits him to support his politically radical habits where anyone is fair game. Of course, it doesn't hurt that the judges are much more likely to protect First Amendment freedom-of-speech rights for political causes than for smut so it doesn't hurt to intermingle them.

Al has paid his dues. He's been arrested 19 times but always got off. 'I like being busted. It's exciting,' he says. 'I love it when somebody gets arrested in the business. It clears the riff-raff out. I'm the only one who beat the federal government in Wichita, Kansas. I'm probably the only person who beat the federal government on obscenity.'

'Don't forget Adam and Eve, they won too,' I say.

'You're right,' Al concedes. 'Phil Harvey's a fighter. I paid my dues. I got ulcers. I'm a wounded warrior.'

Our food arrives. I feel guilty eating a low-cal seaweed salad when he still has 100 pounds to go. If I lost 100 pounds, I'd practically disappear. Maybe I'll get a side of celery sticks.

Before the porno wars, Al was an English major in college. His son was accepted to Harvard Law School and just won a scholarship to Oxford.

Al comes to LA because LA does not come to him. This is where porno is at and Al has a busy schedule: 10 a.m. television interview, 12:30 lunch interview (me), 2 p.m. cable, 4 p.m. video, 6 p.m. prostitute, 8 p.m. dinner with Ron Jeremy.

'He's always thirty minutes late,' Al says. 'But I tell him if he's more than 15 minutes late, he picks up the tab so he's never late with me. I ask a girl "Would you fuck Ron Jeremy?" They say "Yes." I say "That's like saying you practice bestiality." I love Ron but I wouldn't fuck him if I was gay. He's a hairy fat Jew. He's a long dick. You gotta give him credit. He's an anatomical miracle. He can cum on cue. His dick works all the time. He loves being called a celebrity. He's like a dick in motion looking to get laid.'

'What percent of the female performers do you suppose would have sex for money?' I ask.

'A lot of them consider themselves "sexy actresses",' he says. 'Forty per cent you call up and offer them $200 to screw and they'll do it. The other sixty per cent you gotta get a video camera and say that you are doing an 'amateur video'. The girls are here with the delusions of being the next Michelle Pfeiffer. I love to come here. I love to get 19-year-old pussy. I shoot an amateur video and eat nice pussy. I give her $200 and the girl goes home. I love LA.'

'I like the women in the business,' he says. 'I like the fact the women in this business understand men. They know we're dicks. We're sleaze. There's no self-deception. I listen to these talk shows and these women say, "He's looking at pornography." The women are shocked. Why are they shocked? He's a man. And they are always disappointed in us. Women in *this* business are like the guys. They are detached, practical and all they want to do is cum.'

Despite his dirty mind and the dirty talk, Al believes the real porno money is in soft-core.

'Hard core will never be a real player in the big game stakes in our lifetime,' he says without hesitation. 'It's just not going to be. Pornography is the bastard child of entertainment. Look at CES [the Consumer Electronic Show]. Pornography is the reason people bought VCRs before Hollywood filled the vacuum. And now they're pushed aside.'

Forget the high-tech CD-ROMS and the Internet, too.

'I don't use computers and I have no interest in cyberspace,' he says. 'I still can't use my VCR to record.'

The waiter reappears: 'Anything else?' Maybe Jello?

'Yes, get him a big plate of lard with cream and butter and extra cholesterol,' Al says. 'You Little Fuck.'

✱ New York's infamous *Screw* editor Al Goldstein, plus big cigar and Harris from Paris

CHAPTER 27
VICE SQUAD

The Los Angeles Police Department Administrative Vice Division handles commercialized and conspicuous vice, including porno, throughout the city's 18 divisions. On the shady side of downtown Spring Street derelicts clutching wine bottles in paper bags lie on the sidewalk across from the building. It's kind of a dangerous neighborhood. The police really should move to a safer area.

In the entry, a well-built young man in a crisp uniform is checking himself out in a window reflection. He turns around and speaks with such a heavy Spanish accent I have trouble understanding him. I sign in. He checks clearance and sends me upstairs to Vice.

With 5,000 video titles to review each a year, I'll bet the place is jumping, experts with magnifying glasses, studying potentially illicit material in slow motion. The best and brightest studying the down and the dirtiest. Privately, everybody knows policemen like the stuff as much as anyone. In Vegas, when police busted stripper team, Blondage, for 'crimes against nature' they asked the girls for autographs before locking them up.

To my surprise the offices are clean and spacious, calm – empty to be exact. The walls are pastel green, and left blank. Computers on every desk have replaced piles of paperwork. I wait on a couch, and check out the coffee table's magazines. Nothing good, if you catch my drift.

LAPD Chief Supervisor of Vice, Lieutenant Ken Seibert and I are going to do lunch at the Musso & Frank Grill, a detective hangout years ago when real men ate meat and potatoes. And wore fedoras.

Seibert comes out of his office on time, wearing plain clothes: gray slacks and a striped shirt. He towers over me. A burly guy, he looks like a football coach, with a full head of silver, straight hair. He is friendly and open. None of the 'Who are you? What do you want?' third degree. He laughs when I suggest we check each other for concealed weapons. Everybody knows that's what you do. It's what they do in the movies.

'No pin-ups on the walls?' I ask as we shake hands.

'We used to have pictures on our desks,' he sighs. 'That was kind of common throughout the department. They made us eliminate those a while back. The pornography section was the last bastion for this stuff. Even us, we had to eliminate all that.'

Not even a 'Ten Most Wanted Porno Stars' poster?

'You mean you guys used to have more fun?' I ask.

'If you're referring to the 1950s when police couldn't wait to confiscate the imported Brigitte Bardot movies so they could have stag parties with them, I'm afraid that was before my time,' he says. I sense a note of regret. It was before my time too.

So where's all the good stuff?

As if reading my mind, we head to the stash. There they are. My mouth waters. Donuts. It's true, all cops love them. Even porno cops. A box of white powdered donuts rests on top of the refrigerator. I'm about to snitch one as a souvenir when I see something better.

An official Vice Squad mug on the kitchen table. One side displays a detective's badge, the other side shows the four vice symbols of prostitution, Internet, gambling and pornography. I donate $10 to the year's-end Christmas party and pick one up.

We enter the storage room: one tall filing cabinet after another. He smiles. I smile. He opens the first cabinets to display virtually the entire collections of *Playboy*, *Penthouse* and *Hustler*.

'Training purposes,' he says.

'You mean how to?' I ask.

'How to enforce it at the Academy,' he says. That's where rookie Vice officers learn how the line of acceptability has changed over the past two decades.

But that stuff anybody can get. I want to see what nobody can.

He pulls open a drawer filled with porno videos. I glance at the video tape deck across the room. How many people get to spend an afternoon watching banned movies? He reaches for the first cassette.

Just then another policeman enters the room. In one smooth motion, Ken nonchalantly returns the cassette and closes the drawer. He introduces me to his assistant, Bob Navarro, a fit-looking man in his 40s.

Ken Seibert joined the police force in 1968 and has worked in almost every department. When he first started in Vice, he had much less experience than Bob, who has specialized in obscene material.

The LAPD is the only city police department in the US that enforces an obscenity law, because Los Angeles County produces most of America's pornography. The rest of the country deals only on the state and federal level. New York, San Francisco and Los Angeles are the only places in the US where producing 'non-obscene' porno films is legal. What constitutes obscene is the never-ending question and always-changing answer.

'So why show the rookies such mainstream stuff?' I ask.

'To show the transition from the old bikini-clad pin-up in the garage, to topless with covered nipples, then exposed, then more down below. Now everything's exposed,' Ken says without emotion.

'And little by little they started showing naked men, then started showing men with erect penises, then they actually had, *almost* actual sex acts being committed in these magazines,' Bob adds with a hint of nausea.

And?

'The whole basis for what they're doing is to make *money*,' he says. 'And when that is your motivation, you're going to have these people that want to get to the biggest *pile* they can and you're also going to have people who are willing to do more to make money. Over the years, the *so-called*, 'adult industry' has time and time again put out a product that *degrades* women, that has fallen over into the line of *obscenity*, which is *not* protected by the First Amendment and therefore they get *prosecuted* for it. And the motivation is *money*. They want to satisfy some sexual *addict* that needs something a little *harder* so they continue to get *harder* and *harder*. We've constantly pushed that line back at them, trying to get them to steer away from those products that could *cause harm* to our society.'

You mean Bill Margold is not the only one who believes money dirties pornography?

'There are people who think that products that are put out today – the *hard core, semen on a face* - is sexual conduct presented in an *offensive* way and it has *no appeal whatsoever* or literary or scientific value. But the other side has kept putting out this *perception* that it is *acceptable* to most people - and *it isn't*.'

'A lot of people are buying porno,' I say.

'That's *not* necessarily true,' Bob says. 'You will find that a small percentage of people buy a large percentage of that *pornography*. There are huge collectors.'

'Do you see any kind of impact that may have where men no longer can deal with *reality*?' he continues. 'They have to *fantasize* and *masturbate*, rather than dealing in relationships? I want my son to realize that a relationship with other people, with a woman, is the most important aspect of his life. And sex is part of the *blessing* that comes with that *relationship*.'

Gee, I had trouble dealing with reality and relationships before I knew what porno was. Ditto for a lot of my school friends. We were too concerned about getting our sexual act together to worry about a relationship. Better to do it with a stranger. I suggest that it wouldn't be such a bad idea if every father took his son to a legal Nevada brothel for his 16th birthday. Then kids would grow up preferring real sex with a real woman instead of gawking at magazines, fast-forwarding video cassettes or mounting plastic dolls. Ken chuckles. Bob doesn't.

'When your children are not eating properly and would rather have the candy bar, are you really supporting them becoming *strong* individuals?' Bob asks. 'You support what's *good* for people. You support what's *healthy* for people. And you support and *stand* for what's going to make our society a *better* place to live. We as human beings need to do this.'

'That covers a lot of ground to monitor,' I ask. 'Why specifically pornography?'

'One of the *strongest* drives that we have is the sexual drive and if we're *masturbating* to an image of some woman tied up and the impact that has at the height of our *orgasm*, it's certainly going to have an affect on our *attitude* towards woman,' he says. 'Is that going to play a role in my *raping* somebody? Is that going to play a role in the way that I treat women in the workplace? If we have videos of a man and a woman and the intent and the interest is to build a relationship between a man and a woman and sex is part of that relationship, great! But that's not what the porno industry's all about. They're about making *money*, about *titillating* men as *fast*, as quick as they can.'

Gee, I thought everyone fast-forwarded this stuff.

'Our job is to look at material that goes so far that it's really going to have some *obvious* detrimental affects in our society. Let's not let that get out for God's sake. Let's at least stop it there.'

Stopping what where is a never-ending debate. Society is constantly changing and very few things remain obvious.

'We are all brothers and sisters in this world and we have to watch each other,' he says. 'We have to let people know the *toxic* affect that this material is having on us, just like smoking and drinking,' he says. 'It's not a question of "*Does* it have an effect?' It's a question of "*How much* of an affect does it have?" They're being held in check by our enforcement efforts now. But if allowed to run free with no fear of enforcement whatsoever, there's no doubt in my mind, it would get much much worse than it is. Pretty soon you go from bondage, to maiming, to a snuff film, just because they want to see what will sell.'

A snuff film is a movie which depicts an actual murder for the entertainment of the viewer. 'How many have you seen?' I ask.

'We've never seen a snuff film,' Ken says.

That's not to say they're not out there. But they certainly don't exist for commercial distribution. Everyone knows a professional killer can be hired for money in virtually every country in the world. If more money were offered, would ethics prevent them from filming it?

'In teaching class, we have to show if the material has any serious literary, artistic, scientific or political value,' Bob says. His voice full of sarcasm, he holds up a video box cover. 'This one might make it on the literary field: *FUCK MY PUSSY, BANG MY ASS, VOLUME III*. Do they have any considerations what effect this would have on a 13-year-old child?'

But you have to be at least 18 to enter an adult bookshop so what's the issue? Bob figures kids will find everything their parents hide. Ain't that the truth. Even Bob admits he found his dad's porno book, called a 'Tijuana Bible'. He's apparently recovered from the damage done and has led a productive life though no doubt that can't be said for everybody.

He lifts up another video.

'Here's a story about how women want to orally copulate with you,' he says. 'They *absolutely* love that. *Except* your wife. She doesn't want to do it. But every other woman wants to do it. Women want to have you *climax* on their face. They *love* it. They want to *lick* it off. They want to have *sex* with the next-door neighbour's wife. They want to have a *lesbian* relationship. They want an *orgy*. *Except* my wife. Something's *wrong* with her. These story lines, it's big lies that are being told to people and they're buying it. They're buying it.'

He means literally and figuratively.

'If you look at the figures for child molestation, they're on the upswing. If this stuff is so wonderful, why hasn't that gone down? Why hasn't the *rape* rate gone down? Why haven't all the crimes associated with *prostitution* gone down? Why hasn't prostitution itself gone down? We have more crime arrests than ever before.'

Ken must be getting hungry because he interrupts.

'A lot of people do see that as a thing done in the privacy of your own home,' he says. 'So why should we even have a squad to do pornography? We fought for our lives several times in budget cuts. People say "We got murders out there. We got robbers out there. Take those guys from the pornography sections, put them on the street and use them." They don't realize the proliferation of this stuff causes all these other crimes to go up. We showed a hundred times, when you get rid of that, the other things go down. We don't need as many guys on the street in uniform.'

But he's referring to street-walkers. Pornographers don't live in those kind of neighborhoods.

'Our job is to enforce the law the way the bulk of the citizens want the law enforced,' says Ken. 'This is a law that involves community standards which is rare for any law. Our job is to walk down the middle of the road and enforce the law the way it should be enforced within the city of Los Angeles. We just have to go with what's prosecutable and what the guidelines of the City District Attorney gives us. Our job is not to take an extreme position one way or the other but just to enforce the law. And that's what we try to do. We try to maintain that line and stay in the center and bring some rationality to this.'

Bob has a lecture to give. Chief of Vice and I have a lunch to do.

CHAPTER 28

HE'S ONLY DOING HIS JOB

Ken Seibert and I head for Hollywood, to the Musso & Frank Grill, an old hangout of the 'Hat Squad', the tough-guy, fedora-wearing detectives who dined before an evening of cleaning up the town on their own terms, back before the days of Miranda Rights and Citizen Complaint Offices. We pass by Cherokee Ave where Jasmine performs every night in her window.

'You hit an emotional chord with him,' Ken says.

'Who me?' I ask.

'Yeah, you brought out his worst,' he says. 'His expertise is in the encroachment area. But he did get off on a tangent. I'm second-guessing here but I think he thought you came off as very liberal on the subject and he wanted to give you the really right-wing approach to it. He normally wouldn't do that unless he knew you a lot better or it had been a longer session, although our session did get kind of long there. That's why he really opened up.'

Just doing my job.

We park in the back and enter unannounced through a narrow hall, past the kitchen. Inside, the room is dark mahogany-panelled, filled with padded red-leather circular booths. Professional, old, waiters pass by, hearing, seeing and speaking nothing.

Ken is the diner type, not familiar with the expense account menu. I recommend the roast duck.

Seibert joined the force right out of college. Ironically, Seibert and Bill Margold attended California State College in Northridge at the same time. To rise in the ranks requires a wide range of experience. Seibert's career covered uniformed patrol, Metro Division riot squad, undercover street work disguised as a wino. 'I loved it. They were exciting times,' he says.

He worked in internal affairs, investigating complaints against police officers including street misconduct, alleged beatings, guys threatening their wives and off-duty embezzlement. He oversaw one of the LAPD's worst scandals which involved 30 police officers sponsoring the 15 to 17-year-old female Hollywood Explorer Scouts, and having sex parties with them. A number of officers were prosecuted and dismissed.

'By the time I left two years later, I was absolutely convinced that anything a crook had ever done, some policeman had done,' Seibert says.

He next supervised the Narcotics Division, where the real action was. They had daily search-warrant raids, all suspects armed, all entries forced. Every day, narcotics enforcement agents experienced the rush of adrenaline, routinely kicking in doors, weapons loaded, never knowing what's on the other side. Now, he's in charge of raiding porno movie sets.

'This is the same kind of feeling only you don't fear as much that you'd face

✱ LAPD Vice Squad Supervisor Lieutenant Ken Siebert with Harris in front of the Musso and Frank Grill

a gun, you'd fear that people would be running around and going crazy,' he said with a chuckle. 'It's kind of an exciting time. We're actually taking them down in the middle of their porno shoots. And you talk about the fun part of enforcement, that's the fun part.'

Supervising Vice is more prestigious than the title implies – this is where an officer encounters the greatest temptation, when dealing with informants, prostitutes, bars and gambling. Here the officer:supervisor ratio is 4:1 versus the normal ratio of 10:1.

Seibert was Sergeant of the Wilshire Division Patrol when *Deep Throat* was released, the first porno movie to hit the theatres. Before that, porno was mostly 8mm films sold out of the trunk of a car and shown in sleazy bars. When *Deep Throat* opened, so many people crowded into the mainstream theatre that the police had to administer crowd control. What a switch. They used to arrest people for watching. Now they were helping them safely see it. The grateful theatre management gave local officers automatic free passes.

'I'll never forget that,' Ken says. 'We started getting complaints from all the police that were going down, hanging out at the same theatre where we had just been in charge of crowd control.'

Another early incident involved a theatre showing a film depicting urination, which starred 'Little Annie Sprinkle'. When an officer reported a possible violation, Ken instructed him to proceed, watch it again, write up each scene, put it in an affidavit for a search warrant, present it to a judge, then return and serve the warrant. As the process was new to everyone, it took a while to get it all together. The officer called the theatre: 'Are you still showing the film depicting the urination scene?'

Ken roars with laughter. 'Sure enough, what he said tipped them off,' he says.

By the time the officers raided the theatre and confiscated the film, the incriminating scenes were gone, just as Ken suspected. He returned and found them in the trash. 'The dummy had it in the same viewing room,' he says, shaking his head.

From an informant or a citizen's lead, they would set up regular surveillance of a movie set, usually in a private residence. If they saw someone familiar like Ron Jeremy, they knew they were in the right place. They read license plates through binoculars, watched movie cameras and lights carried from big vans, let them get underway for a couple of hours. Meanwhile they'd get their search warrant, most of it written in advance, fill in the surveillance particulars, rush it for a judge's signature, return and raid the place., They'd filter through the crew and cast, find where the sex act was taking place, try to observe some of the scene in progress to prove sex and money were exchanged. They'd collect check stubs, receipts, contracts. Back then, everyone was paid in cash. If the big bulge in some guy's pocket turned out to be greenbacks, that usually meant he was the director or producer. Vice would take down statements.

Initially afraid, performers would become hostile as the situation calmed down. The police would warn them: 'If you don't cooperate with us and give us a statement against the producer, then you're going to go to jail for committing the act of prostitution.'. Even Bill Margold admits the porno industry thrives on the misery of others and performers were the first to turn friendly witness.

'"Now they know where the line is drawn,' Ken says. 'At least in LA they don't distribute things involving urination, defecation, kiddy porno or extreme bondage. They know it so well, they tend to leak information to us if they know one of their competitors is doing that. We've gotten several cases because of that.'

'You have to monitor them because even though they know where the line is drawn, they keep wanting to move across it just to see: how is this going to go over? How is this going to sell? Can I make a little bit more money with this? Even the big guys are constantly pushing the line. They know how to push that line gradually rather than in quantum leaps. That's what keeps them clean for the most part.'

Ken's squad pretty much does everything. Out of 8,000 cops in the city, there's only eight officers monitoring porno production and sales. 'This massive billion-dollar-plus porno industry is afraid to cross that line because of a small number of guys,' he says. 'So it has a major deterrent effect. From that standpoint we have done a pretty good job.'

'Are they all true believers?' I ask.

'Bob is probably the most off-the-wall,' Ken says. 'I brought him in for his expertise but he just got off on a tangent. Everybody else is pretty much straight down the line because they know that's the way I am and they try to do what I want them to do.'

Nationwide, the guys in Ken's section are considered experts in the field of obscenity enforcement, being the only local agency group that deals full-time in pornography. All other enforcement takes place on a state or federal level.

'We get calls to lecture,' Ken says. 'It's pretty much acknowledged if you need information about the porno industry you call LAPD and get the experts.'

'I thought you had to call Bill Margold,' I say.

'If you want *that* aspect of the industry, yeah,' Ken smiles. 'Or Ron Jeremy.'

FAX August 16, 1996

Dear Willoughby,

I'll be working round the clock to get the manuscript to you by the end of next month. I'm glad you like chunks of it. I'm still feeling my way through some aspects of this so I appreciate your input.

I got a call from the Kentucky Penitentiary to arrange an interview with the grand-daddy kingpin of porno. He paid one million dollars on a declared four million dollars profit. The FBI nabbed him with the help of the Swiss bank authorities. And he started off selling comic books!

By the way, any news on your web site address? You could have some material today.

Best regards,

Harris Gaffin

Harris

CHAPTER 29

REUBEN STURMAN, PEEP SHOW WIZARD

Ever been to a peep show? Adult bookstores across the US often have individual booths in the back of the shop. At present prices, twenty-five cents buys you twenty seconds and an attendant is always there to change a dollar.

Imagine a store making a living a quarter at a time. Believe it or not, for more than two decades that's exactly where the biggest pile of porno money came from.

For years, nobody really noticed until police started getting citizen complaints. In those days, there were no adult-store zoning laws or regulations.

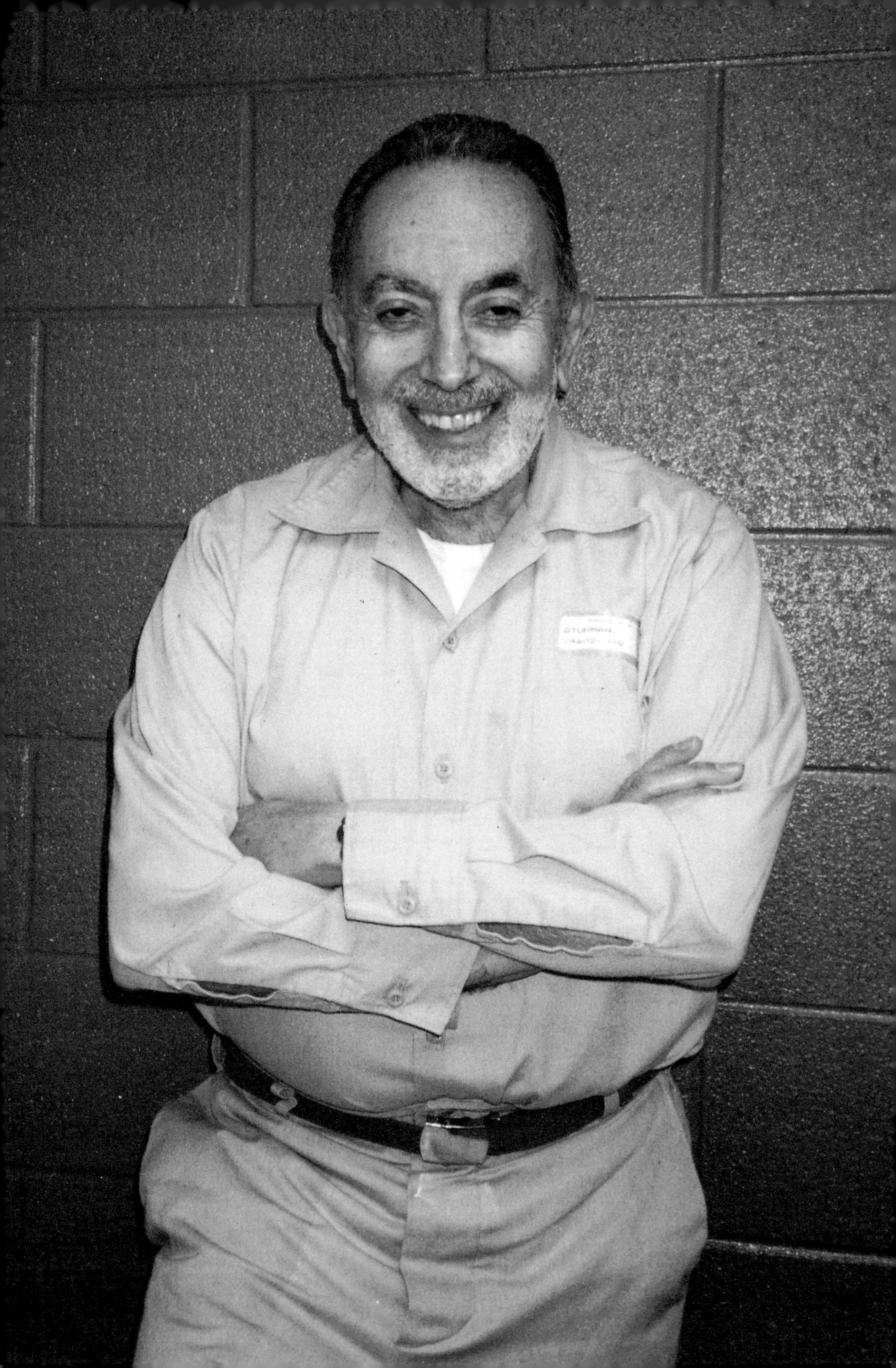

REUBEN STURMAN, PEEP SHOW WIZARD

✱ Peep-show King Reuben Sturman photographed in Kentucky Federal Correction Institute. 'Ninety nine percent of the people in this business once worked for me.'

Some set up shop close to residential areas, *not* because there was any local demand, the neighbors insisted. In LA, Lieutenant Seibert and the Vice Squad were called in and monitored activity. The shops were open 24 hours a day and each store had 15-20 booths. Each booth generated about $150-200 a day - in quarters.

Across the country, depending on the neighbourhood, some stores were subject to strictly enforced hours of operations and had as few as six booths.

In any case, they generated a lot of cash. A guy named Reuben Sturman was the first to realize the peep-show potential.

Before video arrived in the 1980s, these peep-show booths ran 8mm films with an A and a B projector. Anyone who has ever shown home movies knows the headaches involved. There was often a hair in the gate or fuzz floating around the screen. The bulb got hot and blew. When the projector *did* work, it faded the film and turned it pale green. The film often unravelled on the reel and snaked around the projector. Then the operator had to stop the film and cut it with a knife. What a mess. Customers complained. Every day there was a problem. Still, it was a good deal and it did well enough to make the bosses happy and merit police surveillance.

By the 1980s, this system was replaced by video recorders which could show eight films on a machine which almost never broke down and worked like a television. The viewer pushed the button to change the film and pay as many or as few quarters as desired. You could watch EZ Rider tying up Ariana for the price of a bag of potato chips.

Anyway, these peep shows made more in quarters than all the other porno businesses made in dollars. Reuben Sturman was the peep-show king and made sure he got his first.

The bookshops also sold a selection of books, magazines, newspapers, movies and sex gadgets distributed by, of course, Reuben Sturman, who covered all the major markets and then some including LA, Chicago and New York.

'We were making big money,' Reuben told me.

How big, I wonder.

Sturman worked closely with over a dozen companies from whom he bought the films; he had 200 shops nationwide which, let's say, averaged 10 booths making $100 each per day and were opened just five days a week. That's 200 x 10 x $100 x 250 = $50,000,000 per year, in quarters. Splitting that fifty-

fifty with the store, Sturman's take was $25,000,000 a year, conservatively. After all, he produced, distributed and sold the product, too.

'He would come in and skim fifty per cent right off the top,' Lt. Seibert says. 'We used to follow these guys out to a big warehouse in the Valley.'

The quarters were kept in 50-gallon drums.

Outer space begins 50 miles above planet Earth, where the atmosphere ends. In 1963, the Project Mercury astronauts astounded the world when they circled the globe and reached a maximum height of 100 miles. Had Sturman emptied out his 50-gallon drums and stacked his peep-show quarters on top of one another, the Project Mercury astronauts would have had to glance upwards to see Reuben stacking the quarters on his column. It would have reached 157 miles high. Each year.

No one could touch him for about twenty years. Finally, the Internal Revenue Service brought him down on charges of income-tax evasion, the same way they got Al Capone. It was the longest running IRS case in FBI history.

I phoned Sturman at the Manchester Federal Penitentiary in Kentucky.

'You did all right,' I said.

'Just trying to make a living,' he answered.

CHAPTER 30

LEARN WITH PROFESSOR BILL

Valley College is an oasis-like campus, surrounded by a grid of single homes and shopping malls. This could be Any College, Anywhere, USA, but tonight's topic most definitely could not. Civil Law 101 has a special guest, a real live porno star who will speak about pornography, the law and himself.

I'm waiting in the biology building, Bill Margold shows up with a haircut so fresh, he's still white around the ears and neck. He's got on clean new sneakers but otherwise, it's the same old Bill, same old faded short-sleeved shirt and jeans.

At 6 p.m. sharp, biology students are replaced by civil law students, an eclectic group from a wide range of backgrounds and lifestyles, some from work, others from home, inner-city girls with rings on every finger wearing colourful sweatsuits, gum-chewing Valley Girls with their hair done up, a short-cropped, muscular guy in T-shirt, jeans and cowboy boots. Everyone is

LEARN WITH PROFESSOR BILL

here to improve themselves with education. Tonight Bill is going to help them in this process.

The teacher, mustached, clean pressed shirt, tie and corduroy sports jacket enthusiastically softens the class up for the experience. Margold gloats in front of the class, his chin held high.

'Lights off? OK, good,' he says. 'Now you can play with each other.'

Ha, ha, ha.

'From 1969 to 1988 I was a lawbreaker,' Bill continues. 'I was breaking this very strange law called "creating pornography". I was considered to be a prostitute – get it up, get it in, get it off, get it out on cue'.

Margold's career has spanned over 500 films since 1969. 'I've become *the* leading authority on the adult entertainment industry in the world. There's *nothing* I can't answer. So no matter how wild your imagination is, I guarantee I can satisfy that and a great deal more.'

He covers lots of territory, drops a lot of names, mentions his Meese Commission's congressional committee appearance, theorizes about the causes of AIDS, nostalgically reminisces about his appearances on big-screen porno and tells what it's like to be a porno star.

'We were hired to say our dialogue then suck a dick or have our dicks sucked,' he says.

I sit up with a jolt. Did he say 'suckadick'? Who says 'suckadick' during a college lecture?

'You may have noticed that I don't intend to mince my words,' he continues. Some of the students smile. Some blush. Others jot down notes in case there's a test later on.

'The X-rated industry is designed to create masturbation and if it doesn't create that then you go on to find something else to get you off,' he says. 'Hopefully, you all do know what masturbation is, if you don't you're missing one of the great pleasures and cheapest dates of your life. It's the ultimate in safe sex.'

He passes around porno tapes and a porno star photo calendar. 'In this calendar you will see naked pictures of me which I am very proud of,' he says. 'Besides being an actor, a director, a writer and a critic, I ran the biggest nude agency in the world for nine years. I met ten thousand women. Nine thousand of them went out of the business. Of the thousand that stayed in, I made about a hundred of them famous. I am one of the last outlaws in this business. Most of the pioneers have grown old and fat and are chewing their cud in the high field. We exist because America has a dirty mind. The porno industry should be in the gutter where it belongs because people perceive sex to be dirty and our society wants us to live in this kind of frustrated guilt about sex. Our industry allows you to relieve a great deal of that guilt. That's our purpose.'

'This industry has allowed me to be, in some strange ways, the adolescent I never was,' he says. 'I still get a big kick out of it. Although, I don't do any real penetration porn anymore. I did a couple of jack-off scenes recently and they were really cute. Massive cum shots. I have a wonderful dick and it's been my best friend for a long time. It's never let me down. But I do this business for only one reason – the glory, the immortality. What I've done will never ever go away. My name is all over the world, from the Library of Congress to hundreds of magazines. I get such a big kick out of it.'

The students aren't sure how to take this rebel. If a rebel is an authority, does that make him still a rebel? They have lots of questions but shy away from asking what they really want to know.

'Have you ever been a stunt man?' someone asks.

'I've done stunt-cock work, but I don't like doing it because it psychologically scars the poor man you're stunt-cocking for,' Bill explains. 'A cum shot in the face is the ultimate shot in the history of this business. These are money shots. If the sperm's good, then it's good for the skin. I've cured stretch marks and scars.'

'What are the disadvantages?' a young woman asks.

'The downside to the X-rated industry is that while you are in it, it's very hard to maintain a relationship. The industry does not attract happy people. There's a certain misery involved which I am above. Within the industry, people tear into each other. It will eat its own as fast as it can.'

Finally, Bill shows us a porno tape in which he plays a deranged chef who penetrates a cooked chicken. The performers in the film look even more surprised than the students in the class. No doubt the scene was not scripted.

A couple of days later, I'm still digesting the chicken story, when my secretary arrives with my transcribed tapes. She drops the disk on the desk and rolls her eyes: 'This guy sounded like he wanted to be the industry's voice of authority but I'm not convinced that he is.'

'He *gave* the impression through the way he spoke: "Oh I know it all. I've done it all. I've seen it all. I've talked about it all. I've intellectualized it all. I've philosophized it all. I just know everything."' she says 'But you know, any time you're in a situation when somebody's saying "I know everything", you know they don't know everything. You just know this. He really spoke for shock value. As many "dick", "cum shots", "fucking dead cooked chickens", anything that he could possibly throw in, he would.'

Bill Margold lectures on the porno industry at Valley College

Come on, women love that stuff. Everyone knows that. She must be a feminist.

'This guy was so full of himself,' she continues. 'He says that he's done everything – "I made a hundred women famous." He's a one-man show. Saint and saviour for the entire business. The apparently unlimited medicinal qualities of his cum: "cures acne, aids digestion, wonderful as a facial mask", I mean, the man did not stop!'

I have to get a new secretary.

CHAPTER 31

AVN: THE COLOUR OF MONEY

Adult Video News, the industry's major trade magazine, is read by virtually the entire adult retail store community, so producers are keen to reach them through advertising. Pro-industry, pro-business and pro-making money, *AVN* enjoys a powerhouse reputation. The mainstream press goes to them for information. Journalists come on set, say 'I'm *AVN*' and are cleared without even mentioning their names. The *AVN* annual awards night is a formal, black-tie affair where performers and producers accept trophies for everything from 'Starlet of the Year' to 'Best Anal Feature'.

AVN's publisher Paul Fishbein is ambitious and respected, even feared. His is considered a no-nonsense name in a cold-hearted business. He's also on the Free Speech Coalition Board of Directors. Funny, I wonder why Margold never mentioned him.

Printed on slick, glossy paper, the magazine's ads are read just like a fall fashion magazine's. Companies like Vivid, VCA and Wicked advertise prominently.

 AVN is located in a newly-built cement-block building in a Valley industrial zone. Inside it's clean and spacious. I wander past the receptionist, past glass walls surrounding an interior garden, stepping over extraordinary floor tiles. The bathroom floor rates five stars. Every tile in the kitchen is different. No joke. This place must have been used for an Italian tile showroom.

There's EZ Rider, wearing bifocals, labeling filing cabinets full of slides. So this is the place he calls 'the morgue'. Years of photos taken at festivals, award ceremonies, etc. have yet to be properly labelled – it's basically skilled grunt work. Usually slides in a photo agency are labelled as they are shot. Looks like they're just getting their act together. It's a time-consuming, expensive process but necessary if they are to be useful. What good is having great slides of Houston in the bedroom if you can't find them when you need them?

In the next room, a bunch of guys are circled around a desk having a good laugh over a magazine layout. A new porno starlet's photos? I work my way through. It's the latest *AVN* issue, opened to a picture of Bill Margold blowing up a long, thin balloon. It looks like he's doing something else. They don't like him because he don't like them, someone whispers. They made fun of his counselling service which even Bill admits unfortunately attracts male fans anxious to meet performers and performers more anxious to find work than seek counselling. Anyway, *AVN* succeeded in making him look ridiculous but in their haste, got their facts wrong. 'Hey, does this libel him?' someone asks. There's a nervous silence. Naw, they conclude. It just makes him look stupid.

I head upstairs to Fishbein's office. His waiting room is large enough to be a pool hall. The lonely receptionist with a pierced nose has a desk and computer and I suspect is flirting on-line with a singles bulletin board somewhere. She is sexy as in young and free, not sexy as in porno star. I take a seat on a lone couch on the other side of the room. We have to shout across the room to hear each other.

Fishbein arrives. That's him? He who intimidates everyone? He looks more like a college kid than a publisher who strikes fear in the hearts of pornographers worried about a bad review, or worse, being ignored. In his thirties, he's wearing a short-sleeved sport shirt, jeans and sneakers and has a full head of shiny, dark hair, years away from even a touch of distinguished grey. No wedding ring. He's thin and jumpy as a teenage tennis player. He has an intense, focused look. Where Margold's eyes are accepting, Fishbein's stare never relaxes.

The windowless office is white, too white. *AVN* has just relocated here and the walls are blank, no paintings or porno posters yet. He plops down behind a huge desk, swivels his chair and grabs a couple of diet sodas from a stack of cases behind him. He holds all calls but his employees keep wandering in asking questions about production. Fishbein obviously knows every aspect of his company's business.

'I was predestined to be a publisher,' he says enthusiastically.

By the age of 14, Fishbein was already writing articles and publishing a professional wrestling magazine. He majored in journalism at Philadelphia's Temple University, published another magazine, learned streetwise distribution, worked his way through college. One of his jobs was managing a big video store when video recorders were the latest thing. Customers often requested adult movie recommendations so, with $900, he and two friends started an eight-page newsletter reviewing adult films and advertised subscriptions in men's magazines. But a funny thing happened. Most subscribers were adult bookshop owners. It gave him an idea. Get porno producers to place ads in a magazine geared for retailers. *AVN* began in 1983. It was the right idea at the right time. Paul has since expanded his influence by joining several porno-related committees.

'When you look at the statistics, what do you see?' I ask.

'Six hundred million rentals a year!' he exclaims. 'That does not include adult stores, sales and mail order. With product as cheap as it is, buyers are buying this stuff in tons. Six hundred million rentals in regular video stores is 10 to 12 per cent of the entire market. One out of every ten tapes is an adult tape. That's amazing. How much of this stuff can people watch? I can't get through ten minutes of a tape without fast-forwarding it or turning it off. But they can, apparently.'

'And where do you fit into all this?' I ask.

He hesitates, like he's not sure if he should say what he's thinking. 'I'm sort of a spokesperson for the industry,' he says. 'When the *Wall Street Journal* is writing an article on the business, they use my statistics. When the *New York*

Times needs a quote, they call me. When *Hard Copy*, *Entertainment Tonight*, E! Network, CBS or *20/20* or one of those shows needs somebody, they come to *AVN*. When there were some bills up in the California Senate, I spoke to the Senate. There are very few people in this business that can articulate the issues, that have the statistical information to back up what they are saying or that have real understanding of what a censorship law is and what First Amendment law is.'

'How can *you* be the spokesman? I thought Bill Margold was,' I ask.

'Bill Margold is not taken very seriously,' he says. He leans forward to speak clearly into my microphone, like he is talking directly to Margold. 'You can tell him that I said that. He's a shoot-from-the-hip, foolish kind of person who has his own agenda that is "Hey, it's sex, it's fucking. Whoever doesn't like it, fuck it, we're the pariahs of society so let's act that way." He's pretentious. My attitude is this is a multibillion-dollar industry and multibillion-dollar industries shouldn't have jackasses speaking for them, which is basically what Bill Margold is. I spent a lot of time with him on the Free Speech board. I respect him only as a personality to raise money from the dregs of the industry.'

Anything else?

'He abhors money. Quote: "I abhor money." He's just a self-inflated, foolish guy who's actually completely insecure and it's the perfect example of how dumb this industry is that fools like him can actually have a place in it.'

'He has a good heart. He really cares about the talent in the business. His intentions are probably very good. I don't think deep down inside he's a bad person. If you shed the pompous, boring, exterior, there's probably a good heart in there. I don't think he would hurt anybody. But he can't be taken seriously. He doesn't really have the pulse of what's going on. He's not interested in the economics of the business, so how can you take him seriously as a businessman?'

'He'll say "*AVN*? It's a piece of trash." It's jealousy. Margold hasn't made any impact in this business so he hates *AVN*. But in the meantime, every issue of *AVN*, I give Margold's Free Speech, his Free Speech II and his PAWE three pages. Not only that, but *AVN* has raised so much money for the Free Speech organization and given away so many free pages of advertising. Did Margold ever say "Thank you" or "Good job" or "We really needed *AVN*?" We *only* reach 87,000 people and every retailer in the business. We're responsible for raising all this goddamned money. Fuck him. He's an asshole. He's there. I don't know why he's there. He doesn't add anything. He doesn't subtract anything. He's just there. You sit in a meeting with him, he just sucks the energy out of the room.'

Will the real spokesman for the industry please stand up? Margold and Fishbein network around the same people, both enthusiastically support the business. Margold grew up with porno as a rebel thing and wants it to remain there. Fishbein sees porno as a mainstream thing and wants to move it there.

Now, what about this *AVN* Awards Night? The *AVN* Awards are the biggest splash in the business, the porno equivalent of the Academy Awards or the Grammys. (Though they have a few hundred prizes, like they're trying to give a prize to everybody.)

The mainstream movie industry puts out 400 films a year. Porno puts out 3,000 a year. 'There are real cinematographers, real editors, real gaffers, real screenwriters, real directors, real, well I won't say real, actresses, but people who are trying to act,' he says. 'There's really hot sex. There are people creating marketing campaigns. They're doing boxes. It's an industry like any other industry and you need to celebrate if you're working hard all year long. It's nice to have a time to celebrate what you do.'

'Like the award for "Best Spanking" tape?' I ask.

He sighs. 'When I look at the "Best Spanking" tape, I wonder why I went to journalism school. How do we decide? You line them all up and see which people's asses got the reddest? I don't know, except that I have twelve people who review spanking tapes that say there's a definite art to it and they vote on it. Who am I to argue? I sit there and, you know, I shake my head.'

CHAPTER 32

THE BOTTOM LINE AT SHADOW LANE

I'm lost in a Valley hotel, trying to find Shadow Lane Productions, a production company specializing in spanking. The receptionist says she knows nothing about spanking, Shadow Lane, or a film shoot.

Some weird-looking guys are lugging lights and bags of equipment into an elevator. That must be the crew. I jump into the next elevator and follow them.

I run into the owner, Eve Howard, who explains why I got lost: the shoot was listed under a different name and located in a private room which was then switched. Apparently, reception is very good at keeping secrets.

Eve has thick glasses, looks matronly, not very attractive but sort of sexy, like a no-nonsense school mistress, exuding a tension between sexual energy and discretion. She's wearing a tight but businesslike suit, stockings and lacey Victorian pumps.

She prefers to shoot in a hotel room because it's much more discreet and sensual than a movie set. Today she is combining a male spanking club member with a seasoned female performer.

One of the crew immediately volunteers he is *not* part of the scene. Another says he definitely is. The guys tower over Eve, the boss, who tells one well-built guy wearing ballet slippers to move the coffee table into the hall. He goes to move it on to the balcony where it's raining. Eve corrects him but again he moves towards the balcony. She blocks him and finally he takes it to the hall. This guy deserves a spanking.

The room is crowded: three crew, two performers, Eve, myself. Equipment consists of a four-poster bed, two VHS cameras on tripods, two microphones on boom stands and two sets of lights, one placed on the bed where it could tip over.

The story is about a couple who have been corresponding for months and now meet in a hotel room to do a scene. The characters include an attractive tall brunette woman in flirty skirt, stockings and high heels, and a blond, handsome young man wearing an Oxford blue button-down shirt and beige chino pants.

It's hot in here. The performers are thirsty and nervous and open the bottle of wine reserved for the scene. The woman gulps hers down and gets a refill. The young man, Stephen Price, is sweating under the heat of the lights and downs another glass too.

As a kid, Stephen Price was the class clown. Whenever the teacher took a student out of the class to be spanked, Stephen took his girlfriend to the front of the class and spanked her with a Bible in front of the other students. In high school he noticed that when the football team won, the players spanked the cheerleaders in front of the crowd. 'The wildest cheerleaders were the preachers' daughters,' he says.

Now he has to spank from a script Eve expects him to memorize.

Spanker (Stephen): I'm glad you finally got here.

Cut!

'Speak up' Eve directs. Stephen gets more nervous. He can only remember one line at a time. Eve starts and stops if one word is changed. She wrote the script and wants it said correctly whether he has acting experience or not. He's sweating.

THE BOTTOM LINE AT SHADOW LANE

✻ Eve Howard reviews a spanking script with her (conservatively dressed) performers

✻ Spanking begins

✻ The session over, the spankers show their true feelings

'I didn't know it was going to be this much work,' he says. 'I thought it would be a breeze.'

'It will be, once we get to the spanking part,' Eve assures him.

Action!

Spanker: You know, Maggie, I'm finding it hard to believe you're submissive.

Cut!

'Damn. Why am I so nervous?' Stephen says.

'And *you* don't even have to take your clothes off,' I reassure him.

It's hot under the lights. The woman is facing our way, flipping up her skirt to get air.

Eve feeds them their lines because they keep moving between tossing the script on the ground and trying to move forward. Every time someone forgets their lines, they have to pick up the script and start again.

'I see you completely ignored my suggestions for wearing blue jeans.' The line requires five takes.

'May I have some more wine?' the woman asks.

'After your spanking.'

'I'm getting a spanking?'

It's confusing which lines are scripted and which are conversation.

'Why did you decide on me?' he asks Eve after screwing up his lines again.

'Looks alone,' Eve reassures him.

He takes his partner over his knee. Spank! Spank!

'Oh! Stop!' she cries.

He stops. She was acting because the camera was rolling.

'No! I didn't mean to stop!' she reprimands him. Now he has to spank her again. She's getting impatient.

'I thought I was hurting you,' he says.

'No, you weren't,' she answers.

'Good,' Eve says. 'Lift her skirt.'

The woman then gets upset over the way she's getting spanked. 'You have to cup more,' Eve says. 'You have to figure out what part of the hand to use if we're going to continue. Bounce it off the model. It doesn't look good. Focus on her bottom. Spread it all out and rub and deliver a sting. The problem is he's thudding. Spread the impact.'

Eve and the model disagree because what looks good on camera and what feels right on the behind apparently are two different things.

The crew suspects the model is just giving the new guy a hard time.

Eve Howard majored in literature at Vassar College. While her head was in Chaucer, her heart was in Hollywood. She moved out to Los Angeles in 1976 and wrote hard-core male-oriented porno text.

'I was good at it, but it was killing my soul because I didn't like to write those kind of things,' Eve says. 'It's extremely vulgar and it's all tailored to the male fantasy, a very old male fantasy.' She began freelance fetish writing, a niche full of trimming and fancy costumes. But her real love was spanking.

While the hard-core porno market consists mostly of men, Eve's soft-core market is mostly women. Shadow Lane specializes in spanking for women who love it: literature, videos, instruction, weekend spank-ins. If it relates to red bottoms, they do it. It's kinder, gentler kinkiness. Set up in 1986, Eve has soft-sold the company so well, mainstream magazines will accept her advertising and mainstream bookstores will accept her books. Not even Vivid has done that.

Customers are part of the social life, too. Shadow Lane coordinates personal ad publications and parties. 'Bondage & discipline' support groups or clubs scare them. 'They want to wear their street clothes and be in nice places and do discreet, charming, spanking games,' Eve says. The girls usually wear cocktail or prom dresses, and other fancy clothes, though some leather fetishism sneaks in too. Most play happens in sexy, cozy, private rooms. People often meet at the parties after corresponding for several months.

'We bring a different sensibility and it's more grounded in the movies, the TV shows, we saw growing up in the '50s, *I Love Lucy*, with a strong charming masculine figure who's a bit paternal and a clever, witty, naughty, mischievous female counterpart who basically gets her own way, although she might have gotten a spanking along the way,' Eve says.

'As far as the women go, I guess because it is a patriarchal society, we are stuck with our old-fashioned patriarchal fetishes. We accommodate feminism in our own independent way. But we kind of cling to the Clark Gable/Gary Cooper image, upstanding men, a little bit stern. That's the turn-on for a girl into spanking.'

In the expensively glossy magazine *Stand Corrected*, nudity is kept to a minimum, and there's bare bottom and covered bottom spankings. The romance is in slowly undressing and unpeeling the layers. A lot of women into spanking are also into corsetry, garters, high heels, stocking, silk and satin underclothes.

'The whole issue of sexual violence does not really enter into our scene because it's all consensual,' Eve says. 'The women in the scene desperately want to play. They've tried to find straight partners who are sympathetic and most of the time they are not.'

Fetish is different from hard-core straight sex: fetishists are consumers who write letters and socialize much more among themselves than do straight-sex people. Also, there's more opportunity for women in fetish. They can write and produce what they want. Production quality is not as demanding. It's shot mostly documentary style without trained porno stars or heavy financing.

'They're so loyal. They're wonderful. They shower us with love,' Eve says of her customers. 'They buy our products. They write to us, they help us form a little community. It's a wonderful thing.'

Sounds like telemarketing religion, 'Send love! Payable to us!'

The spanking community is only about ten years old. Before that spankers and spankees were isolated with only a few scattered male masochism-centered publications. Most Shadow Lane customers are well educated and know what they want.

'That little Cosmo girl who's 22 and is thinking about getting a spanking,' Eve says. 'She's going to get our catalog and see this cute boy's picture with his blond hair and blue eyes and think "This is what I want. I can have this? All I have to do is write an ad? OK." And she'll do it. Next thing you know, she'll come to our parties and she'll be the prom queen.' And get spanked.

'Getting a spanking involves some degree of pain,' Eve says. She is always nervous working with a professional model who is paid but not enjoying it. That kind of pain hurts. 'I don't feel at ease,' Eve says. By contrast, 'To someone who's into spanking, that pain translates into a pleasure sensation. Even when it's an intense scene and they are kind of whimpering a little bit, mentally they are into that. I feel very good shooting with a woman like that.' Of course, the problem with those who are really into it is that they tend to forget their lines in the heat of a good paddling.

Performers don't rehearse in advance because it's all done in one day. Eve warns them not to arrive on a full stomach before going over someone's knee.

Most people into spanking were not abused as children. Rather, it's associations with other erotic things. It happens to girls somewhere between ages three and five and for boys between four and seven, an obsession that begins even before an awareness of sex, although the child definitely knows it's something to hide and only share with friends willing to be naughty with you. Fetish, like foreplay, is an augmentation to sex.

Eve notes the term 'fetish' was brought into popularity by Von Kraft Ebbing about a hundred years ago when anything that wasn't absolutely ordinary was considered deviant. 'We're working with practices that are so old, so ancient. Terms like sadomasochism and fetishism came to life during the Victorian era when the morality was so repressive and oppressive,' she says. 'Who's to say that we should call these things fetishes at all? Why aren't they just affinities?'

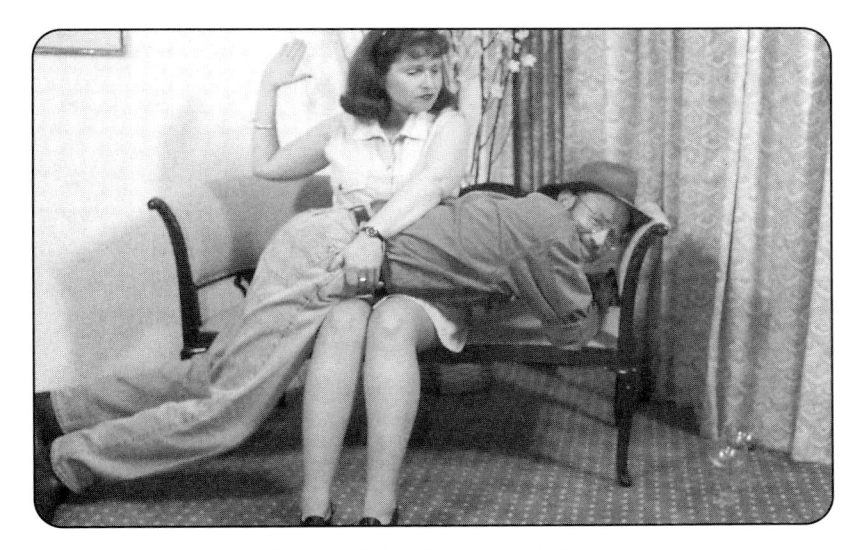

✳ Eve Howard gives Harris a spanking lesson

✳ Harris puts his training into practice

CHAPTER 33
THE GAY LINE: FROM THE BOTTOM TO THE TOP

Jim Steele directs gay videos. He is the only gay at Vivid and directs all their gay films. Vivid's a straight company but gays know Vivid has a gay line while many straights aren't aware they do.

Jim Steele is a pretty macho-sounding name. What's he like? A bruising football player? An army drill sergeant? His place is located in a tough downtown Los Angeles area, in the real world, away from the gay community, film community and porno community. So far so good. I buzz. He lets me in.

To my surprise, there's nothing hard about Jim Steele. In fact, he's kind of soft around the middle, wearing a monotone light grey ensemble. He looks like a regular film director.

'How come you don't live in the Valley?' I ask.

'Because I would rather die,' he answers.

Inside, he has an amazing area all to himself including two buildings with a big covered over parking space between. In effect, the area is a garage, warehouse, studio and basketball court. It's a funky place. There's a lounge area, studio with a high ceiling, and an extra apartment where 'the boys' stay if they're from out of town. That way he can keep an eye on them. As long as they can make it home, Steele knows where they are on shoot day.

The best part is the kitchen, custom-made, wall-to-wall galvanized steel. All the furniture is hand-made and has funny angles as though out of *The Cabinet of Dr Caligari*. The kitchen passes muster: the basics for serious cooking all present and correct – olive oil, garlic, lemon and a full set of steel pans. It's not a bachelor pad. It's a home.

'Most of the guys appreciate the fact that it's a nice place,' he says. 'They don't trash the place which they do in a lot of studios. The crew that works for me knows that it's my house. This is not a rental studio.'

The gay viewer is more up-market and videos command a higher price. Gays have money, don't have kids, don't have to pay alimony, drive nicer cars.

'We certainly dress better,' he says. I beg your pardon.

The gay market is a lot smaller than the straight market. There are fewer productions and they hold their price better. Video prices are stable at $60 per film. No performer can make a living from doing just gay videos.

'It's a great second job,' Jim says.

Once a performer's 'star' image is established, as the women turn to dance, the men turn to escorting, charging $150 an hour. Gay mainstream executives pay for the privilege to meet them, take them to dinner. The aura is greater around the gay stars. They're better at playing the prima donna role, more unapproachable and good at intimidating their clients who are often grateful just to meet them. They know how to work it.

'Would you say that gays are more savvy at selling internationally?' I ask. 'A lot of straights have no interest or inclination to sell outside of the US.'

'Our stuff is definitely available worldwide,' he answers. 'It must be so nice to be able to throw away money.'

In a straight film, everybody knows what the girls do and what the guys do. With a gay line, there's a progression. There's more intrigue in gay performances than in straight porno films. Besides who's in it, fans want to see who's a bottom and who's a top. A lot of guys don't do everything.

Jefferson, VCA's gay art director, is trying to explain how it works. He doesn't mind me getting personal as long as I don't mention his last name or his hometown state where everything that he is doing here is illegal and immoral.

VCA doesn't show any full frontal or rear nudity. They are all pretty soft-core so they can get into more video and bookstores. There is no gay cable market.

'Actors start off posing as straight models; a lot of times they are straight in their personal life so they don't have a problem with topping in a gay video,' he says. 'But they won't suck dick. They won't get fucked by any means. They'll do anything else.'

The nuances of gay films are subtle. For example, Ryan Idol has made a whole career of prolonging. In a five-year period, he didn't do anything but fuck for the longest time. Then he finally sucked dick. VCA and Ryan made a two-picture deal. He will suck but not fuck, then fuck and maybe suck.

It gets more complicated. One gay performer lives a married, straight life. Yet, he's only a 'bottom', never a 'top'. However, he's considered the best which makes him a top bottom. Straights who play gay say it's the pay. In straight porno, everyone wants to see the girl. Guys in straight films are just props. In gay films, guys buy gay to see straight guys play gay or gay guys who say they're straight. In any case, gay guys pay to see guys play gay which explains why gays gets more pay.

The right guy can make $1,000 minimum just for getting sucked. So straights say they do gay just for pay. Does that make them straight or gay? No one is ever really sure. The mystery sells videos and gives the performer a better negotiating position. A straight gay for pay can demand more money because the producer knows a guy who likes to play gay won't insist on his way about pay. There are many angles to work. On the set before a scene, a lot of them look at a girlie magazine and pretend they're straight so they can up their rate.

'I suspect that they are enjoying it just as much as anyone else,' Jefferson says. 'It's all an act. They make quite a production out of it. They want you to know that they are looking at a girlie magazine. They want you to know that they are straight. They want you to know that they've got that wife at home. They put on a show even when there's just me, the photographer and the makeup guy.'

These guys demand $2,000–3,000 a scene. 'And when you pay them that money, all they want to do is fuck,' he says. 'They don't want to suck. They'll let the other guy do the other stuff. But if you have two straight guys they won't suck each other's dicks. And forget it if they are two tops. You can't put them together.'

An agent specializing in top gay performers has a hard time booking the performers in LA nightclubs. 'In LA, people are not likely to pack a club here to see a porn star – you just saw him in the shower at the gym,' Jefferson says. They see him walking down the street and it's not that big a deal. The agent handles all the major gay stars like Ryan Idol, Tom Katz, Scott Ransom, Chad Connors, Steve DeMarco. He books them on the dance circuits all over the country, where they make most of their money.

But even the hottest guy on the dance circuit doesn't have the draw of a performer who's been featured in adult video. Then 'a star' is coming to the club. Fans will pay for that. And when the boys are in town, they meet their potential clients for the night. The major money is in the escort business where they can make $5,000 a night with one client. An ideal gig is to be 'kept' by a wealthy man for a few years – a 'full-time gig'. This happens on occasion, usually after they leave the business.

In their free time, they're busy, taking pilot lessons, going to college, travelling all over the world. Escorts travel a lot. Men will scoop them up and take them to London for a couple of weeks. 'Some of these boys would never get to see the world without being kept,' he says. 'It affords them a pretty nice lifestyle.' Though it never seems to last very long.

The gay porno infrastructure is in LA but Falcon, Hot House, Steven Scarlborough, the major players in the gay industry, are in San Francisco. Falcon is the biggest company. They constantly launch nationwide model searches and fly in models from other cities.

The lifespan of a gay performer is pretty short compared to that of a straight porno girl. Virtually no one's lasted longer than five years. Ryan Idol, who's got a very good look, has done less than ten movies total. The marketing strategy is 'less is better'. They might do one thing in one movie, wait a year to do another, and make more than $20,000 a movie.

Some guys have full-time jobs. Porno is the perfect second job, though dancing and escorting could be full-time. Being an escort is not necessarily about sex. Some boys get hired just to take off their clothes and flex their muscles. Some have clients that don't touch them. Many do very little. A lot of them take their clothes off, their clients get off, and that's it. The aura of the star is inhibits the fans from expecting more.

'Porno stars are very intimidating to the client because the ego on these boys is so out there,' Jefferson says. 'But they are really the most insecure people. They come off as being very egotistical and it's all a façade. They constantly need to be stroked. This whole thing is about attention. It's like being a den mother on every one of these productions. I've heard of porno stars walking off the set because they weren't getting enough attention. I would not want to be a director or producer. I would not have the tolerance.'

CHAPTER 34

BOYS' NIGHT OUT: SAILORS AND SUPERMEN

Saturday night is gay night at Club Axis. Tonight is a special event honoring porno director and performer Chi Chi La Rue. My name's at the door thanks to Jim Steele. Porno people are VIP people in the gay world. Tonight that includes me, a straight, mainstream, gay porno, journalist.

Gay clubs are scary to straights unfamiliar with the scene but when you think about it, they're places where a guy can feel right at home. Just don't talk about girls. A single guy going to a straight nightclub gets treated like a dog. At a gay club, a single guy gets treated like a lady, or a gentleman. Anyway, he feels welcome. A guy is one of the boys. So I figure it will be a breeze to do a bunch of interviews.

Upstairs, guys are wearing classic, Village People, macho outfits. When I was a kid, I had them all: Superman, cowboy, soldier, fireman, baseball player, football player, sailor, even policeman. They're all here tonight. Gay guys can wear them for fun but straight guys can't wear them unless they are serious.

Maybe that's why some macho straights resent macho gays – they're being mimicked. With flair.

There's a pool table, bar and dance floor and a roped-off section across the room for VIPs. I hand the attendant my card. He goes away, returns and lets me pass. Merci, garçon. There's Jim Steele, though not in costume. He's in shirtsleeves, jeans and sneakers, like he just came from work. He's the only one who looks straight possibly proving a social theory of relativity.

Welcome to the VIP 'Love Lounge'. Jim does the introductions. Here's the Marlboro Man, with black Stetson, a black leather vest revealing a well-tended physique, tight jeans and rattlesnake cowboy boots. He's offended because I didn't know he's a big star, though he's said so himself. I run back to Steele like I'm running back to my mother. He assures me the guy is neither a real cowboy or a real porno star. Next, the new porno star boys – they're very popular, even among the blasé VIP section. A very drunk manager pulls me aside and kindly suggests that now is not the time to do interviews. 'Don't take it personally,' he says. 'It's a Saturday night party. Don't expect anybody to be serious.'

Chi Chi La Rue – one of the gay market's leading porno celebrities – is big and burly and dressed like a fairy godmother. He is holding court and everyone comes by to pay their respects.

It's showtime. We follow Chi Chi on to the packed dance floor. He gets up on stage singing, '*We're going to have fun tonight/ If you're old enough to drive, then you can drive me crazy/ You're so young, you don't have to shave/ And I love to spank your ass when you misbehave/ If you don't come by I'm going to start to cry/ I'm gonna rob the cradle. Do it to it while I'm able/ Gonna rob the cradle.*'

'If you don't know how to do it, you watch one of my movies and learn,' he addresses the enthusiastic crowd. Chish introduces porno star Tom Katt, seen in Chish's movies *Total Corruption Part 2* and *One Night in Jail*: 'Let's bring on Mr Tom Katt, the hot superstar of porn!' In case we don't recognize him, we're informed Tom is the hairy one.

They toss videos into the crowd. The guys go crazy.

'Hey whores, suck *that* lollipop,' Tom says.

Later, I ask the manager, 'How many here tonight?'

'What's my count?' he shouts over the phone. Exactly 974.

He tells me they only rope off the Love Lounge for porno stars like Chi Chi. Otherwise, it takes up too much space and cuts down the number of paying customers they can admit. On Saturday night, only Chi Chi La Rue is working. And of course, the straight, mainstream, gay porno, journalist.

FAX August 30, 1996

Dear Willoughby,

I've just received your fax. I'm counting on your comments to guide me through this project so don't worry about breaking my flow or sounding negative.

My contacts in this business now number well over a hundred people and counting. I'm sorry for the delay but I'm trying to get a solid understanding of all aspects of the business; it's a bit like peeling an artichoke. I've not met anyone in the business who confirms a Mafia porno connection. In fact, the only people who say there is one *aren't* in the business.

This week, a photographer friend from Paris is in town who does beauty coverage for all the top fashion magazines. He wants to direct a soft video to go with the book showing me as a journalist learning from two porno girls how to make a film.

I look forward to hearing from you.

Best wishes,

Harris Gaffin

Harris

CHAPTER 35

SPOT THE DIFFERENCE

Susan Yanetti invites me to the opening of Club Porno, a Vivid-sponsored Sunday night straight porno nightclub, where some of Vivid's contract girls can be seen on the dance floor. The idea is to associate socially acceptable nightclubs and dancing, with pornography and attract the young and hip. If conventions are any indication, it will attract mostly guys who want to mingle with the porno stars. A disco full of guys, what could be sexier? I think I'll pass.

SPOT THE DIFFERENCE

A friend from Paris, Ken Petard, is in town and wants to go out. 'I'll take you to the newest, hottest club in town,' I say. 'All the top porno stars hang out there.' He's impressed. I call Susan and get two VIP passes.

Just as I figured: it's all guys though at least no one's wearing Superman or cowboy outfits. There's Susan on the dance floor; there's Janine and Nikki Tyler on stage, doing stimulated simulation. Nikki is crawling on her hands and knees chasing after Janine. Janine is whipping her hair around. They're hot – very sexy and energetic and attracting everyone's attention.

'Yeah, but what kind of a fantasy is that?' I say to the guy next to me. 'I heard Janine only does women.'

'That's her image,' he says like he knows. 'If she ever picked you, make out your will, get life insurance and say good-bye to all your friends. She is so hot she will fucking kill you.'

Upstairs in the VIP lounge Steve Hirsh is sitting with guests and other Vivid girls eating Chinese take-out.

My friend Ken's a glamour photographer, works for all the big magazines. I tell him I know Vivid's owner and publicist and can probably arrange the girls. We could do a photo essay for a mainstream glamour magazine, for exposure. He could work with the top porno girls. I would document it. Everyone's happy.

We get a catalogue of the Vivid girls. Each girl has exactly the same hair and make-up, shot from the same camera angle using the same lighting style. They are almost indistinguishable. Ken keeps flipping back and forth trying to see the difference. He works with raw beauty and has a very discerning eye. He gives up. He can't tell them apart. 'They could show a coordinated corporate image and still maintain the personality of the individual models,' he asks. 'Look at the Calvin Klein ads. Let's do a casting and I'll take a look at them.'

'It doesn't work that way,' I explain. 'These are Vivid Girls. I don't know if they will do a casting for you.'

'I don't do shootings with models who don't do castings,' he says and walks away to watch the dancers.

CHAPTER 36

JOY KING: PUBLIC SPIRIT

The office of Wicked Pictures is very neat, too neat. Everything's stacked in neat piles. Four piles on the cabinet, three on the desk, five on the bureau behind. Publicity director Joy King is a good-looking, athletic woman in her mid-30s with long, wavy California blonde hair. As she greets me, the air conditioner blows some paper on to the floor. When she bends over to pick it up, I do something I've never done in my entire professional career. I lean forward, reach out and stick my hand right into one of those piles.

I knew it. In the middle are all different colors and note sizes. I'm sure she took all the messy papers and stacked them into piles to cover them up. I do it all the time.

'Did you clean up before I arrived?' I ask.

Joy blushes and confesses. I'm flattered. No one ever did that for me. I like her already.

'There's a call from *Esquire*, New York,' squeals the intercom.

She looks at me, leans back in her chair. She touches the machine with her hand and speaks into it: 'Tell them I'm in an important meeting.' Not everyone gets this Class A treatment, her look implies. I believe her.

Joy sweeps her long locks from her face with one hand and lifts up the stack with the other. All these piles? They're requests, all wanting time, all clamoring to meet their young and beautiful exclusive porno star, Jenna Jameson. Several letters start off 'I'm writing a book.'

'We never know,' Joy says. 'Is this person going to publish a book about how seedy and disgusting we are?'

Isn't that the fun of it?

Her locks tumble again. This time, she blows them away because both hands are holding another pile of handwritten letters on typing paper, stuffed into tiny 3x6-inch envelopes with no return address.

'There's just so many of them,' she says. 'I never really know who's legitimate or someone's who's just trying to meet a girl in the business, just trying to get their dicks up. We tend to be very apprehensive when people approach us from outside the industry. We've had plenty that seem legit but aren't.' The porno publications, she knows what to expect. It's the mainstream she has to watch out for.

In 1995, a certain journalist representing *Bikini*, a hip, young,

✱ Jenna Jameson poses in front of poster for her big budget film *Conquest*

mainstream magazine, contacted Joy. The guy wanted to do a day-in-the-life of Jenna. Joy checked out the guy, the magazine, the publisher and spoke with the editor. Then she met with Jenna who liked the magazine but not the journalist who she knew personally and had wanted to date her. They cautiously decided to go ahead.

'This guy had been all but stalking her to try to get in bed with her,' Joy says. 'His motivations were clearly not of a journalistic nature.'

When the article came out, he bashed her, said she was a jerk. He wanted to stick his foot up her ass. 'This is what winds up happening,' she says. 'He thinks he's going to enter the porn world for one day and get fucked by some gorgeous chick. He was pissed off because he didn't get laid and trashed her in print. There have been plenty of guys who have tried and failed.'

Even the guys not looking for sex still want something for nothing. Those *not* requesting interviews, write 'I'd really like to get into the business. Can you help me?' Others ask 'I'm getting out of prison soon. Can someone meet me at the airport?' or 'I'm getting discharged from the army. Can I stay at your place until I get set up?'

'It blows my mind,' Joy says. 'The problem is it's a fantasy to these guys who have trouble relating to reality. They look at her as someone they know.'

I'm beginning to understand why the porno people keep to themselves. But Joy assures me she is not mainstream-shy. She and a bunch of other porno people blow off steam competing in a mainstream bowling league every Wednesday night.

'Probably half the people don't know they're bowling with a good portion of the porno industry,' she says with a smile.

Joy, a 15-year veteran in the business, also runs Jenna Jameson's fan club, an unusual situation in that most companies don't want anything to do with a fan club. Joy is a level-headed business woman, the kind of partner every porno star should have. She's from that new generation that grew up with video recorders and porno rentals, who see porno as an extension of the entertainment business. She does her job with pride and feels no need to hide it from others.

By promoting Jenna, she promotes Wicked Pictures. Both are done on the Internet but it isn't all it's cracked up to be yet. A far more effective tactic has been putting the fan-club address at the end of the movie.

Joy constantly monitors the fan-club list, thinking up all kinds of ways to generate revenue and promote her client. For example, if fan club members haven't bought anything and their account is dormant for three months, she might send them a free magazine and a 15 per cent discount certificate. It's really a publicity device because it's not as lucrative as it might seem. After all, about a quarter of all Jenna's fan mail comes from prison-record people who cannot receive all the material and have a limited income. A very limited income.

'A fan club is a business and you can't make money from someone who has no money,' Joy says. So, as loving and caring as most porno stars seem to be, they usually throw those letters away because the guys have no money to spend.

' Realistically, the girls don't have time to read the letters, let alone answer them all,' she says. Not to mention, no desire to, either, though they often make an exception for their more exotic type of fan: 'Foreign guys really break with the cash,' Joy says. By contrast, American guys don't.

'I don't know if these guys think she's made of money for free photos, postage etc.' Joy says. 'She would have to be independently wealthy. I don't understand this. Do you write Budweiser and say that you want a free six-pack?'

Other than guys wanting to get into the business, prisoners needing a lift, GIs needing a couch, there's always the vice squad to break up the daily routine. Joy has survived several 'visits'. Police raids come and go, depending on the political administration. Republicans believe in less government interference in the personal lives of citizens, unless it's about sex. The last raids occurred in the late '80s and early '90s under the Reagan and Bush administrations.

'They came in. It wasn't the first time. We all knew the routine,' she says. 'Everybody goes to the lunch room and they take a copy of your driver's license. They take a Polaroid. They talk to you for a couple of minutes and then you go home. Then they sit there with the owners and maybe the accountant and go through some records. For most of the guys, this is just a job. They have to be there. After a while, they loosen up. You know darn well that these guys are watching the movies just like everybody else. But they have a job to do. It's a bummer.'

On the way out, I step around a rubber mold of Jenna Jameson's buttocks.

CHAPTER 37

HOLLYWOOD BOWL

That evening I stroll into a bowling alley in the 'burbs. This place is, like, so American. There must be 40 lanes, all packed, noisy. There's Steve and Joy from the Wicked team. There's Betty and Russ Hampshire from VCA.

'You want something to drink?' Russ asks, with an East Coast working-class accent.

'A beer,' I answer.

'A beer? They have names, you know,' he says. 'You gonna ask a waitress for a beer?'

'OK. Miller,' I answer.

'Miller? What kind of Miller?' he says. 'They got Miller Lite, Miller Dark, Miller Genuine Draft.'

'Hey Marge!' Russ shouts over the din to the waitress. 'The guy wants a beer!'

'What kind?' she shouts back.

'See, what I mean?' he says.

'Genuine Draft,' I say.

He shouts the order to the waitress. Now he's happy, she's happy and I'll be happy when I get my beer.

'So, what do you do?' I ask innocently.

'What do you mean, what do I do?' he asks, annoyed already. 'I'm VCA.'

'What's that?' I ask, like I never heard of it.

'It's a video company,' he answers. He's getting angry. This is fun.

'And what do you do there?' I ask.

'I own the place!'

'Oh, I thought you worked for Betty Hampshire,' I say.

'Hey, Betty! This guy just asked me if I work for you,' he shouts.

Before he knocks my block off, I tell him I'm joking. He calms down.

'You want something to eat?' he asks.

Not this again. He buys the team a round of hot dogs with everything.

Russ says he joined the army right after reform school.

'Why reform school?' I ask.

'Temper,' he says. 'I'd get so mad, I'd forget what I got mad about.'

Once out of reform school, his life sounds like a Bruce Springsteen song. In the army, he earned a bronze medal in the infantry in Vietnam. Then he worked assembly-line jobs. Finally, he graduated from McDonald's Hamburger University in Chicago, Class of '78, majoring in Hamburgerology.

'Everything I learned about porno, I learned at McDonald's,' he says with a proud grin. 'Everything was timed. Little margin for deviation.'

Betty joins us after bowling a strike.

'People always asked "What the hell does working at McDonald's and flipping burgers have to do with this?"' she says. 'Precise timing. That's what made it work.'

Porno fans get more beef for their VCA buck. Each porno flick runs two hours and has precisely seven sex scenes.

'When I worked at McDonald's, we had a certain temperature for the French fries,' Russ says. 'We had a precise temperature for the grill for the meat. This is the way it was done – we even measured the Coke by the ounce.'

'He runs his business that way, very militant McDonald's style,' Betty says. 'Some people find it old-fashioned, a little condescending, maybe. But it works.'

Russ is up. Strike followed by another strike. One of the best bowlers in the league, he's high scorer tonight and his team is going to win.

'Go husband!' Betty cheers Russ on. 'No bad beef here!'

Between turns, Russ cleans up the counter and the surrounding area. 'I can't stand the mess,' he says.

Steve Orenstein stops by. He's bowling in another lane with Joy King and Tony Cleary from Metro, a manufacture and distribution company. Other porno companies are bowling also.

'My team always does better when I'm not here, if that tells you something,' Steve says. 'I'm away for two weeks – they win every game.'

Now, with the league games over, the guys play for bets.

'Come on Paul, you putz,' Russ shouts. 'I got a bet he chokes under pressure.'

Paul chokes under pressure, scores a zero gutter ball. Betty rolls her eyes.

'Even if it's for a dollar, he gets serious,' she says.

The guys are betting for $2. Russ shines under the pressure, bowling an impressive 226. He gleefully collects the money from everyone, including his staff, clearing almost $10. However, before he can pocket it, a little girl hits him for Girl Scout cookies, takes all his winnings and then some.

After bowling, all the porno folks gather at the bar. Orenstein's there with his mother and father. Joy is there too with her sister, who now also works for Wicked. Russ picks up everyone's tab plus several 'last-call' rounds because he and Betty have to leave before their favourite restaurant closes. Guess where?

'Chickenburgers at McDonald's,' Russ says. 'They're having a two-for-one special.'

CHAPTER 38

WICKED, MAN

There are a lot of successful manufacturers out there but the same three names keep popping up: VCA, Vivid and Wicked. I figure the youngest must be the hottest.

Wicked is located in the Valley in a new industrial park, the kind that have trees and grass, not barbed wire and chain-link fences. I'm meeting Steve Orenstein, president of Wicked Pictures.

A brand-new black BMW sits in front of the building. His, I'll bet. New rich. Big spender. So far, so good.

I open the glass door and immediately face a no-nonsense, gray-haired old lady behind an ordinary office desk.

'I'm here to see Steve,' I say, expecting to breeze past.

Not so fast, young man.

'What is your name? What company are you with? Do you have an appointment? What time is your appointment? What is this is in reference to?' She wants to know everything.

Who are you, his mother?

I'm still answering questions when publicist Joy King pops out of her office and leads me down a narrow corridor to a windowless office that looks more like a hands-on manager's workspace than a corporate CEO's ivory tower. In other words, a dump, furnished with a desk, couch and two chairs. The kind I can afford. That's it. No shelves. No files. There's papers strewn all over the couch and on the floor. I can't even see his desktop there's so many papers, a bunch of them held down by a paperweight which reads 'Jenna's Favoritest'. Orenstein's not ashamed of the mess. In fact, he's proud of it.

'You have papers everywhere I can see,' I say.

'Come over here,' he says with glee. 'I have some under the desk too.'

He's right.

'That old lady sure is a pain in the ass,' I snigger.

'That's my mother,' he says.

'Very efficient and professional,' I add.

The biggest hotshot in porno works with his mother?

'Twenty years ago, I worked for her,' he says with pride. 'Now, she works for me.'

Behind him hangs a signed Peter Max lithograph. The kind I can't afford.

Orenstein owns Wicked Pictures 100 per cent. He's unpretentious, barely 30, with short curly red hair, and wearing a David Letterman sweatshirt, jeans and sneakers. He has a kind, innocent face, which might be masking just how shrewd he really is. Steve's a nice boy, the kind a mother would be proud of.

The company with a larger-than-life reputation has just six employees and no creative director.

'How come everybody thinks Wicked's so big?' I ask.

Before he can answer that, porno model manager Lucky Smith passes by, obviously cleared by Steve's mother. Without bothering to say hello, we watch him open a metal cabinet in the hallway and take a chocolate cookie from the cookie jar. 'Just came by to get one of these,' he says, then disappears.

We look at each other. Lucky returns with Juli Ashton, VCA's contract girl and unquestionably one of the best-known porno stars. In a way, she reminds me of Peaches. But Lucky's girls play for real, show up on time and get top rates.

They're on their way to Reno to shoot a Playboy video, a company which traditionally disassociates itself from porno stars and strippers. But they love Juli and overlook her less than girl-next-door performances. Lucky is so grateful, he's worn his best black T-shirt. He's obviously washed and combed his waist-length hair. And he almost shaved.

'Your underwear is showing,' Steve says to Juli.

'It's supposed to,' I answer.

'Now he's going to write what a geek you are,' Lucky sniggers.

It's so nice to be considered part of the mainstream press.

They've got a plane to catch and disappear after swiping a couple more cookies. The last time I called Lucky's management agency, Risqué Business, his answering machine said, 'This is Lucky. There was too much pressure. We just all went on vacation and may not come back. You can leave a message, if you're the optimistic type.'

So when *Playboy*, *Penthouse* or *Esquire* want to contact some of the top porno stars, they deal with Lucky and his answering machine. No one's ever accused *him* of kissing up to authority.

Steve is second generation in the business. Back in New York, he worked summers part-time in a porno magazine warehouse where Mom was the bookkeeper and Dad was the manager. 'I was very embarrassed by it all,' Steve says, recalling how he cringed whenever the warehouse workers called out a title: 'Hey, Steve, we need more *Super Boobs*.'

At 19, he managed adult bookstores with arcades and peep shows, stayed up front in the bright lights by the cash register, afraid to venture out to the dimly lit back where the seedy types loitered.

For ten years, Steve worked in sales and distribution, learning the ropes, meeting the players and becoming a hot-shot, know-it-all salesman in the process. Now, he's an old pro. But he recalls his early 'don't take no for an answer' enthusiasm when he first encountered porno heavyweight, VCA owner Russ Hampshire, a guy known for his direct approach.

'Who the fuck is this guy?' Russ had shouted. 'I want him out of my warehouse right now!'

They became best friends.

Years later, Russ makes Steve an offer he can't refuse. The chance to have VCA contract girl, Juli Ashton, in a Wicked picture.

Steve set up Wicked Pictures with virtually no creative experience and no pretense of having any. He hired talent as necessary, which is what all the top companies do as well as virtually all major mainstream powerhouse studios. The real money is almost always in distribution.

Steve's start-up strategy followed an almost classic little-guy approach. He did what Vivid did. He could not compete on price with established, big companies like Vivid and VCA who release at least one movie per week. They'd locked up the lion's share of cable rights when there was much less competition and wholesale prices were triple what they are today. By now, they were producing most of their work in-house.

When the big guys got going in the 1980s, every mall in America had a donut shop and a new video store with a booming X-rated section. All the 8mm films went into the closet; the video cassette deck reigned supreme. Fans mobbed the conventions to see the stars in person and buy tapes at the same time. In those days, a single store might order 150-300 tapes at $50 each.

'Now we get $15 on a good day,' Steve says with a sigh. 'Those were the days. Now, there's only so many products people can handle. Everyone's sales have gone down. The world population is up. There are more markets too. But actual physical tape sales are less.'

So, what could Stevie do? He put all his eggs in one basket. And watched that basket. Competing on quality was the *only* choice for long-term survival. Have a unique product, hold the price and enter with a bang!

Wicked has been called a Vivid wannabe because it mimics Vivid's slick advertising campaign and contract-girl promotions. But there is a difference. Vivid's philosophy emphasizes the company. It's an honour to be a Vivid girl. The girl is part of the Vivid package, like the Playboy bunny is part of the Playboy identity. Wicked's philosophy puts more emphasis on the contract girl. 'Wicked has this girl' goes the advertising, not 'This girl is a Wicked girl.'

'It's basically "This is the girl you want to know about and this is where she is,"' Steve says.

The first thing he did was get that unique product. Lucky brought in a girl named Chasey Lane; Steve signed her up to an exclusive contract. Pretty as a picture, she looked great in advertising, on the box cover and in the movies. Best of all, when buyers wanted to see the girl who was getting all this publicity, she could only be found at Wicked Pictures.

Next, Steve hired a production crew, got a script, usually prepared by the director, budgeted a high-quality ad campaign, established a presence at the conventions, advertised in *AVN*, sent out flyers, invited journalists and porno magazines to meet the star and visit the set, and gave them lead time to print their news.

Then he got ripped off.

He wanted to be the best so he took the highest quote without questioning it. The director justified it by saying it takes more time to do a better job. The guy hired the cast, crew, equipment and costumes for a second day, shot two movies and secretly kept one for himself which he immediately distributed under his own name.

'So you called your friends in the Mafia who broke his legs, right?' I say. I know it works.

'No. I never hired the guy again,' Steve says.

What a wimp.

Wicked released other movies starring Chasey. They waited. And waited. Six months went by. Nothing. Then suddenly, the fax started creaking. Chasey finally had become a hit.'When's your next Chasey movie coming out?' the distributors were asking.

Too late – Chasey Lane was now a Vivid girl. Now, the new girl you really want to know about is Jenna Jameson and Wicked is where she is. Orenstein promoted her at the 1995 Cannes Film Festival with a double-page ad and a close-up portrait opposite a white page with one line of text: 'Come Meet the New Adult Star.' Every television and cable station showed up to meet her.

Orenstein promoted her one Wicked film, *Blue Movie*, before its release. At the *AVN* Awards, it won 'Best Picture' and Jenna Jameson won 'Best Performer'.

Now he's on the map – everybody knows Wicked and orders are pouring in. It beat the giants and everybody assumes it's a giant too. Suddenly, they're saying 'VCA, Vivid and Wicked'.

Recently, Wicked moved across the street, doubled their warehouse space and doubled their staff from three to six. Yes, the BMW out there is his. It's leased.

'Now I'm at this level where I'm this little guy that's somehow got this reputation that I can't believe I got,' he says. 'Now, I have to really think about keeping it.'

CHAPTER 39

VCA: PORNO FOR THE MASSES

It's another bright sunny California day, so, just to get out of the house, I drive up to Chatsworth, further out of the city and deep into the Valley where VCA has set up shop.

VCA is the giant. That's what they say. You've seen one warehouse, you've seen them all. That's what I say. I pull up to a couple of long, single-storey, white warehouses gleaming in the Valley sun. They're surrounded by perfectly manicured lawns, beautiful shrubbery, trees and flowers, which are in turn surrounded by a chain-link fence. In other words, a no-nonsense, mainstream corporate America-style building. All the expensive-model cars in the parking lot are washed and waxed. A white Porsche looks great next to my faded blue '84 Honda Accord. Hey, mine's paid for. Then again, so possibly is hers.

In the entry, an attractive, professional-looking receptionist pushes buttons on a dozen or more phone lines. On the coffee table in the lounge are mainstream magazines and flowers. Cases to the side display a few dozen trophies for excellence in pornography. That's what's left, the receptionist says. Most were destroyed in the 1993 earthquake. The local preachers blamed the porno industry for making God angry. Also displayed are the myriad golf trophies awarded to Russ Hampshire, VCA's owner.

VCA is the world's largest porno premises. Nothing comes close in size to its 30,000 square feet.

The receptionist, headset over her ears and tattoo around her ankle, buzzes me in. Debbie Rupio, the publicist, meets me at the door so I don't get lost.

Debbie dresses Madison Avenue advertising agency. Guys here wear neckties. In fact, everyone here is smartly dressed. In Debbie's office, she's tacked twelve files, perfectly aligned, four across, three down, to a bulletin board, each file representing one month. Her desk is clear, nothing out of place. She has budgeted two hours for the warehouse tour. I can return for interviews later.

As we pass the creative section on our way to the warehouse, I notice two art director's offices, one for the gay market, the other for the straight market. Both execute concepts originating from the overall corporate identity director working in yet another office. VCA's international sales and licensing agreements are negotiated by an autonomous company, Antigua, located behind the double doors.

The public relations documentations section includes rows and rows of shelves holding boxes of files of slides, art work, screenplay and press clippings for VCA's 5,000 titles. Wardrobe storage is more organized than a Paris fashion designer's atelier, each garment labelled and referenced should any scene need to be reshot.

Next comes the mail-order room where a dozen people, each with headphones, sit at their desks, working their phones. Altogether, they clock in over 40,000 hours of sales annually.

The storage room contains hundreds of thousands of empty cassettes, miles of blank tape and forests-worth of cardboard boxes for shipment.

'You ain't seen nothing yet,' Debbie says.

The next room is off-limits to non-essential personnel. Like a maternity ward we can watch through the picture windows and see what no other porno company in the world has. Track Tech, a division of VCA, has the largest video-cassette duplicating facility in Los Angeles. By making cassettes and having a professional duplicating service, VCA via Track Tech, is guaranteed to get a tiny profit of the millions of porno, and mainstream, tapes duplicated.

No matter how many producers enter the market or how low wholesale prices drop, VCA will earn a share. Computers run the facility automatically, loading blank videotape of any programmed length into empty cassettes in a sterilized atmosphere of purified air, all temperature and humidity-controlled.

The actual duplicating process begins in the 'master control' room; it looks like a television network control room with stacks upon stacks of wired flashing digital video equipment. Eight different porno films are duplicated simultaneously playing on eight different monitors. This room is empty, too. Where could everyone be?

Next door. Here, three guys, drenched in sweat, are running around like headless chickens in the duplicating room copying videos in 'real time': a two-hour movie takes two hours to copy. Making 2,000 copies would take at least 4,000 hours, or 2,000 machines would take two hours. Track Tech has around 2,000 top-of-the-line video cassette decks, stacked eight high, aisle after aisle after aisle, row after row after row. The room is a temperature-controlled 68 degrees for maximum performance. The three technicians load the blanks and unload the copied tapes as fast as they can – orders are backed up. The machines run 24 hours a day, seven days a week as different shifts come and go.

The volume is overwhelming compared to most of the industry. However, compared to a major mainstream operation, this is small potatoes. A major success in porno is 10,000 copies. *The Lion King* sold 30,000,000 copies. If Track Tech's machines worked round the clock, seven days a week, it would take them nearly two years to fill that order.

Next door, a full-time mechanic whistles while he works, repairing, maintaining, oiling, greasing, tuning-up, whatever needs to be done all day long to keep a happy ship sailing smoothly.

The duplicated cassettes get labelled, put in box covers, then stored in cubby holes by title in the warehouse which is larger than all the other areas combined. It's floor-to-ceiling tapes, tens of thousands of tapes. Workers with computerized print-outs wheel industrial-sized shopping carts, dodging fork lifts. They cruise down the aisles, pulling boxes off the shelves by the dozen and handing them to the loaders, who pack them into cardboard boxes, seal and address them and drop them on to the two-wheelers of the UPS shipper. He goes back and forth all morning long, loading them on to his open truck backed into one of three loading bays. They work like ants at a picnic.

Naturally, computer-savvy VCA has its own web site. 'I'm here to fulfill and satisfy all your visual sexual needs,' the net surfer is greeted. At this site, 150 video titles can be ordered, or you can participate in cyber forum interviews with porno star Juli Ashton, naked on a couch, tapping on a keyboard.

While most companies hire a college student to maintain their Internet site, VCA has a full-time web master plus two other computer whizzes good enough to take on mainstream work and pay for itself, just like the cassette duping business. That doesn't include 'David King', resident computer genius, who played piano at age three, got a computer for his Bar Mitzvah, cleared $50,000 a year in high school designing programs on weekends, dropped out of Yale to 'make money', and now designs and programs an adult computer game every two weeks. These guys have all kinds of technical equipment at their disposal, like Silicon Graphics machines – a 35mm motion copy machine that transfers picture images to digital graphics.

I'm gettingt a serious case of information overload. I'm offered a Mountain Dew; I'd prefer two aspirins.

Wendy manages the record-keeping room: row upon row of cabinets. Taped to the walls are sayings such as 'Sexual harassment in this area will not be tolerated, however, it will be graded' and 'I survived Catholic School'.

While producing pornography is legal in Los Angeles, producers are burdened with paperwork. The federal government requires documentation of all performers, including photo i.d., in order to make sure no one under 18 is used in a film. Every time a film or a photo is sent to someone for any reason, that person must also keep an exact duplicate record. If photos are sent to an art director or a printer or a magazine editor, in theory they must all have copies. The system is redundant and needs to be streamlined, but virtually the entire industry is complying with this law. Someday down the line when the government is in a bad mood they should be able to find somebody somewhere who has at least one record missing so they can nail them. Wendy's kick-ass copier uses lots of paper.

'How many copies of records do you have?' I ask.

'I can't say, but I'm sure it's destroyed many a rain forest,' she says.

VCA has in-house state-of-the-art digital editing equipment and a complete recording studio with a sound booth for creating original music scores. That set-up alone is worth a hundred grand or two.

Down the hall, framed, autographed, jerseys of great American sports heroes decorate the pristine white walls: Joe Namath, Pete Rose, Michael Jordan, Dick Butkis, Gail Sayers, Nolan Ryan, Hank Aaron, Gordie Howe, Wayne Gretsky, Shaque O'Neil, Ted Williams. It's part of the boss's personal collection...

A big, fit-looking man wearing a Sahara Hotel golf hat, a Hawaiian sports shirt, Bermuda shorts, and white socks and sneakers, comes bounding down the hall. Meet Russ Hampshire, owner of VCA. There he is, Mr America. Bronze-medal decorated Vietnam veteran, photographed with President

Carter. A Connecticut Yankee. Wears a baseball hat to work. Bowls every Wednesday. Eats at McDonald's. Drinks beer from the bottle. Married, kids, grandkids. Contributes to Little League, donates old equipment to charity, attends PTA meetings. Face it, America's number one pornographer is as American as apple pie.

My tour finished, I visit Betty Hampshire and then Russ, whose office is next door. Betty's bulletin board also has the 12-page schedule, four across, three down. On her desk sit bottles of vitamins, bottles of liquid 'Tippex', a typewriter and a TV/VHS unit. A framed Betty Boop cartoon, family snapshots and wedding pictures stand on her bureau. Flowers and houseplants decorate the room.

Betty knows everything about the company – she ran it herself when Russ got busted by the FBI and spent nine months in a minimum security prison in Boron, California. Much to everyone's surprise, the company thrived when Betty took over. She'd been Russ's secretary for nine years before, much to her mother's chagrin, she and Russ got married.

'Aren't you afraid to be married to a guy in the business, surrounded by beautiful women all the time?' Mom asked.

'It's like artwork,' Betty reassured her. 'You can admire it in a museum. But you don't need to take it home.'

Prior to his arrest for selling three porno videos in Mobile, Alabama, Russ was known for his temper. 'He used to have a baseball bat and when he was mad, he would pound that baseball bat and people would shiver in their shoes. Then he would forget about it,' Betty says. 'When he came home, I was worried about how he would react to everything being so good. He is so emotional.'

But Russ simply picked up where he left off.

'I used to go out to the federal prison camp and I would have bags under my eyes,' she says. 'I was stressed and he'd walk into that room all tanned and handsome and I'd think to myself "Who's incarcerated, me or you?" The rest did him good…'

Just then from the other room, the sound of a baseball bat crashing on to a desk shatters the quiet.

'What kind of a stupid thing was that to do!' Russ is screaming.

I look at Betty. She looks at me and shrugs her shoulders.

'See what I mean?' she says. 'Where was I? Oh yes, the rest did him good.'

I think I'll see Russ another time.

She and Russ seem to play good cop, bad cop with their team of 150 loyal employees. I don't stay much longer because Betty has orders to fill, problems to solve and employees to comfort. They must be doing something right:

they've got people who've been with them more than a decade, getting health insurance, vacations, all the things regular companies used to do.

VCA is totally opposite to where I started this journey. What a contrast between Bill Margold and Russ Hampshire, two complete opposites with nothing in common.

I head to the parking lot and there standing outside are the two of them, having a meeting in the warm California sun.

FAX Sept. 21, 1996

Dear Willoughby,

I was on a pirate ship over the weekend and revitalized my skills as a photographer. I've certainly have overcome any shyness about taking pictures on set. It's funny, by now I'm a regular and see quite a difference between myself and someone on the set for the first time.

One thing that keeps coming up is the number of people in the business who put it down. None of the big players say they enjoy their product. They're only in it for the money. Half the guys think all the girls are really whores who only do it for the money, which is exactly what the religious Right says. Whores all!

The other sentiment I keep coming across is 'You don't have to be nuts to work here, but it helps!'

When you've had a chance to read what I've just e-mailed, let me know. I've got some queries for you. Keep in mind I'm working with you and have no objections to reworking anything that can be improved. Any setbacks to the schedule can really be attributed to the wealth of material I'm coming across.

Best regards,

[signature: Harris Gaffin]

Harris

CHAPTER 40

GIRLS AT SEA: *CONQUEST*

I'm on board a made-for-Hollywood pirate ship for a 'big budget' film by Wicked Pictures. The ship is the exact size as the *Santa Maria*, as used by one Christopher Columbus in 1492.

The budget is $100,000, about ten times larger than the average porno budget. Everybody knows that porno involves so much money. But big is relative. There are big mice and there are big elephants. Wicked owner Steve Orenstein could shoot one such 'big budget' movie a month for 50 years, his son could shoot one movie a month for 50 years and *his* son could shoot one movie a month for 50 years and there would still be $10 million in change before they would approach the budget for the mainstream shipwreck *Waterworld*.

We set sail one foggy morning from Long Beach Pier, though, technically speaking, we're engine propelled. We've a good three hours' sail before we start shooting but I'm already in costume, complete with three-cornered hat.

On the boat are three of the top porno stars in the business: Shayla La Veaux, Juli Ashton and Jenna Jameson. The three, in bikinis, are sunning themselves together while talking to a bald macho-looking Italian pirate named Claudio. He smiles. The girls smile. We all smile.

'Everything is better in America,' he says.

The pirate extras are bummed that there's no beer. They sing:

We're friggin' in the riggin',
Friggin' in the riggin',
Friggin' in the riggin,'
Cause there's fuck all else to do.

The crew includes four stunt guys and the fight choreographer who will teach the extras how to punch and fight for the camera, sometimes using real weapons, on a rocking boat.

Jenna Jameson is one of the most recognizable female faces in the business, Wicked Picture's 'star' and their only contract girl.

'When I was five I was a very *independent* young girl,' she says.

Jenna grew up in Las Vegas, came from a loving family. Mom was a stripper. Dad was a Vegas cop. They married and had little Jenna. Mom died when Jenna was four. Dad raised Jenna and her brother. Jenna and Dad do talk shows together.

Jenna was a good, adorable, kid – Dad nicknamed her 'Heartbreaker'. She never got into trouble and did well in school. She started stripping as soon as she was old enough to work in nightclubs, just like Mom, and with Dad's knowledge and support.

'My father knew that I was smart enough and *independent* enough that I could take care of myself,' Jenna says.

She declared her dependence on a guy.

'It happens to every girl in this business,' says an older and wiser Jenna. 'The girls are vulnerable when it comes to that sort of thing, especially at that young an age, meeting a guy who says he knows it all. He tells you, "OK, I'll take care of you", and then slowly manipulates you.'

Independent stripping wasn't all it was cracked up to be, either.

'You go into it thinking everybody's going to be watching you, admiring you,' she says. 'You're thinking "Oh my God, all these guys are going to want me" but in truth, you go through a lot of rejection. You ask the guy if you can a dance and he says "No, you're too skinny for me."'

So after a year or so Jenna couldn't stand stripping, or men. 'I hated them,' she says. 'It's the worst side of men you can see. I mean, they just think that they can treat those girls like shit. A lot of guys are just obnoxious fucking assholes.'

Next she turned her pretty face to pretty-girl magazine layout and got a new boyfriend.

'Did he manage your career?' I ask.

'Yeah, the asshole,' she says. She got a lot of work and made a lot of money, appeared on about a hundred magazine covers.

Onward and upward. Next came porno films. 'I *knew* I would be good at this,' she says. 'I knew I could act. I always wanted to be in movies. I love being in front of people so hey, why not?'

She switched her 'evil boyfriend' for an angel girlfriend, Nikki Tyler. She did a couple of movies, but stopped abruptly.

'I have to say they weighed heavy on my shoulders,' she says.

'Were those early films classics?' I ask.

'I'd like to burn every copy of every movie,' she says. At least she learned what *not* to do.

She returned to porno, contract shopped, alone thank you, visited company after company, let them bid against each other and finally picked the best offer at Wicked. And had it put in writing.

'I say what I want to do, when I want to do it and who I want to do it with,' she says. 'More and more people are realizing what a good career this is and how much money we can make. It's a stepping stone because in the years to come, more and more girls in this business are going to cross over to the straight stuff. I know I will. I know I will. I can just feel it. I know that I have that extra something. I'm a very sexual person. I want to have the vehicle to push that forward and let people know how sexual and pretty and talented I am.'

No one ever made it in Hollywood who waited for someone else to promote themselves.

Shayla La Veaux has such a pretty face and cheerful disposition that it's hard to imagine the turmoil that once lurked underneath her smiling face and pert 5'0" body.

From the word go, Shayla was trouble. She skipped school, had a leather-jacketed boyfriend, 'the kind mothers hate,' she says. She dropped out, returned, smoked dope, dropped out again.

'I put my Mom through hell. Then again it's just sort of a product of what you're brought up in,' she says without elaborating. 'She did the best that she could and I did the best that I could.'

Shayla knew she could never stand a job sitting behind a desk all day. At 15, she got a standing job behind a counter at McDonald's, then at Wendy's. At night, she snuck out the bedroom window to strip-tease at bachelor and birthday parties. Mom freaked when she found her first-born's costume in the closet. At 18, she still lived at home.

Eventually, her dancing led to cocaine; most of her earnings went up her nose. She lived to pay her bills and party. Then she came to Hollywood.

'Basically, that's why we're all here,' she says. 'I was pretty much an accident waiting to happen.'

Fortunately, she met Lucky Smith, one of the few serious porno-star business managers. Under the long hair and flip, wise-guy rebel streak is a hard-nose negotiator, with a legal background. He upped her rates, forced her to save her earnings and convinced her to get her act together. 'You're going to be on time,' he told her. 'You're going to be responsible.'

He convinced her she could make it. She was a good kid. She was young and scared and depended on Lucky. She'd picked the right person to trust.

'Lucky very much protects us from all the assholes within this business,' she says. 'We don't have to deal with all the headaches. We can concentrate on what we have to do.'

Now, Shayla gets top rates and is considered one of the best, most reliable, hard-working, cheerful, pint-size, fun-loving performers in the business.

✳ The pirate ship used in *Conquest*

Come lunch time, Joy the publicist turns makeup artist, slapping mud on our uniforms and faces. Orenstein rates a double slap. Half the food supply seems to be missing, so we share tuna sandwiches and macaroni salad. Where's the rest, the pirates ask. The chef isn't on board and nobody can find where he's hidden the food.

Someone notices the pirate flag is missing too. No problem. An art student makes a Jolly Roger with a black cloth and some masking tape.

Mainstream scripts are 120 pages long. A porno script is usually 15 pages of four-letter words. Some shoots don't have a script at all. There are few takes: three is considered a lot.

Everybody right foot forward. Swords at the ready, guns too. When an old pistol is fired we start fighting. A guy runs around the deck with the smoke machine. Steady, fire. Click. Guns don't work. He reloads, Smoke man runs around again. Ready. Click. Five times. The smoke guy is getting tired and we're running low on smoke.

'Forget the gun! Action!' the director shouts. We fight. Cut! Now what? The captain forgot to shut off the motor, a performer forgot to take off his sunglasses, somebody forgot to remove a Coke can in the background. Places everyone. Smoke machine! Action! The pirates charge, laughing and having a ball. Cut! The director's not happy. Nobody is fighting properly.

'I don't want you laughing and smiling,' the director says. 'I want to see full grimaces, snarling, a lot of yelling. Remember, you want to kill each other. We'll run through it a couple of times.' There's more to being a Hollywood pirate than I realized. Eventually we get it right.

Later in the afternoon comes the orgy scene. On a high budget, it's called an orgy. On a low budget, it's a gang-bang. The sun is lower, the air's cooled down. A gentle breeze mildly rocks the boat. Maiden Juli Ashton is presented to four naked officers surrounding her.

The photo op comes before the real action begins, where the star poses for the press. We press photographers fight for position. There are only three of us. The flashes pop. First we do hard-core: 'Lift your skirt! Beautiful! Open your blouse! Terrific! Look dirty! Turn around and bend over!' Fantastic!

Next comes soft-core: 'OK, cover it up! Good! Close your blouse! Fine! Smile! Wonderful, darling. Cross your legs. Thank you.'

The director's dressed in red, pulls down his pants, does a scene with Juli Ashton, pulls back up his pants and continues directing. A man of diverse talents.

Juli gives it and takes it. She wanted a profession she could jump into whole hog. Here she does. Juli loves having sex – she boasts she once took on an entire dorm floor of college students in her freshman year. She's very articulate when she's not having sex, which seems to amaze everyone she meets. Even the soft-core Playboy empire, normally coolly distant from the hard-core world, has embraced her.

Despite lovely Juli's assuming position, the cool air and constant rocking is wreaking havoc on the guys, who are having trouble 'getting wood'. The cameramen are waiting. Juli is waiting. Everyone is waiting except the sun which is sinking.

Years ago, a vital member of the film crew was the full-time 'fluff', a woman whose sole job was to do whatever it took to keep the men ready. Budgets today don't include that.

Finally, one by one, they deliver, except Claudio who is struggling in the cool air. Mosquitoes are now attacking his calves in swarms. I put on my jacket and gloves and continue to watch.

Below deck, performer Alex Sanders is pacing back and forth preparing for a scene with Jenna and Shayla. His only problem is not delivering the money shot inside his pants.

'Ow! Ooh! Ee! Ooa!' Claudio swipes at the insects while trying to concentrate. This is a job for a centaur. At last he delivers and Alex swings into action with the two ready and able young women.

'Towel!' Juli calls.

✴ Juli Ashton during the filming of *Conquest*

'What towel?' an assistant shouts. Where's the lube-and-towel boy? Left on the pier with the towels. The girls are all sticky, gooey and icky. I find Joy hiding.

'Those guys sure had problems on the deck,' I say.

'Alex didn't have any problems,' she answers. Joy doesn't miss a thing.

For dinner, we each get a half of cold chicken without knife, fork or plate. Just like real pirates!

CHAPTER 41

THE PRICE IS RIGHT: NITEWATCH

Barbara Klein, the owner of Nitewatch, can be such a bitch. But it's all done in fun. She loves playing the in-your-face tough cookie; she's a smart cookie, too.

I haven't met too many immigrants in this business but they're obviously around. And as usual, they take the job nobody else wants.

What do you suppose this wise-guy Israeli is selling? Exotic, fantasies of far off places? I imagine the titles: *Middle East Mamas*, *Seven Veils Revealed*,

THE PRICE IS RIGHT: NITEWATCH

Ancient Rites Get Raunchy, *Oasis Orgies*. Fantasy drives this business.

In the industrial area of the Valley, I pull up to a side street where the buildings are separated by wall-to-wall pavement, barbed wire and chain-link fences. Forget the flowers and shrubbery. Cars parked every which way block all free space. No sign on the building I'm looking for. Wait, there's a faded number on the cinder-block wall. A group loudly speaking Hebrew and another one loudly speaking Spanish congregate in the parking lot. From inside the open garage door Latin music is thumping from a cheap radio. It's hot and stuffy and dusty. And in this part of Los Angeles, the air is always bad.

My appointment's not set for any specific time. When I show up, she'll find time.

Barbara is short with straight brown hair, severely pulled back. She's wearing a one-size-fits-all, stiff 3/4-length leather coat and holding a baby monkey that's wearing a diaper designed for premature baby humans. She cut a hole in the diaper for the tail but made it too big. So while holding the monkey, it pees all over her beat-up coat. What a cute pet.

Nitewatch manufactures low-end product. 'I don't even care for the quality,' she says. 'You pay for what you get. You pay shit, you're going to get shit.'

What the client wants, the client gets.

Nitewatch's niche is price, not exotica. If the market can't tell quality, what difference does it make? If the market judges the porno by the cover, why bother at all with content? Make the box cover dirty and move it. Forget being the best. Screw the awards. Forget the high-priced contract girl, shooting on film or Betacam. In fact, forget any quality pretence. Price and price alone drives this hard-core market niche. Everyone's prices are spiralling down, cutting corners and costs is the key to survival. Barbara and her husband find ways to lower their overheads and pass the savings to the wholesale distributors who trickle it down to the consumers. Lower price means greater sales.

We go out back to her own private junkyard so she can have a smoke. 'You see anything you want, take it,' she says. I consider a filing cabinet with broken shelves but it won't fit it in my car.

This street-wise, fuckadis and fuckadat-speaking Israeli hunts for every possible savings. For example, video duplicating machines go for $2000 new, $300 used. She got a steal at $75 and grabbed 500 of them. Where they came from, she don't want to know. She buys 'one-pass' T-60 or T-120 standard-length cassettes, meaning second-hand, used by a major video store or a mainstream distributor stuck with unsold movies. The tape is erased and recorded over. She buys them in bulk, bringing the wholesale price costs down from $.55 to $.35 a tape. No air-conditioning means lower electric bills, so they leave the garage open. Immigrant labor means easy come, easy go. A Mexican electrician wires up the 500 duping machines.

Low mark-up, high volume, minimum production costs. The 500 old duping machines don't like the heat and break down. Barbara blames the technician.

'The guy is really intelligent but he has a problem,' she says, lighting up a new cigarette. 'You sneeze next to him, he's sick. That's it. I have to call the paramedics. Yesterday, somebody sneezes next to him. So therefore, I have to wait. Tomorrow, and I pray to God that nobody sneezes next to him or says anything about sickness.'

She's laughing. She must be making it up.

'This is not a joke. I know, it sounds like a joke but it's not,' she says. 'I'm dealing with that kind of people. I'm laughing, but sometimes, I just want to hammer his fucking head in.'

Barbara's safety net is her husband's fortune, made in the garment industry. A shrewd businessman, Joe directs the company from his second-hand desk. A couple comes in with a master tape they produced. A good one. Joe feigns disinterest, offers them $750 cash. They stomp out.

They return a few hours later hoping to renegotiate. Good luck.

'Look, I'm taking a risk. I don't know if I can move it. The market is tight. Take the cash,' Joe says. They take it, not realizing his shtick is standard buyer's *kvetching*. They have no patience or negotiating savvy. Barbara shakes her head and smiles.

'Why are they so stupid?' she wonders. 'It was a good tape. We'll make 10,000 copies and sell it at $10 each.' That sounds a bit optimistic.

Long ago, manufacturers and distributors realized it's often cheaper to buy film rights than to produce fresh material. Find a dead company's old stock, hire an editor, cut it up, make compilations, or simply change the box cover and re-release it.

Other tricks include trading tapes for services, a cost-cutter prevalent throughout the industry. Pay bills or buy advertising space with tapes. It is an outlaw, quick-buck mentality everyone disparages and wonders when the *other* guy will stop doing it.

Lighting up as fast as she can smoke, Barbara inhales smoke and exhales statistics. Catalogue is down to $1.75, about half the price of the big boys. Direct sales are 30–50% below them, too. Suddenly it dawns on me, I'm surrounded by boxes of porno and we haven't mentioned one word about sex. Come to think about it, hardly any money people do. Barbara likes it like that and she likes meeting the other company owners. 'When you meet with them they're not talking about all the beautiful hookers and beautiful girls and how they're going to get laid and all that bullshit,' she says. 'This is business.'

Isn't that what made America great?

We tour the warehouse. There's tapes for the black, Hispanic and white markets. Nitewatch is an equal-opportunity smut peddler. Barbara's market includes low-income fans, her tapes are available at all kinds of stores, liquor, convenience, adult stores, truck stops, you name it.

She pulls out her favorite box-cover titles.

'*Forrest Hump* and *The Catcher was a Spy*, I made those up,' she says with pride. So she cut costs on the copy-writing department too.

If it's strictly a numbers game, what's happened to the high-quality theory and the name-promoting game? Out the window, that's where. Talk the buyer's language. Price is music to their ears. *All* big companies quietly drop to catalogue as quickly as necessary to generate cash and turn over product. They mark down quicker than fall fashions.

Doesn't the contract girl have a substantial following, making her worth her weight in cassettes?

'The bottom line is it doesn't matter,' she says. 'As long as you put a pretty girl on the cover. It doesn't matter if she's Elizabeth Taylor. They don't care because most people really don't know who the girls are. Very few know who is who and who is what. All you need is some girls and some really nice action. Everybody's happy.'

'So then the girl doesn't have such a strong negotiating point,' I say.

'She has nothing. She does what I tell her to do,' Barbara says. 'I pay her and that's it. Same for the guy. The guys are a dime a dozen.'

So how does her production team find girls to work so cheaply?

'To be honest with you, I could care less where they get them from,' she says. Barbara hires a production crew who do the casting in her office one day and shoot the next. 'I pay them. Then it's "Have a good life. Good-bye,"' she says.

CHAPTER 42

AN OLD HAND: GOURMET

Years ago, Gourmet was a big name. I want to visit there to see how the past mixes with the present and maybe learned about the 'golden years'.

Joe Spilone isn't feeling too good. At 60, he's recovering from quadruple open-heart bypass surgery. He's about 75 pounds overweight and he doesn't know how he, or his business, is going to survive. Years ago, Gourmet was one of the big names. But since his partner retired, things haven't been the same.

'I'll tell you the truth, business is shit,' he says.

His office, studio and warehouse are all rolled into one. Joe, a rotund, affable fellow with white hair and a belly-full of deli sandwiches, was in the steam-shipping business for 27 years. He comes from 'back east', grew up in the Bronx. His childhood friend, Howie Wasserman, moved out to California, got into porno production and did very well. He was doing so well, he called his lifelong friend and offered him a partnership to help him manage his business expansion. For years they worked together. Joe supported a wife and family.

Just then a fax creaks through somewhere under the piles of of paper smothering his desk. He tears it off, studies it and frowns. A low-end manufacturer is offering finished product to distribute. Joe looks at the price and gasps for air. His hand covers his chest. He can't believe it. They are offering a complete package for $1.65 a box.

'That's below my cost,' he moans.

Joe figures $.83 for a 75-minute tape, $.26 for the box cover, $.50 for duplicating and overhead in addition to sales tax and freight. They are selling cheaper than he can make it.

'And the feds go around saying how rich we are,' he says.

Joe recently got another proposition to buy boy-girl 'scenes', complete for $300 each. Buy five scenes and put together a movie for $1500. His 'low-budget' films average $6,000. When pornography became legal in Denmark, about twenty years ago, prices dropped so low, the entire Danish industry went bankrupt.

How could you survive today? He smiles. Here's what he would do if he was young again and just walking into the business. He would hire all the top new performers, shoot the hell out of them and then just sit and wait. When one of them becomes a contract girl with a company like Vivid, let them do all the promoting. Then, when she becomes a big hit, release all the movies.

That's what he would do.

So with wholesale prices dropping everywhere, how can so many companies survive?

By not paying their bills, that's how. But not Joe. 'I've never written a bad check in twelve years,' he says, with pride. He always pays his bills on time.

That's not like some people he knows, referring to a guy who still owes him $4500. 'I got money. I got money,' he called. Joe rode across town, two hours in traffic. When he got there, the guy gave him a check for $100.

If an Italian from 'back east' can't collect his bills, who can?

Unless you're one of the big boys, you get no respect. Joe complains he never gets the girls he wants from the talent agency. The big guys always get priority, even if he was there first. Take the time he booked talent one month in advance to shoot *Big Bust Babes* and *Double D Dikes*. The day before the shoot, he still had no girls. He got on the phone and hired them himself. The agent promptly sent a bill. Joe got so annoyed he started his own agency. He hired a student to create a computer program. Of course, now Joe has to learn how to use a computer. But it looks pretty good. He's got the categories and rates all figured out: SG (single girl), GG (girl–girl), BG, (boy–girl), BGA (boy–girl anal), DP (double penetration), IR (interracial), BBB (gang-bang).

Once he learns the computer, he has to get the girls, type in their information, call the manufacturers, call the girls when there's a job, negotiate the rates, make sure they show up and send the bills if they do. At least he'll be able to get talent when he needs them. And another thing, agents charge a minimum of $60, even for a $100 job. Not Joe. His minimum will be $15 and scaled accordingly, up to the $60 maximum. If box-cover prices drop, why can't agency fees?

And *AVN*, the 'pro-industry' trade paper, they don't give him no respect, either. Joe shot a movie, *Tricky Business*. He bought an ad. The *AVN* critics still panned it. What kind of way is that to treat a client? They should say nice things. The big guys who buy all the ads, like Vivid and VCA, they never get bad reviews.

Somehow, Joe gets by. He's been married forty years to the same woman, Barbara, who does the bookkeeping. They get a kick out of watching these films together and really enjoy the performers they hire. Like the guy who can take on three girls and deliver the money shot three times in one afternoon. And the girls, they're always entertaining.

'Some are great kids. Some are very intelligent,' he says. 'Others just want to party. Then you got the ones with no fucking idea at all why they're here.'

CHAPTER 43
JANINE: YOU CAN'T TOUCH THIS

Phone rings: 'I got you Janine. She'll call at 10 a.m. Don't move.' Click.

Contract girls usually come to the negotiating table with a hefty outside income source, from their strip-tease dancing or magazine layout popularity, which is why they're offered a contract in the first place. Companies will pay more for a performer with a following because they believe it will increase video sales. Contract girls control more of their shots. No one can make them do what they don't want to do.

In the old days, the Hollywood studios had much more control over their contract players than today's porno companies have over theirs, which explains why they are hard to get hold of.

Janine is Vivid's biggest-name porno star and is a partner in the country's hottest dance circuit duo, 'Blondage'.

I call her dance agent, Marty Foyer, based in Fort Lauderdale. Florida has more clubs, dancers and agents than anywhere else in the country. Hollywood porno's top contract girls usually come from Florida agent referrals. I met Marty in Reno last year at a strippers' convention. Big, bearded, and brought up on New York deli, he's one of the agents with a good-guy reputation.

'Someone like Janine comes along once in a lifetime, like Windows '95,' he says. 'Here's a woman that can turn heads. When Janine enters a room, mouths drop, eyes freeze. She's the most published stripper in history. Second place hasn't been born yet. She's the only adult film performer you can call a 'legend'. You can quote me! She can board an airplane wearing sunglasses and a sweatshirt and no makeup and it doesn't help. Everyone will recognize her.'

I'm sure the Windows analogy is a compliment. I'm a Mac user myself. I sit and wait.

At 10 a.m. sharp, Janine calls.

'Is it true you come along once in a lifetime, like Windows '95?' I ask.

'What?' she asks.

'Tell me about your marketing strategy to get to where you are today,' I ask.

'I had no plans at all. It was a complete fluke,' she says. 'I'm just riding the success.'

"How did you manage to become the most published woman in *Penthouse*'s history?'

'Just lucky.'

'Are you proud to be the best?'

'That's not my shtick to be the biggest and the best.'

'How long will you stay in the business?'

'The minute the fun goes away, I'm gone.'

'Will porno ever go mainstream?' I ask.

'No. If sex was not taboo, we would be out of work,' she answers.

Tall, statuesque, a classic blonde with virtually perfect features, Janine grew up an athletic kid in southern California. She was all-American girl with an all-American story, normal upbringing, normal marriage, kid, followed by normal divorce, all before she turned 18.

As a schoolgirl, she did topless modelling, graduating from nude dancing to porno.

'I just kept on going,' she says without remorse. 'This is how I want to live my one life.'

A contract girl can pick her sex partners and Janine picks only girls, which, for men across America, only makes her more desirable.

While most girls find it easy to spend all their money, for Janine, it's more difficult, possibly because of the great amount she's making. That's not to say she isn't trying. She takes friends to dinner, pays a lot of taxes, bought her sister breast implants and a Ford Mustang, bought herself a pink and white custom Ford Explorer: 'It's my penis, or lack of one,' she says. She takes her kid to sushi lunch five times a week.

Single-parent moms know they're role models: 'I raised him with unconditional love and hope to get the same in return.' Age five, he already notices how sexy Mom dresses to work. He's asking more questions. But even porno mommies are anxious when it comes to discussing the birds and the bees.

'I hope it's a few years down the road,' she says. 'Oh God, please let it be a few years down the road!'

But in the meantime, life is a bowl of cherries, or rather a piece of cake. She loves birthday cakes with lots of frosting.

'I get lightheaded,' she says.

'What kind?' I ask.

'Lemon cake, raspberry cake with whipped cream and chocolate Bavarian cake,' she says. 'I'm getting all turned on by this! Enough!'

Click. Hello? Is my time up?

That's it. I didn't get past Janine the porno star. Experienced Hollywood movie stars often preclude interviews with 'No personal questions'. Porno stars never say that. They just stay in character and keep their private life private.

CHAPTER 44
DYANNA LAUREN: FAMILY VALUES

After hours, I'm waiting in the Vivid lobby, hoping to meet former Penthouse pet Dyanna Lauren, now a Vivid contract girl.

When she enters the room she looks familiar. Do these Vivid girls seem more distant or is it my imagination? I know successful movie stars try to avoid interviews after the novelty wears off. Maybe it's the same thing for the contract girls. After all, some of them come to Vivid with an established following from their dance careers where they make more than from their monthly porno films.

But they want publicity and they get it from doing porno. Dance makes them oodles of money, much more than porno, which is basically editorial, but they only work once a month on a film contract. Some may already have all the attention they need, assuming that's possible for any kind of performer to achieve. The novelty of being interviewed lasts a year or two at most. The mainstream press doesn't help their career unless they are planning to do mainstream work, which they're usually not.

'What do you want?' her expression says.

'Tell me about your lovelife,' I say. Mainstream movie stars always get that kind of question. It gives the interview a personal touch.

'My pig is the love of my life,' she says. 'His name is Benny and he's a black pot-bellied pig with two white hooves. He weighed about 75 pounds at nine months and full grown will weigh about 100 to 150 pounds, if he's fed right.'

'Do you eat bacon?' I ask.

'I'm pretty much a vegetarian,' she answers.

Dyanna and Benny live on a thousand-acre ranch 100 miles south of Los Angeles. Dyanna has two cars, a sedan for the highway and a 1974 Dodge pick-up truck for the farm.

'It's the ugliest-looking body you have ever seen, but boy does it have a good engine,' she says. Who said porno stars are only interested in looks?

When Dyanna is not feeding Benny or doing porno, she might be building fences and rewiring the garage. Her grandparents wanted her to be well-educated so she could attract a man while still making own money, not just spend his.

'I got married which was the biggest mistake of my life,' she says. 'He was a horrible person, very self-centered, very selfish and an alcoholic.'

'Why'd you pick him?' I ask.

'I haven't a clue,' she answers.

Dyanna sings in a rock band, dances at clubs, mends fences, raises roofs, hammers nails, cooks dinner, bangs guys and goes down on girls. 'I'm just a renaissance woman,' she says. Take that, Leonardo.

At 5, Dyanna was a strip-tease prodigy. Using her bed as a stage, she practiced alone, then performed for her babysitters, piling on layers and layers of clothing and then peeling them off one by one. But she never got completely naked. After all, she was under 18. Why?

'Just something in my character, nothing prompted it,' she says.

Apparently, this is common among many young girls. It's just that most don't turn pro. Years later, she danced at clubs, posed for magazines and put herself through college. Eventually, she met the porno people and joined their ranks.

'These people were walking around naked for all of the world to see,' she says. 'I just really felt very comfortable. This was not a rebellion thing. This is where I'm happiest.'

Mom helps with Dyanna's fan club. Brothers, sisters, nieces and nephews know what Aunt Dyanna does for a living. Dyanna doesn't do drugs and doesn't drink.

' They know this is a business,' she says. 'It's a lot healthier for these children to take rather than for me to hide it.'

CHAPTER 45

COMPILATIONS: IT'S ALL IN THE DETAIL

One day, while waiting in the Vivid offices, I hear moaning and groaning coming from one of the nearby rooms. Strange, Vivid does not seem like a hanky-panky type company. People work hard to produce pornography, not screw around. What is going on?

I peek in next door – there's a guy at a desk getting a big kick out of watching a video.

'Go Rock! Yes!' he shouts. 'This guy can fuck like a God.'

Wearing a baseball cap on his head and a tattoo on his arm, Keith Bailey watches porno films eight hours a day, five days a week, rating and categorizing

COMPILATIONS: IT'S ALL IN THE DETAIL

in minute detail every aspect of every item in every scene. This information is used to make 'compilations'. Similar scenes from different videos are compiled into two-hour new releases, each consisting of twelve scenes.

With rating sheet in one hand and pencil in the other, Keith confidently checks 'hot' for action and gives performer Rocko Siffredi a 'Great', for 'Cum shot'. Keith knows his stuff.

The Sex Scene Breakdown Sheet is a datasheet which details movie title, performer's name, sexual preference, race, age, hair length and color, breast size and penis size. There's a checklist to note the guy's circumcision situation, body type, tattooed or not, pubic hair shaved or not. The compilator selects category choices from 33 locations, 25 costumes, 15 props, 11 sexual positions, 30 action ratings from 'cold' to 'burnin', and an amazing 23 categories of 'cum shots'. Only a trained eye with years of experience could possibly discern and appreciate the subtle differences and various nuances.

'I've been watching porno since my Dad bought his first Beta machine,' Keith says proudly. That was years ago. Since then, Keith has become an old pro at watching porno.

'I'm your basic voyeur,' he says.

Keith is not alone. It takes two to compile. Nancy, working from the same room, enters the data into the computer. Once done, she can search any criteria or combination imaginable. What if Vivid wanted to produce a video solely of 'Shaved women with tattoos in a locker room wearing nurse's outfits, playing with shaving cream, doing double pussy penetration in a reverse straddle'?

'No problem,' Nancy says. 'The only difficult part would be creating a title.'

Today, Keith and Nancy are working on several orders including: *Muggs and Juggs* #5 – attractive women with full breasts, *Bust a Nut* #5 – good, hot generic sex, *Butt Nugget* – all anal, and *Monster Facials* #5.

She prints the list for the video editor who will pull the master tapes from the library and 'lay the scenes down', meaning copy them to a fresh master tape to prepare for duplicating cassettes.

At the still photo cabinet, Nancy finds the different titles, selects twenty color slides from the video scenes and sends them to the art director who will create the box cover.

'People like these because it's two hours of straight sex. There's no story line like the features.'

'Has this affected you?' I ask.

'Not at all," she says. 'When I first started working here, it shocked me. But then after watching so many movies I just got jaded. Now it's just a job.'

CHAPTER 46
TIME FOR A REALITY CHECK

Susan Yanetti now works full-time at Vivid, responsible for both their mainstream and X-rated publicity.

Club Porno is now going strong – television news and all the weekly events magazines have covered it.

However, in addition to pitching story ideas like 'How Hollywood Influences the Perception of Beauty' to national entertainment news shows, Susan now handles the down-and-dirty porno magazines' requests for raunchy photos.

This has been an eye-opener. She jumped into it with the same enthusiasm as a first-time stripper. All these guys can't wait to admire us women! Susan, a college and graduate-school educated woman never imagined the market was driven by working-class male fantasy. Hard-core male fantasy. She's back to calling the women 'girls'. In fact, she's taken the blinders off.

'I'm not a true porno person,' she says. 'I know it's not for some.'

She's been on the sets. 'Going to do a scene today?' the crew teases. Not this time, fellas. The glamour part is still great. Publicly, she is the envy of all her public relations associates. Need any help?, they ask. Privately, she has learned the limits though she is still just as cheerful, still wearing her funky look of sneakers, black tights with racing stripes and a purple top.

'This is fun. Let's face it, we're still talking about sex,' she says.

Her office is deep inside the Vivid warehouse where she is currently moving from a small office to a slightly larger one, so both rooms are in a complete, let's say, state of transition. She throws some junk off the couch and offers me a seat while pulling up a chair.

'I want to make Vivid to video what Campbell's is to soup,' she says. 'That is my goal.'

She's really cooking. She got Vivid to spring for a $2,500 one-day media training seminar. She's gone after the counter-culture products and the mainstream media rebels. She invited the press to cover the making of *Intimate Secrets of the Kama Sutra*, filmed in Jimi Hendrix's home. She got the girls on a 7 a.m. radio talk show. Jenteel has visited fans up at the University of Wisconsin. Vivid is using soft, soft-core boxes to sell hard-core in mainstream places. She's got the contract girls advertising gigs promoting Fresh Jive fashion, Warp, an alternative Japanese snowboard, Van's sneakers, Black Flies sunglasses and handbags. Hard Candy cosmetics is sponsoring a nail colour called 'Porno'.

Little by little it's all adding up. It's very impressive and no other porno company is doing any of these things but compared to mainstream, it's still small potatoes. There's a reason: 'I haven't run into one performer who wants to be mainstream,' she says.

Porno performers never expected to be taken seriously and most of them don't even try. Susan dreamed of molding them into her image of 21st-century feminists, sexy bitches who do what they want when they want it. Of course, they already can do that but not with the results Susan anticipated.

'They can't tell the difference between a mainstream publication and a porno magazine,' Susan complains. 'If I tell them I can get them an interview with *Rolling Stone*, it doesn't mean anything to them. If I set them up, I get "My boyfriend's father is in town" or "I can't, I have to go to the mall" or "I want to play with my boyfriend." I'm thinking "What kind of bitch are you? What the hell do you care about your boyfriend's father? This is your career!" They don't see it that way. With the folks I have now, their dream is to be a headliner at the Pink Poodle and that's it for them. They think they are already at the top of the ambition ladder. They're happy. They are not out to parlay this into a multi-million dollar career. If I represented a Hollywood actress and told her I could get her an interview with *Rolling Stone*, she would respond "Let me at them!" Instead, these girls ask "Is it paying?" It's a cash-and-carry mentality. There is no such thing as long-term planning. They have no long-term perspective.'

Despite the roadblocks, she pushes ahead. *I'm* the one whose high expectations have been disappointed.

'It's strange, I came to Vivid first for the performer's profiles,' I say. 'But they seemed to be the most resistant. For example, even though it was all confirmed beforehand, when I met St Croix, he let a performer stand by interfering. The he just shut up and ate his lunch.'

'It must have been Dyanna,' she says matter-of-factly. 'She and him are dating.'

What am I covering, the high-school social beat?

'I thought Benny the pig was the love of her life,' I say. 'Nikki was impressed with Vivid's walkie-talkies and Janine dreams of getting in a sleeping bag with birthday cake. Did I miss something in the translation?'

'The problem is, they need a formal introduction,' she says. 'That's the way it should be done. You have to warm up the performers. Let them know how important the interview will be for their career and for the company. You have to protect them. You don't just throw a journalist unescorted on to the set. They need more media training. That's why I'm here.'

CHAPTER 47
KRISTINE'S ARE FOR REAL

Bondage expert Kristine Imboch has moved into a new apartment which will double as a set. At first glance, everything looks hunky-dory normal. In the living room are two black couches and a coffee table. A photo of her parents rests on the fireplace mantle though no pictures hang on the walls. Then there's a frame for suspending a willing victim in the living room. Kristine's handyman dad built it for her. It's easy to assemble, fits into a hatchback car and can be carried by one slight, 110-pound woman. And it can easily be camouflaged as a plant holder should the conservative in-laws pay a sudden visit. And as long as they hide the Old World-style stocks in the dining room, everything odd will appear normal at the Smith residence.

'It was always strange knowing the real you is not welcome,' she says.

Some of Kristine's fingernails are long and red and some are short and unpolished. Yesterday, she was in a movie and she put on her fake nails with 24-hour glue. But instead of taking them off after the job, she lets them fall off naturally a day later. It sounds okay but it looks strange.

Despite all her enthusiasm for bondage, believe it or not, it is not an end in itself. Her girl–girl movies are about sex and wherever possible, her performers have real orgasms which, she maintains, most 'straight' porno-shoot female orgasms are not. A woman needs far more preparation time than a guy and there are no indications that they get it. Noise is not a way to tell. Yet most men have no idea. Kristine bases this on her experience as a director and as a woman.

For a period of five years, starting in her late teens, she was inorgasmic and that led her to all kinds of study about sexuality, researching the female orgasm.

A lot of people don't know that women don't have orgasms and don't know that they need them. Her boyfriends were obsessed with it only because it reflected badly on them. Some play it down. How would a guy feel if he didn't have any? Women will go through the whole sex act inorgasmic, an hour of moderate to extreme arousal and have no outcome and that's worse than not even starting. Besides much more frustration, there's also subconscious anger at the partner because they're the ones who seem to get all the fun. The guy rolls over and goes to sleep.

She visited a gynaecologist who hiked up her pill dosage, which sent her arousal level sky high, but didn't solve the orgasm problem. Otherwise, she was a healthy woman in her early twenties.

She went to a college counsellor. 'Sex may be very big in the culture but it's not all that important in real life when you factor in that almost no minutes of your life are actually taken up with sex,' the counsellor said. 'It's such a small piece of who we are. It's not that important.'

Later, she asked models for vibrator recommendations. They reported that guys cautioned against their use. 'You can get hooked on them,' they warned, meaning the guys didn't want competition.

'Most of them are for guys because they have those goofy little animals on them and stuff,' Kristine says. 'I don't really think a woman would buy a flourescent green caterpillar dildo vibrator.' Women buy 'back massagers' at the local drugstore.

Finally, a sex counsellor delivered results in five sessions. The problem was mental. Kristine was emotionally holding back and orgasms are a matter of letting go of control. Control is a loaded topic for bondage people.

'I had a problem with losing control and low self-esteem,' she says. She wasn't reaching orgasm because she didn't think she deserved one. Her mother was like that too. She catered for others and her whole sense of self-worth came from serving and bringing pleasure to other people. 'You don't get any bonus points for doing something for yourself or for doing something that gives you pleasure," Kristine says.

She came out about bondage after she came out about orgasms.

'Bondage had its own big guilt thing, feeling the disgusting part of me that was into something that others weren't into and shame on me,' she says.

Ideas of control and power go beyond bondage and cover most of the general population, including, of course, the porno population.

'When men make porno, they like proof of the woman's arousal as proof of her vulnerability,' she says. 'If she's aroused, then she's been taken down a notch. One thing, they're into is copious lubrication. Exaggeration is a natural searching for the orgasmic image: if one thing is sexy, the next step up is sexier. If breasts are sexy, then bigger breasts are sexier.'

Bondage may be wrapped in the sexualization of power and control over the other, but even those not into bondage like to control arousal. 'They think they just like getting her excited but maybe it's not just because they're a giving, caring man and they want her to have pleasure,' she says. 'Maybe they like the power and control.'

Not that there's anything wrong with it, just don't call bondage freaks weird. Now that that's all straightened out, Kristine could concentrate on making videos. Besides the bondage, there's also the female orgasm which she maintains distinguishes her product from those made by guys.

'As a director, my biggest problem is finding a woman who is able to have an actual orgasm in a shoot situation with the camera staring at her and a director waiting,' she says.

I thought it was easy.

She tries to set the mood, finds suitable female pairs and avoids pressuring them. Men are not allowed on the set during the orgasm scene. It's easier when they aren't around. 'The performers don't feel like they are being evaluated,' she says. 'The main thing is to create a safe environment for a woman to have an orgasm. I'm sure some of them have to fantasise. They have to withdraw into themselves, focus on their sensations. It is like trying to get that "money shot".'

Guys don't feel like they are giving up themselves when they have an orgasm. 'I've never seen any guys self-conscious,' she says. Even the meekest guy goes "Ha! Ha! Here I come!" They never feel ashamed or feel like they're revealing themselves. But for a woman, being intimate and having an orgasm with someone is like sharing a personal secret. Unless of course, she's an exhibitionist. Then all bets are off.'

To men, a silent woman is not considered a dynamic, responsive, person. Yet she may very well be the one achieving the orgasm. 'I don't even know if regular porno directors can deliver unself-conscious orgasms out of women,' she says. 'Professionals have trained themselves to make more noise but are they achieving orgasm? I think that male eye bearing down on you is adjusting your reality.'

During a real orgasm, women will stop moving and stop talking and will hold still. In porno films, when there's no movement, it means she's bored.

'The patterns of my women, they hold their breath totally,' she says. 'They are not repressed but these are not patterns I see on a porno set. For a women approaching a sexual plateau, they act close to death. And right after the orgasm they hold still. Their nipples don't get hard. Hard nipples are just cold nipples.'

The Hollywood orgasm version goes 'Uh, ah uh, ah' for ten minutes. Rarely does a woman freeze and stiffen beforehand. Before a normal female orgasm, there is a silent, rigid 30 to 60-second time period. She looks like she's about to be pushed off a cliff, that feeling of being almost there, that anticipation. There's no build-up if someone is yelling and screaming and thrashing around. 'Your body isn't ready to have spasms so it's holding back and yet the accumulation is leading you forward,' she says. 'It's a beautiful little power struggle, its own little story. And nothing's happening. All you can see is her teeth gritted, her hands fisted and her toes pointed or curling. You don't get that with the theatrical version. *Then*, there is a letting go of control.'

Women can fake an orgasmic contraction. But in an orgasm close-up, Kristine includes the perineum contraction which is almost impossible to fake, as well as all the physical effects. 'After a real orgasm, the woman's face is flushed with a marvelous sweat sheen,' she says. 'It's an afterglow. Her face has a healthy, lit-up glow. She's panting a little bit. That is a really sweet moment. She is very vulnerable and very feminine. That you can't fake. It takes trust for a woman to share all that.'

'It's funny that our culture values a woman for being a sexual creature but other times tries to make you feel sorry that you are,' she says.

Well, I can't say I noticed any of the above when I visited sets. Maybe, I didn't know what to look for. In either case, making movies was more like, well, making movies.

'I thought being on a set would be more sensual,' I say.

'You were thinking about erotica when you were really dealing with porno,' she says.

Kind of reminds me of pro wrestling.

CHAPTER 48

A HARD ACT TO FOLLOW: BUTTMAN

Year after year, the 'Buttman' series has outsold the best the big companies have to offer. Buttman enjoys the highest compliment in the industry: it has never gone to catalogue. That's like a fashion designer never having a post-season sale.

What kind of guy can year after year produce Hollywood porno's most popular series? John Stagliano is the producer, director, writer and cameraman of Buttman. His style is an unusual combination of childlike innocence and X-rated action. His point of view is like a lost kid's and audiences identify with it. Low angle, looking up, just as he might have done at the age of his first sexual sensation.

What makes Buttman's creator tick? I figure a guy like Stagliano must be uninhibited, crass and insensitive. Someone who always seems to get what he wants. The audacious guys get the audacious chicks. Nice guys finish last. Being a gentlemen is for the meek and timid.

In the Evil Angel office, I'm ushered upstairs and meet Jeffrey, who had convinced Stagliano to meet me. While I wait for Stagliano, Jeffrey entertains me. Jeffrey's mother was a Rockette at New York's Radio City Music Hall. He launches into a burlesque tap dance, balancing a top hat on a cane, flipping it up, rolling it down his arm and plopping it on his head. I'm pretty happy when Stagliano is finally free.

Here he is, Mr Never-Went-To-Catalogue, inspiration for a generation of porno makers. John Stagliano looks a little like Tom Jones, well-built, handsome, dark curly hair, a warm but shy boyish smile.

John grew up in a loving, conservative Roman Catholic family in the suburbs of Chicago. Dad was a garbage collector who never talked much. Mom was the dominant figure in the household.

John's first sexual awakenings began at age four; whenever he climbed a tree or straddled the jungle gym he felt a sensation between his legs.

He started collecting pictures of sexy movie stars. At 12, he was a school crossing guard, wore a yellow belt and helped little kids cross the street. At lunch time, he'd sneak home, take *Photoplay* and *Coronet* into the bathroom and make it with Racquel Welsh in a white bathing suit.

✱ 'Buttman' John Stagliano

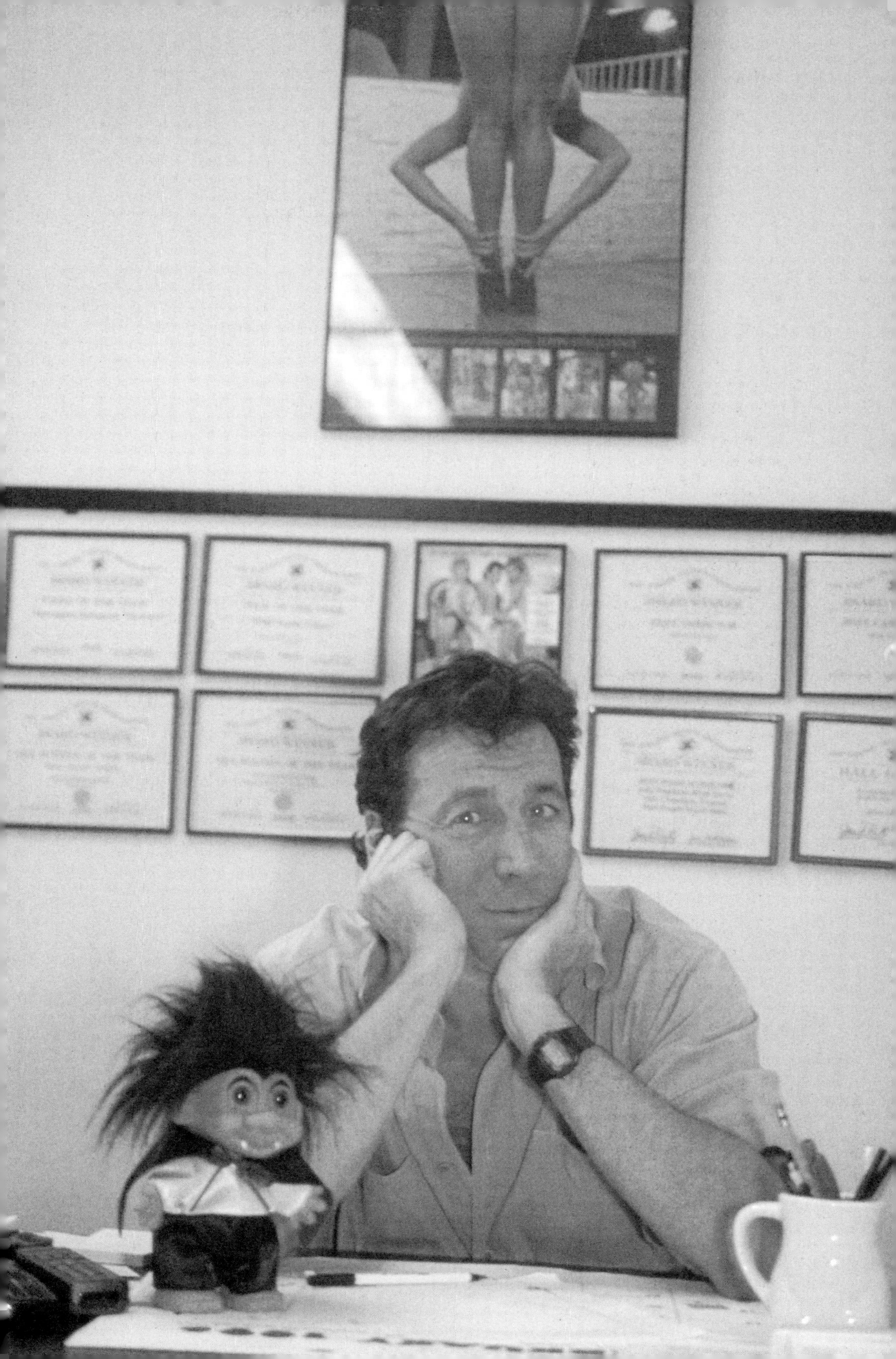

He bicycled into Chicago, found sexy girlie magazines at the newsstands. Soon he hopped buses to 77th & Western where he found a liquor store with racier magazines. He was obsessed with this stuff.

One day, he found porno magazines hidden under Dad's car seat. Every night after that, John checked the car. At 16, he visited his dad at work and he found boxes of pornography upstairs. Dad let him take home half a dozen magazines.

But even that wasn't enough. Fantasy competed with reality. John climbed up on a neighbour's fence to peek into the bedroom of the 16-year-old daughter, when she came out of the shower. Suddenly, she screamed.

'Maybe she touched something hot in the room and she really wasn't screaming because she saw me,' John hoped. 'Maybe she wouldn't recognize me even if she did.'

She was and she did. Her father talked to John's father who cut off his porno supply.

John's other neighbours included two boys his age in seminary school studying to be priests. They were a bad influence. They taught him about Robin Hood who stole from the rich and gave to the poor. Since John had no money, he was poor and could steal. He preferred nude photo books at the Evergreen Shopping Plaza's bookstore. Dad caught him but didn't punish or turn him over to the sheriff. The books mysteriously disappeared.

Too shy to have a girlfriend, John wore big horn-rimmed glasses and wasn't very good-looking. At 16, he worked as a dress shop stock-boy. In the back room, he fondled the mannequins' breasts, squeezed their behinds and came all over the place. 'It was pretty exciting,' he says.

I can't believe he's telling me all this. I can't think of any profession in the world where people would be so unself-conscious about their most private experiences.

Not until his senior year in high school did he get his first girlfriend. It was the first time that he actually related to a woman as flesh and blood.

'I was obsessed with her because she had an incredible butt,' John says.

At 17, Mom taught John the facts of life. She knocked on his bedroom door one evening. John hid the magazines.

'You know about the birds and the bees, right?' Mom said.

'Yes,' he answered.

'Good. Don't do it,' she said and that was that.

He was inspired by the novels of Ayn Rand, with their individualist heroes defying convention and taking control of their lives. He decided to take personal responsibility for his life, become 'independent'. So he dumped his girlfriend, paid back the bookstores, quit the state-run college and ended his 'dependency' on pornography. He filled the void with modern dance classes.

'These girls would be in leotards that would be creeping up their butts which would drive me out of my mind,' John says clawing at his face. Singing sirens tormented Ulysses. Great butt tormented John.

He had to escape. Temptation was everywhere. He transferred in his junior year to UCLA, dropped economics and took up basketball and tennis. But the itch remained.

At age 19, he got contact lenses, cut his hair and for the first time in his life, liked what he saw in the mirror.

He studied photography but quit within a week. He changed his degree subject seven times in two years. His obsession tormented him; he watched peep shows and snuck into strip shows. Meanwhile, he worked 80-90 hours a week all summer as a Good Humor Ice Cream Man, saving his money, planning to attend Northwestern University. But it was always hard, especially whenever he saw a girl in a bikini. When Northwestern rejected him, John returned home.

He was accepted into the University of Illinois in Chicago and moved into an apartment on the North Side, his old stomping grounds. His old strip club was within easy walking distance and the old adult theatres were now showing hard-core movies. His addiction to porno really wasn't that bad, he rationalized, because he didn't feel guilty about it. He wore a raincoat to the porno theatres and came out relieved. John knew society considered his addiction a perversion. His girlfriend proved it. He confessed his sins to her. She called him a pervert and left. Had John stayed in the closet with his raincoat, he might have kept his girl friend.

In 1972, John had his first real sexual relations with a girl he met in the park where he played baseball and football. She taught him the ropes.

'Remember to play with their asses,' she explained. 'Girls like that.'

At the age of 23, John moved back to California, attended UCLA, and took more dance and acting classes to overcome his insecurities. 'Stop worrying about looking like an idiot,' he told himself over and over again. It worked. He had talent and good rhythm.

In 1979, he became one of the first of the Chippendales male strip act. By now, he was dance and theatrically trained, good-looking and the only guy not gay. The ladies substituted for pornography.

Meanwhile, John secretly contacted porno makers, posed successfully for pictures but failed to 'get wood' in movies.

In 1983, he won $2,500 on the Playboy Channel's 'Shake it Sexy' male strip contest; with his winnings and $8,000 in credit-card cash advances, he teamed up with porno maker Bruce Seven, made his first porno movie and sold it to VCA for $23,000. Bruce Seven, a porno guru, is considered the best teacher in the business, with a background of mainstream Hollywood set design. He taught John how to execute, edit, and pace a video.

'If you don't edit your own movie, you don't learn from your own mistakes,' he told John who now ate, slept and lived porno. In a business famous for partying, he worked day and night. He studied the camera angles that excited him and added them to his productions. He couldn't get enough. His work was his life. He scoffed at emotionally detached, soulless porno directors just in it for the money. 'It's perverse,' John says. 'You have directors that don't watch porno movies.'

After editing, he learned how to do sound and lighting. Obviously some things he already knew how to do himself. He used available light and eliminated the crew. He left the microphone on the camera and eliminated the need for a gaffer and extra wires and equipment. He shot the still photos. His technique for working alone became known as the 'Buttman' style.

'There's no point to production value unless they enhance the sexual value of the film,' he says. 'To try to entertain people on a level other than a sexual level is pretty much futile. People who rent a porno tape don't want to see conflict or crying or a love affair gone wrong. They want to see sexual buildup. If it doesn't work for the sexuality of the film, it shouldn't be there.'

In 1988, John started Evil Angel Video with $80,000, $60,000 from cash advances on 13 credit cards and $20,000 from foreign agent sales advances. In 1996, Evil Angel sold about half a million videos.

Today, the Buttman series is still considered a porno classic and has outsold all the big company productions with their huge advertising budgets. Buttman has *never gone to catalogue*, the ultimate porno industry accolade. Despite the incessant outpouring of competitive material, he has never had to lower his price. Wholesale price has stayed firm at $15 a box over the past seven years. Many manufacturers start at $12, drop to $8 after a month and within three to six months are down to mail-order catalogue sales, at $3 to $5.

'I always wanted to do a buns fetish thing,' he says. 'I always wanted to do something where the girl is looking right into the camera and I put the two of them together and put myself in there as the cameraman. I'd do a sex scene myself and save money. I had no idea it would be that successful.'

'For the hard-core video fan, porno is getting harder and nastier,' he says. 'You've got better porno than ever before.' Yet Buttman videos hold their value. And famous contract girls have nothing to do with his product. He doesn't use them.

'I don't believe that on our end, the hard-core porno end, the star system is real profitable because our orientation is good, hard, nasty sex and people like variety and new girls,' John says.

Now that he's rich, he can afford live home entertainment. He flies all over the world, to Rio de Janeiro or to Amsterdam to get off. His life has progressed from bicycling to the dirty bookstore, to flying anywhere he wants to watch nasty table dances. He hasn't changed. He is still single. Recently, Finnish porno starlet Sabina visited and worked on him every night providing only temporary relief. When she left, John picked up where he left off.

FAX December 3, 1996

Dear Willoughby

We're almost there. I've had a few promotion ideas. Every January and July there is a video software dealers' convention in Vegas. At this time, Bill Margold organizes a press conference for the many female porno stars. It's what you might call a hands-on affair. It would be a good opportunity not only for research contacts but also for book sales. I'm going to go to the next one after Christmas and do a bit of research. Keep it in mind. I can see the starlets giving autographed kisses on the pages where their names are mentioned or their pictures shown.

Also, given that the majority of wired computed users are male, I wouldn't be surprised if we had a big potential audience on the Internet.

You should now have *everything* by January, promise!

Best regards,

Harris

CHAPTER 49
SEX AND AGGRESSION IN LOS ANGELES

The VSDA – Video Software Dealer's Association – Convention, is being held at the Los Angeles Convention Center. A huge *AVN* sign hangs over the entrance. It looks like they own the place. Inside, the hall is filled with various manufacturers' booths.

Vivid and VCA each have their own 20' x 20' booths. At Vivid, there's Susan Yanetti, St Croix, Jon Dough, Steve Hirsh and all the Vivid girls, including Nikki, Dyanna and Janine, signing autographs and posing for pictures. At VCA, there's Russ Hampshire and Juli Ashton. GVA, the country's largest distributor, sponsors several manufacturers in one large booth including Nitro (Hi Houston!), and Wicked. There's Joy and Steve and Jenna Jameson promoting *Conquest*. Rebecca Lord looks like a fashion model, dressed in orange with red silk gloves and green platform shoes. Nina Hartley is promoting her sex education series for Adam & Eve. There's Ron Jeremy who certainly doesn't look like a fashion model.

Dick James is here, the conservative Iowan turned Californian libertarian. We're discussing double-standards. 'I don't get it,' he says. 'Murder is illegal but it's OK to film it. Sex is legal but it's illegal to depict it. They believe an image of sex is a worse sin than sex itself.'

'I guess they're concerned about people getting too aroused,' I say. 'You get excited by sex, not by murder.'

'It's funny how religions are totally unwilling to accept lust,' he says. 'Even among the most religious groups, if the man did not get an erection, there would not be religious kids. Society would die off.'

'Take cheerleaders. It's an unspoken rule in society that they are expected to sexualize by wearing brief outfits and showing their panties. This is an acceptable provocation, which is totally dependent on the denial that it is sexually stimulating. That is a denial of reality. This is what's happening. The girls' support of the team is based on sex.'

At Bill Margold's Free Speech booth, an elegant-looking woman, Charlie LaTour, is signing autographs. In the 1970s, Charlie was a performer and 'fluff', keeping the male performers ready to perform on cue. It's a lost art. 'It was the era of free sex, free love and drugs,' she says.

Charlie loved her job and was really good at it. And she wasn't a snob. She didn't just do the performers. She did the director, the producer, the accountant, anybody who needed a helping hand, Charlie couldn't refuse. Being a preacher's daughter, she gave new meaning to the gift of giving.

We take a walk along the glass-walled, sunlit hallway and sit on a bench. A woman from the mainstream part of the convention is sitting at the other end.

'Why do you think films are trying to get more and more outrageous?' I ask Charlie.

'The "more" they are seeking is not a visual "more",' she says. 'There is no "more" that you can show. The "more" that they are seeking, that they can't find, is the sensual. They're looking for the internal "more" of sexuality. And that is what they are not finding."

Charlie misses the films from back then – *The Devil in Miss Jones*, *Girls, USA*, *The Private Afternoon of Pamela Mann*. In those days, only a handful of movies were made each year.

'When you watch a classic film, you feel your own sexuality swell within you,' she says. 'It titillates every sense in your body. It drives your sexuality.'

'The type of men we had in adult erotica and in pornographic films, they were men who were allowed to be sexual. Jamie Gillis, Ron Jeremy, John Holmes – these men knew how to sexually *be* with a woman. They knew how to touch. Did you ever see Jamie Gillis stroke his cock? You could sit in a movie theatre and actually orgasm watching that man stand above a woman, the woman is lying on the bed and he's just standing there staring at her with this look on his face. You could pop in the movie theatre just watching that.'

'When you see the videos of today, you are talking mechanical. You are talking spread the legs. You are talking a woman's genitalia and a man's genitalia.'

The woman sitting next to us abruptly gets up and leaves. Charlie and I look at each other.

'Genitalia?' I say. Charlie laughs.

'I was trying to be discreet,' she says. 'Otherwise, I would have said "They stick the dick in the cunt. They pump a little. They go 'Ohh. Ahh. Ahh, Ohh. That feels good. Hump me more. Harder. Faster.' Bingo. Orgasm. It's over." And to them that was sex. That is not sex.' She pauses.

'I hear some of the male actors complain – I've witnessed this on a set – where the girl says to the guy "We're getting ready to do penetration. You go off into that corner and stroke your cock. When you're hard and ready, you come back over and we'll go do the fuck scene."'

'That is wrong. When you tell someone to stroke their own cock and get it hard and then come over, that's not sexuality. That's mechanical. That's like saying "There's the food line, go get your food, fill your tray and then bring it back and we'll sit together when we eat." You don't have the intensity on the sets today that you had back then.'

'I used to review videos, ten a month,' she says. 'That was all I could endure. At one point, I was sitting in my bedroom and I was watching these and I came flying out of my room. "I can't take it anymore! I have to get out of here!" Because you were watching mechanics. You were watching that chug-chug of the train but you weren't going anywhere. So I stopped doing reviews. It was enough to turn the most sexual individual cold. I have my own sex life to keep a fire in the furnace. People say to me "I feel so horny and I have no one around, how can I cool down?" Just go watch an adult feature. You'll chill out real fast.'

Even a rebel Mom can have rebel kids. Her son is studying to be a minister but Charlie preaches to the tune of a different drummer.

'What I have unfulfilled is the desire to bring to the upcoming generation, the awareness of true sexual identity. Of teaching them and showing them how to become expressive. And to feel secure in their own sexuality. To help them realize sex is not a politically correct part of your persona. It is what and who you are. You have to be able to express it. And allow it to flow with ease.'

'When I go out I will pursue my sexuality to my last breath. And when I go out, I hope I will go out in full orgasm. It shall be with the highest orgasm I can possibly attain.'

We head back to the hall where I meet Mike Albo from *Hustler*.

'Are you the guy who said Margold's FOXE convention was filled with "geeks and freaks"?'

'Definitely not,' he says. 'I called them "geeks and losers". I said it was a stalker's convention.'

Albo is a porno critic. He wants to know who I've interviewed. I say Bill Margold. 'My best friend!' he exclaims.

Albo says he's a playwright and teacher gone bad. Made a mess of his career before pulling himself together with a regular gig at *Hustler*.

'Working in porno is cool,' he says. 'The chicks dress a lot sluttier.'

Albo isn't jaded. Like Margold, he enjoys attacking, especially the porno performers who do a lame job. Some of them are only concerned with their dance career; they do the minimum necessary to earn the title porn star only so they can get better pay as a feature dancer. Sometimes, the critics change their names. The girls go bananas when they get panned and call up all irate. Albo always is sympathetic to their complaints. 'Who him? I had the guy fired. He isn't here anymore,' he tells them. They thank him – he gets back to work.

'Our fans are from the federal penitentiary, another segment are military people,' Albo says. 'We're seen at finer liquor stores everywhere. On Friday night they buy a porn mag and a six-pack and think "I'm dating Houston."'

Albo believes sex is dirty, that porno should stay underground and not go mainstream. 'It should be kept hidden in the sock drawer like normal people do,' he advises.

While I'm visiting Margold's booth, a big fat guy dressed in white, wearing wraparound green reflective sunglasses, comes over to Margold. He looks very serious. All he lacks is the fez hat to look like Sydney Greenstreet in *Casablanca*.

'Have you interviewed Jim Holliday, porno historian?' Margold asks.

'Never heard of the guy,' I say. 'What does he look like?'

'Never heard of me!' the big guy thunders. Writing a book and not have me in it! What kind of book would not have me in it!'

I assume he's joking but it's hard to see through the sunglasses. He's not smiling, that's for sure.

'How did he know about it?' I ask Margold.

'I'll bet Albo set him up,' he seethes. 'I despise Albo. He's one of my own children gone bad. He forgot his roots. He suddenly, unprovoked, attacked the fans.'

'I told him you were famous,' Margold says to Holliday.

'OK, I'll interview you right now,' I say.

'No. If you never heard of me, you don't deserve to interview me,' he says, then adds. 'I'll make sure that book gets a bad review!'

'Who the fuck do you think you are?' I scream at the top of my lungs. People circle around, ready to watch a schoolyard fight. I'm ready. He's ready. Actually, neither one of us is really ready because, without saying a word, we part ways.

'Well, it will probably be difficult to interview him now,' Margold says with regret. I thought he loved fights.

'What's with him?' I ask.

'You didn't genuflect to his greatness fast enough,' Margold says. 'I feel sorry for him. I've never met a man who takes himself more seriously. Life for him is a quest for supreme recognition. I care for him. But he is a bully because he uses his perceived fame as a bludgeon.'

AVN's Paul Fishbein stops by the Free Speech booth and greets Margold.

'How are things going?' he asks.

'Fuck you, you're an asshole,' Margold says. 'You're not a good publisher.'

Fishbein leaves before finding out if Margold is really ready or not for a

* Sofia Ferrari and Claudio schoolyard fight.

'Why did you say that?' I ask. 'He was being friendly.'

'People come to me to be lacerated,' Margold says. 'This is a man who has no spine. If he ever takes a bust, he'd change *AVN* to 'Auto-Video News.' *AVN* is worthless. It's so slick you can't even wipe your ass with it. "Fact" is a foreign language to them.'

On the other side of the hall, all is peaceful in the female domination section. For example, San Francisco's Kim Wylde is not necessarily a sadist. It really depends on who's her partner. Some people she likes to beat. Others, she prefers them to beat her. It's a game of give-and-take. This mature respect for individual needs makes for a happy relationship.

Trish Brown's company, California Wildcats, specializes in women fighting and tearing each other's clothes off. It's not really hard-core pornography because penetration isn't shown. Trish made *The Best Chest in the West*, starring the Boobsie Twins and Venus de Light, a former Miss Nude and a formidable boxing and wrestling champion. Nearby is a tough-looking woman named Hollywood, a professional street-fighter. She doesn't need a ring. She prefers the spontaneity of real life. She'll do bodyguarding or start a fight, whatever the situation calls for.

'Where were you when I needed you?' I say.

I wander around the booths and greet Wicked's Joy King.

'I heard about your encounter,' she laughs. 'You probably figured out by now Holliday has an ego as big as Margold's.'

Sex and violence. This place is, like, so American. Where is it safe? There's the Italian section. I see Claudio Bergamin from *Conquest* and Gina Rome signing autographs. They introduce me to another Italian porno star, Sophia Ferrari.

'Which is better, sex with your husband or sex with Claudio?' I ask Sophia.

'Sex with everybody is good,' she says.

At last, here, everybody is happy and laughing.

CHAPTER 50

THE DINNER PARTY

Claudio from *Conquest* and Gina Rome have invited me to a dinner party at their home. What are these people really like when not working? When not in character, are they freer sexually than most, or do they have the same regular inhibitions?

How to dress for the occasion? Obviously, dress like I am visiting friends – but what's friends to them feels like guests to me. And what if I have to *un*dress? Anyway, what difference does it make? I've been around enough to know that whatever the Italians wear will be right and whatever I wear will be wrong. I get a little dressed up, not a lot: torn black jeans for friends, a black shirt for guests, fancy underwear for looks and white socks for comfort.

Unlike most porno stars, who come from a blue-collar background, Claudio and Gina come from a solid middle-class background and that includes being financially secure enough to pursue their dreams. They have rented a big, beautifully furnished, three-bedroom house with a heated swimming pool lit up in the backyard. It's large enough to shoot a movie in. I'm impressed.

'Most porno people don't live like this, I can assure you,' Claudio says while giving me a tour. He's wearing a polo shirt, shorts and boat shoes, while Gina wears a flannel man's shirt, shorts and high-top sneakers. They are dressed down for friends, not dressed up for 'company'. I wanted to impress them as friends. I was right. I got it wrong.

We start with a Negroni, a mixed drink (Martini, Campari and Gin).

The dinner guests are a mix of Italian performers and porno-loving friends. The first course consists of antipasti, a gift from a neighbour who owns a gourmet food shop. When Claudio and Gina moved into their home a year ago,

THE DINNER PARTY

they were naturally cautious about telling the neighbours what they did. But before too long, Claudio had spilled the beans. The neighbour turned out to be a big fan. From time to time, Claudio brings him a few porno videos and in exchange, is inundated with all kinds of gourmet delights, like the salami and $24.95-a-pound smoked salmon before us tonight. Claudio breaks out the wine, a special deal he found of Chilean Chianti, only $2.98 a bottle.

Claudio is a mining engineer from Trieste, in northeastern Italy. He came to the US to get his pilot's license; while here, he pursued porno performing. 'This has always been my dream,' he says.

A guest from Tuscany teases Claudio about his wine selection. It tastes fine to me. Soon we are on our second bottle. And third. Claudio assures us that the wine cellar is full.

From the start, the conversation is about work and business. In other words, sex. 'Some guys do it four times a day, every day,' Claudio says. 'It's incredible.'

We straight guests, excuse me, friends, rat-tat-tat questions at the porno people like it's a press conference.

'I heard porno companies are shooting 35mm again,' I say.

'They tell the lie,' says Joe d'Amato, from Rome. He has directed both porno and mainstream films and now lives and works here. 'They usually shoot 16mm and call it 35mm. They shoot High-8 and often call it Betacam.'

'What does it take to direct porno?' a woman asks.

'You just take your camera, you take your wife and you make the movie,' he answers.

'What makes a good movie?'

'I need the tact, not just the fuck. Please excuse me. My English is fucking bad.'

'What kind of person does this in front of a camera?'

'Normally, the woman is better than the man,' Joe says. 'A man, to be doing this, is not too intelligent. Is hard work and a low pay. A woman, is easy work and a high pay.'

Claudio serves the *primi piatti, orecchiette con cime di rapa*, pasta with olive oil, anchovies, Parmesan cheese, parsley and ground black pepper. He also brings more wine. While he's in the kitchen, Joe whispers, 'I no understand Claudio, he smart but he do this work.'

The conversation switches to Rocco Siffredi, one of the best Hollywood male performers. However, he's not American and doesn't even live in Los Angeles. He is a happily married Italian living in Rome, available by special appointment only. He strikes terror in the hearts of the American performers:

not only is he handsome and reliable, he is also charming, funny and suave, all the things Italian men are reported to be. And of course, there's his equipment.

'The man, to do this work, must be an exhibitionist,' Joe continues. 'Rocco is the worst exhibitionist. He have a big pecker and he like to show it. Always he take it out. After two minutes in a scene, he take out the pecker. Impossible to do a love scene like a regular movie with the kissing and the touching because all the time is ready, goes up, up, up. Even he make the dialogue, the pecker, it go up. It's unbelievable. We are very proud to be Italian for Rocco.'

'So the men do it for fun.'

'For sure, the man, he do it for fun because if no fun, is impossible to do this job,' Joe says.

'They do it to date the women,' Claudio interrupts.

'And the women?' I ask.

'I don't know many woman who do this for fun,' Joe answers.

'Could a mainstream male perform on a porno set?' I ask.

'Absolutely not. I try many times. I use a regular actor to make a mood but all the time is trouble with the pecker.'

'What would you advise a young director?'

'Always do the sex scene first,' he says. 'Because if the man cannot perform, then you don't waste the film with the other scenes.'

One of the female guests is concerned about the exploitation of women and their being abused by men.

'You have to be nice, otherwise the woman she mad and the pecker, it no work,' Joe assures her.

The group debates porno market saturation. Is there a place for new material? We turn to Joe.

'Is room because for ten years is the same movie all the time,' he says.

What about the plot? Is it really necessary? Again we turn to Joe.

'America, it wants the sex,' he says. 'The rest of the world, it wants the story.'

Claudio carves and Gina serves the second *piatti* of barbequed beef, with grilled eggplant and peppers.

Gina looks like a college student, so normal and innocent. I've seen her pictures. Maybe normal but definitely not innocent. She recently had an unusual job with director Kristine Imboch.

She played a security guard, who witnessed a woman being kidnapped and tied up by the all-female 'Organization'. Gina watched to gather evidence but got so aroused she took off her clothes and played with herself. Close-up on the perineum contraction. The 'Organization' caught Gina and tied her up, too.

But she escaped and spanked her captors while waiting for the FBI to arrive.

'Did the FBI guys come?' I ask.

'No, because then she would have to pay for more actors,' Gina says.

Claudio and Gina's friend Sophia Ferrari is also Italian. She's sexy-looking, with frizzy long hair and is wearing a lovely low-cut lingerie top. She gets a lot of work and is married to an American.

'Does your husband get jealous?'

'No, because he likes to fuck around, too.'

'Do you separate your porno image from your regular life?'

'You have to separate yourself unless you're completely empty-headed,' she says. 'Let's face it, it takes your soul.'

Claudio kisses Gina between courses, getting bolder with each serving. Everyone smiles. Everyone is jealous.

'Which do you prefer, sex with Claudio or sex with a younger man?' I ask Gina.

'You know after eight years with the same guy, of course, a new guy is better,' she answers. Everyone laughs but everyone is still jealous.

'Is work difficult?'

'I don't like work when there's no work and you have to call for the work and they say "There's no work",' Gina says. 'And when there is the work there is the waiting. They say 8 a.m. but we don't work until 10 p.m. Should be two prices, one for long and one for short.'

'Is this a bad job for a woman?'

'To work in a mine, I think is worse,' she answers.

Everyone is totally smashed by the time dessert is served, home-made tiramisu followed by fresh fruit, followed by espresso. We sit round the dining-room table, slowly finishing the remaining bottles of wine. Claudio is looking for something under the table near Gina. Some of the porno-friendly guests prepare to leave. After they're gone, Claudio closes and locks the door. It's party time! In an instant, someone is on the kitchen floor, a couple are on the sofa, others dive into the swimming pool.

A man and a woman climb up the stairs to the bedroom. In no time at all, the woman comes down. 'Let's go,' she says to her partner who quickly gets dressed. Upstairs, somebody is snoring.

CHAPTER 51
ADULTDEX: THE FUTURE IS ON-LINE

It's been a year since the last Las Vegas Adultdex Convention. All is not well in the adult CD-ROM world. Vivid, VCA and GVA have all cancelled their booths. Many of the survivors have returned to simply clear out their old stock at reduced prices.

'Downsize is the word and those that got hit the hardest did not,' says Adultdex organizer, Fay Sharp.

There are half as many booths as last year. That's the bad news. The good news is the space has been taken up with Internet providers. Last year's hottest new technology is replaced by this year's.

Ray Pistol rented one of the booths but he's too busy to attend and too busy to invite Margold and me to dinner this time, too. In fact, business is going so well, he's bought the House of Lords restaurant he wined and dined us in last year. He's also bought the web server company that launched his site and promoted his strip club.

Margold has set up a booth to collect funds for the Free Speech Coalition whether they want him to or not. If he didn't do it, nobody would. Margold is selling calendars. Anyone who's birthday falls on the same day as a porno star, gets the $10 calendar for $5. There's plenty of baseball cards, too.

'You play with your own bat when you get home,' he says.

There's a long line of guys between the CD-ROM-on-sale and Internet-is-happening rooms. Wow! What are they giving away? It's Houston! In glamorous Versace no less. Her corporate sponsor is an Internet company called IEG, who is also sponsoring another performer named Felicia. For some reason, there's an abundance of Felicia T-shirts and no Houston T-shirts so Houston is autographing and giving away Felicia T-shirts. The guys don't care: hey, it's a free T-shirt.

Houston invites me to join her while she signs autographs. Things have really been going well for her. For example, she recently had her vagina molded in plaster of Paris. This is the porno equivalent of Graumann's Chinese Theater where mainstream movie stars achieve immortality by leaving their handprints and signatures embedded in the cement sidewalk outside. In the porno version, the mold of Houston's vagina will be incorporated in a useful plastic doll.

Houston is now on the road 26 weeks a year, booked as a Triple-X

Superstar. She was just in New York. Next week it's off to Detroit, then Quebec. She travels with four trunks filled with light beacons, fog machine, props, merchandise and outfits. It's all carried by Christine, her LP – 'luggage pimp', and she's accompanied by 'Q', her DJ.

'I just had a bad week in New York,' she says. 'It was really rough.'

'Guys hassling you?' I ask.

'No, guys watching the World Series,' she says. 'It was really rough getting them to watch me.'

'Are you still Mr and Mrs Smith around the neighbors?' I ask.

'Nah, they know,' she says. 'They've become fans.'

Even Mom's boyfriend has all of Houston's movies.

Houston's been getting nastier, too. She works enthusiastically on the set. When the director asks, 'Who wants the pop shot?' she is the first to raise her hand. 'Me!' she screams. 'The fans love it,' she says. And they come to see her on the strip club circuit where she can really get nasty. Her eyes are alive. She's full of excitement.

When her autograph hour's up, she switches off with Felicia and goes up to the 'Web Site Hotel Suite'.

Upstairs the suite is filled with guys. At this convention, everyplace is always filled with guys.

The suite was rented, the computer installed and Houston hired to attract prospective web site advertisers. But it is filled with young guys who just want to drink beer and flirt with Houston. They make themselves comfortable on the plush couches. They try and talk to Houston but fumble through their sentences, either because her powerful sexual presence intimidates them, or else they're so bombed from IEG's open bar they can hardly speak. To Houston's amazement, a couple of guys grab a few bottles and head into the bedroom, where they flop down on the bed, and watch the football game on the television.

A guy named John is supposedly in charge. But he's obviously more a computer type than either a public relations administrator or a bouncer; he has no idea what to do. In fact, he has mixed feelings about the whole thing. He thought he was hired to be a computer hack but now finds himself smack dab in the middle of the porno business, surrounded by a room full of beer drinkers joking about sex and talking about porno. He looks like he wants to hide. He defers all questions to 'Seth'. 'Seth can answer that,' he says. 'Wait until Seth gets here.'

✱ Houston on duty at Adultdex

IT'S THE REAL THANG!

Enter a pint-size guy, Brylcreamed hair, wearing grey slacks and a crisp check shirt. Maybe he reaches Houston's shoulders. This is Seth Warshavsky, from Seattle, also home of Bill Gates and Microsoft. A computer whiz and owner of the www.clublove.com web-site, at 23, Seth has already made his fortune in the phone sex business and is now poised for the next high-growth market. He has a web site where for $20 a month, a subscriber can access all kinds of sex-related activities such as conversations with Houston, live strip shows, one-on-one peep shows.

But Seth sees the future. He is preparing for the Internet to go cable. When the quality arrives, this guy will have his own worldwide sex-related cable station. He has the computer savvy. He has the infrastructure. The phone sex companies are all geared up to receive and process credit cards on thousands of calls simultaneously. IEG has T3 links to the Internet with eight SGI challengers and twelve full-time computer employees. It means they've got power. Now they need content.

Companies like Vivid and VCA have their own web sites. But Seth's web site can draw from a multitude of manufacturers and offer far greater variety so Vivid has signed on with him. So has Nitro. He'll be a giant worldwide distributor, only he won't need the huge VCA-type warehouses: movies will be downloaded just like movies are ordered in a hotel room on a pay-per-view basis.

Consumers can sign up the world over at $20 per month. The potential is far greater than a local cable or television station. He hires advertising agencies in other countries to create and place ads in adult consumer magazines to promote web site subscriptions. The race is definitely on for the next empire builders.

Aside from an occasional strip-club lap dance, Seth is not a porno type of guy.

'It's a sick business but I like it,' he says. 'I'm a high-stress guy and the craziness keeps me sane.'

The whole system is based on web site 'hits'. IEG averages 100,000 hits per day, though that doesn't necessarily convert into dollars. It's like registering the number of window shoppers at Harrods.

Seth's strategy is to build a broad content base. It's still in its infancy. Stay tuned next year. Already he has 45,000 subscribers a month. He could be the next porno giant and he won't be from Hollywood.

Meanwhile on the Adultdex floor, the porno people are on their best mainstream behaviour, and following all the Sahara Hotel's rules and regulations. Performers are discreetly covered or wearing modest bathing suits.

No one is smoking. It's so tame, it's so boring.

This is not lost on Bill Margold. He brings in a beautiful young woman wearing a raincoat and high heels. She opens it. Oh yes! She's wearing nothing underneath. The guys go crazy. So many guys circle around Margold's booth the girl gets lost in the crush. The CNN video crew rushes over. By the time they push through the crowd the girl has covered up. 'What naked girl?' Margold says. 'The crowd came to see me.' He gives them a sound-bite for the 11 o'clock news. Bill Margold, spokesman for the industry.

That evening, it's Margold's turn to pick a restaurant. We go Italian. It's lousy. Good. He won't make fun of my ribs place anymore. Anyway, it's gone out of business. This place won't even serve us extra bread. Margold opens the grated Parmesan cheese and eats one spoonful after another right from the glass shaker. When the meal finally arrives, he dumps the rest of the cheese on his plate. That's OK, I didn't need any. My pasta is overcooked and the tomato sauce is watery, just the way I like it, not. After the meal, Margold carefully licks all ten fingers searching for additional flavour. We return to Sam's Town for coffee and rhubarb pie.

'That girl in the raincoat was really cute,' I say. 'Why don't you ask her out?' He looks shocked.

'People use the industry to avoid relationships' he says. 'My life belongs to the industry. I'm like a monk: my office is my monastery. I can't share my life with anyone.' Bill Margold, spokesman for the industry.

HARRIS *from* PARIS

AFTERWORD
WHERE ARE THEY NOW?

AVN has launched two new magazines and reports 7,000 new video releases in 1996, up 15 per cent from 1995.

Buttman's bought a new raincoat.

Conquest won an award.

At the age of 61, EZ Rider's become the father of twin boys.

Free Speech made the 6:00 news for legislating lobby.

Greg Dark featured in *Premier* magazine in October, 1996.

Houston's bought a brand new white BMW 321i.

Kristine Imboch has become multi-orgasmic.

Nina Hartley was honoured with the Hot d'Or 'Hall of Fame' award at the Cannes Film Festival.

Ray Pistol's bought the rights to *Deep Throat*.

Rebecca Lord's bought some new coffee.

Ron Jeremy has had his name in lights on the Las Vegas strip.

The Boston Globe did a front-page story on the porno industry.

Mainstream film distributor Columbia Tri-Star released the porno biopic, *The People vs Larry Flynt*.

Mainstream New Line released a porn-inspired film *Boogie Nights*.

US News and World Report's cover story for February 11, 1997 is 'The Business of Pornography'.

Peaches seems to have gone back to Atlanta.

Bill Margold is still Bill Margold.

FAX

December 29, 1996

Dear Willoughby

Well, that's it. I'm sending you the final chapters by Fedex and E-Mail. Don't see anything about the book as yet on your website...

When we first talked about this project, you suggested I might use **The Right Stuff** as a model for my Gonzo view of the porno industry. Now it's complete, I've been thinking once again about the similarities.

What is the "right stuff" anyway? Remember the Tom Wolfe book, when John Glenn started positioning himself as the moral voice and divided the ranks? It's the same thing, only society doesn't want porno people to be role models. John Glenn criticized the others' sexual pranks but in porno the technicians are condescending to the astronauts as well as the consumers who buy their product. It's as if the technicians spent their time saying "I would never go up in one of my rockets. You must be nuts..."

My greatest hope would be to pit two self-appointed 'spokesmen for the industry' against each other and have some fun. Margold, for instance, takes the rebel point of view. The others - the new generation - see no need to rebel and just want to be in a healthy, legitimate, money-making business.

Porno is going more and more mainstream. Soft porno is already in computerstores where it was once banned. And in every convenience store. Recently, shock jock Howard Stern appeared on the Jay Leno show with two Vivid porno stars. What will happen when porno crosses a certain line of respectability?

My agent points out that a cheque is due on delivery. When is publication? As you know, I have a wealth of ideas for marketing and promotion.

Best regards

Harris Gaffin

Harris Gaffin

INDEX

This index is compiled on a word by word basis so that, for example, San Francisco precedes Sanders, Alex. Illustrations are entered in bold print and titles in italics. Titles without further description are films.

Adam & Eve, mail order company 37, 100, **101**, 102-4, 112, 190
Adams, Michael 22-3
Adultdex Convention 95
agents 30-2
AIDS 127
Albo, Mike 74, 192-3
D'Amato, Joe 196
Antigua, production company 54
Ariana 18-19, 125
Ashton, Juli 153-4,158, 162, 166, **167**, 190
AVN (Adult Video News), trade paper 30, 34, 129-33; Bill Margold's opinion of 194; and Joe Spilone 172; at the Video Software Dealers' Conference 190

Bailey, Keith 176-7
Benny the Pig 175, 180
Bergamin, Claudio **194**, 195-8
The Best Chest in the West **194**
Beverley Hills Playboy Mansion 8
Big Bust Babes 172
Bikini, magazine 147
black people 59-61
Blatt, Todd 53, 54-6
Blondage 114, 173
Blue Movie 156
Boan, Red 36-7
Bobby Sox 47
Bon Vue, production company 16
bondage 16-19, 83-7, 180
Boogie Nights 204
bookings 31
Boston, Massachusetts 13
Boston Celtics 80
Boston Globe,newspaper 204
Boston Red Sox 81
Brooklyn, New York 97

Brown, Trish 194
Buttman 39, 184, 204
Buzz Coffee Shop, Beverley Hills 71

Cabinet of Dr Caligari 140
California Valley Girls Take it to the Max 32
California State College 119
California Supreme Court 32
Cannes Film Festival 156
Capone, Al 126
Casablanca 193
Central Juvenile Hall 97
CES (Consumer Electronic Show) 113
Cherokee **58**
Chi Chi La Rue 143, 144
Chippendales 187
Cinnamon, production company 24
Cleary, Tony 53, 151
Cleveland, Ohio 44, 95
Club Axis 143
Club Porno 145, 178
Columbia Tristar 106, 204
'Combat Zone', Washington St., Boston 14
'Comdex', computer exhibition 92-3
Conquest 148, 190, 195, 204
contract girls 31, 173-4, 175

'Daniels, Evan' (psuedon.) 51
Dark, Greg 35, 70-3, 72, 204
Davy, Peter 34, 38
Debi Does Dallas 105
Deep Throat 121
Demoan, Mona 50
Denmark 171
The Devil in Miss Jones 105, 191
DiMaggio, Joe 81
DOM (Direct Order Marketing) 35

Double D Dikes 172
Dough, Jon 47-51, 190
Douglas, Jeffrey 96

Ebbing, Von Kraft 138
Esquire, magazine 147
Estuary Channel (cable) 111
Evil Angel, production company 71, 188
Evita 24
EZ Rider (Peter Gallant) 16-20, 18, 33-4, 125, 204; at AVN 130; becomes the father of twins 204; at the FOXE awards 130

Fabulous Flasher 40
Fascination 108
female domination 88
female orgasms 180-3
feminism 100
Ferrari, Sofia **194**, 198
fetish 34-5, 138-9
First Amendment 32
Fishbein, Paul 130-3, 193
Fleiss, Heidi 105
Florida 173
For Your Thighs Only 105
FOXE (Friends of X Entertainment) 10 Awards 73
Foxx, Kitty 78-9, 78
Foxxx, Shayla 53-4
Foyer, Marty 173
Free Speech Coalition 29, 93, 96, 130, 199, 204
Freeman, Harold 32
Full Metal Jacket 94

Gaffin, Harris (the author) **2**; background and introduction to porn 13-16; with Greg Dark/John Stagliano 72; with Kitty Foxx 78; with Sharon

206

INDEX

Mitchell **91**; with Nina Hartley 101; with Ron Jeremy **106**; with Al Goldstein **113**; with Lt. Ken Seibert **120**; gets into spanking **139**
Gallant, Peter-see EZ Rider
Gate's, restaurant 97
gay pornography 140-4
Gillis, James 191
Girls 191
God's Daughter 98

Goldstein, Al 107, 111-3, **113**
Gourmet, production company 171
Green Apple, comic book store 80
Greenstreet, Sydney 193
GVA (General Video of America) 95

Hair 24
Hampshire, Betty 150-2, 160
Hampshire, Russ 53, 104, 150-2, 154, 157, 159-61, 190
Hardcore, Max 35
Hardwick, Floyd 57, 59
Hartley, Nina 91, 96, 98-100, **101**, 190, 204
Harvard University 97
Harvey, Phil 102-3, 112
Head to Head 23
Hendrix, Jimi 179
Herrera, Robert 9-13
Hightower, Ron 59-62
Hirsch, Steve 21, 44-6, **45**, 146, 190
Holliday, Jim 193, 194
Hollywood 20, 59, 67
Hollywood Press, newspaper 8
Holmes, John 191
'Houston'(Kimberley Halsey) 40-3, **41**, **190**, 199-202, **201**
How to Start and Operate a Mail Order Business, book 102
Howard, Eve 133-9, 135, 139
Havlecek, John 80
Hustler, magazine 12, 74, 115, 192

I Love Lucy, TV Series 38, 64, 137
Idol, Ryan 142, 143
Imboch, Kristine 83-7, **85**, **87**, 180-3, 197, 204

Intimate Secrets of the Karma Sutra 179
Iverson Ranch 47

James, Dave 20, 21
James, Dick 35-6, 190
Jameson, Jenna 147-150, **148**, 156, 162-4, 190
Jammer,Kal 29
'Janineî 26, 80, 146, 173-4, 190
Jeremy, Ron 105-9, 121, 122, 190, 191, 204; with the author 106; displaying his Lifetime Achievement Award **109**
Jesus Christ Superstar 24
Jordan, Alex 29, **29**

Katz, Tom 144
Kaufman, Justice 32
Kentucky Penitentiary 123, 126
'King, Davidî 159
King, Joy 147-50, 151, 152, 194
Kiwanis, club 36
Klein, Barbara 167-70
Knight, Madeleine 25, 26

Lane, Chasey 155-6
Las Vegas 10, 78, 92, 114, 162, 189
Las Vegas Adultdex Convention 199
Lauren, Dyanna 175-6, 180, 190
Light, Venus de 194
Little Tokyo, Los Angeles 64
Lord, Rebecca 68-70, **69**, 190, 204
Los Angeles 20, 115, 168
L A Express, newspaper 39
Los Angeles Police Department
  Administrative Vice Division 114-22
  Narcotics Department 120
Lovette 34-5, 75-6, **77**
Lynn, Ginger Allen 21

Malle, Anna 52
Manchester Federal Penitentiary, Kentucky 123, 126
Marcus, Mr 57, **58**, 64-7
Margold, Bill 8-13, 8, 32-3, 71, 83, 108, 122, 161, 189, 204; at the Adultdex Convention 93, 96; picture in AVN 130; background 97-8; criticised by Paul Fishbein 132-3; and the FOXE awards 73, 74 and Free Speech Coalition 199; eats Italian 203; lecturing 126-9, **129**; his office 27; on money 116; and Carol Rouge 37; at the Sahara Hotel 94-5; at college with Lt Siebert 119; at Video Software Dealers Convention 190
Margold, Nathan Ross 97
McDonalds 151
men 61
Metro, distribution company 53, 151
Midnight Blue, cable channel 111
Mitchell, Sharon 88-92, **91**, 107
Monro, Tami **18**
Monroe, Kitty 24-7
Moore, Rodney 34, 38-40
Musso & Frank Grill, Los Angeles 114, 119, **120**

National Obscenity Enforcement Union 104
Navarro, Bob 115-19
New Deal (F. D. Roosevelt's) 97
New Line, production company 204
New Wave Hookers 71
New York 20, 25, 60, 67, 115
Nitewatch, production company 167
Nitro, production company 34, 42, 190, 202
North Carolina 37, 102
The Nuns Bad Habit 90

obscenity charges 32
O'Connell, Brittany 94
One Night in Jail 144
Orange County, California 94
Ordinary Couples, Extraordinary Sex 103
Orenstein, Steve 53, 151-6, 162, 165
orgasms, female 180-3

207

INDEX

Paramount pictures 106
PAWE (Protect Adult Welfare) 29, 132
peep shows 123, 125
Pendavis, Jasmine 56-7, 64-7
Penthouse, magazine 36, 115, 173
Penthouse Pets 26, 175
The People vs Larry Flynt 204
Petard, Ken 146
A Picnic of Pain 89
Pistol, Ray 93-5, 96, 199, 204
plaster of Paris 37, 199
Playboy, magazine 36, 115, 153, 155, 166
Playboy Channel 22
Polaroids 31
Powers, Ed 77
Premier, magazine 204
Price, Stephen 134, 136
The Private Afternoon of Pamela Mann 191
Project Mercury 126
Pussy Fest of the North West 40
Pussycat Theater 98
Pussyman Auditions 54

Rainbow restaurant 105
Rainer, Janice 88
Rand, Ayn 186
Rayveness 36-7, 74
Red Roosters Swingers Club 78
Reno, Nevada 153
Richards, Peaches 9-13, **11**, 153
Rider, EZ (Peter Gallant) 16-20, **18**, 74, 125, 130, 204
Risky Business, management agency 154
Rolling Stone, magazine 179
Rome, Gina 195-8
Roosevelt, Franklin D. 97
Ross, Larry 34-5
Rouge, Carol 37
La Rue, Chi Chi 143, 144
Rupio, Debbie 157

Sahara Hotel 93, 94, 159, 202
San Fernando Mountains 20
San Fernando Valley 20
San Francisco 24, 115
Sanders, Alex 166
Santa Monica Evening Outlook, newspaper 97
Sawitz, Reb 98

The Source, restaurant 12
Screw 111
Seibert, Lt. Ken 114-22, **120**, 125
Seven, Bruce 188
Sex Freaks 35
Sexual Freedom Alliance, magazine 98
Shadow Lane Productions, production company 133
Sharp, Fay 199
Showers, Rob 104
Showgirls, strip club 94
Skin Trade, magazine 57, 59
Slightly Sinful, lingerie boutique 94
Smith, Lucky 53, 153-4, 164
Snatch Productions, production company 54
South, Jim 29-30, 33, 42, 71, 96
spanking 133-9, **135**, **139**
Spilone, Barbara 172
Spilone, Joe 171
St Croix, Steven 47, 50, 51, 59, 179, 190
Stagliano, John 71, **72**, 184-9, **185**
Star Maker, magazine 88
Steele, Jim 140-1, 143-4
Sturman, Reuben **124**, 125-6
Suffredi, Rocko 177, 196
suicide 29
Sullivan, James 74
Sunset Boulevard, Los Angeles 12, 22, 105
Sunset Strip, Los Angeles 82

Talk of the Town, porno shop 94
Temple University, Philadelphia 131
Thomas, Paul (PT) 24-5
Total Corruption Part 2 144
La Tour, Charlie 190-2
Track Tech Studio 52, 157-8
Tricky Business 172
Truman, Patrick 104
Tyler, Nikki 47, 51, 146, 163

US News & World Report, magazine 204
USA 191

Valley College 126
VCA, production company 104, 152, 156-61; at Adultdex Convention 95; advertises in AVN 130; Todd Blatt's office in 54; owns Track Tech Studio 53; at Video Software Dealers' Convention 190; web site 158, 202
la Veaux, Shayla 162, 164
Veronica 12
Video Software Dealers Association (VSDA) 190
Vitale, Bobby 26, 53
Vivid, production company 19-22, 25, 47, 137, 152, 176-80; at Adultdex Convention 95, 96; advertises in AVN 130; partnership with Cinnamon 24; and Club Porno 145; and Jon Dough 50; gay films of 140; Steve Hirsch as owner 44-6; and Dyanna Lauren 175; raided 104; at Video Software Dealers Convention 190; website 202; Susan Yanetti as publicist 82;
Vivid Girls 21, 22, 45, 70
Voyeur, Vince 24-5, 52

Warshavsky, Seth 201-2
Washington DC 97
Washington St., Boston 14
Wasserman, Howie 171
Welcome to Bondage 17
Wicked Pictures 53, 149, 152-6; advertises in AVN 130; makes *Conquest* 162; offices of 147; at Video Software Dealers Conference 190
Wildman, Donald 105
Williams, Ted 81
Wilson, Paul 74, 76
Wilson, Ray 74, 76
Windows95 173
women 27, 61-2
World Model Agency 29
Wylde, Kim 194

Yanetti, Susan 82-3, 145-6, 178-80

Zee, Ona 96